The Point
of the Deal

The Point
of the Deal

How to Negotiate
When "Yes" Is Not Enough

DANNY ERTEL

MARK GORDON

Harvard Business School Press

Boston, Massachusetts

Library of Congress Cataloging-in-Publication Data

Ertel, Danny, 1960–
    The point of the deal : how to negotiate when "yes" is not enough / Danny Ertel and
Mark Gordon.
        p. cm.
    ISBN-13: 978-1-4221-0233-6 (hardcover : alk. paper)
    ISBN-10: 1-4221-0233-5
    1. Negotiation in business. 2. Negotiation. I. Gordon, Mark (Mark N), 1956– II. Title.
    HD58.6.E78 2007
    658.4'052—dc22

                                                                          2007017285

To Sarah and Nancy,
without whom there would be, for us,
no point to any deal.

Dedication

We gratefully dedicate this book to Roger Fisher. He has been our teacher, mentor, coach, colleague, friend, and inspiration for some twenty-five years. Without Roger, this book would simply never have been written.

While this book aspires to go beyond the "yes" franchise that Roger created when he coauthored *Getting to Yes: Negotiating Agreement Without Giving In*, it embraces and builds on the foundations firmly laid by Roger, Bill Ury, and Bruce Patton in establishing the field of negotiation theory. Pushing beyond "yes" in no way diminishes the seminal importance of the millions of copies of *Getting to Yes* now distributed in thirty languages around the world.

As the Samuel Williston Professor of Law at Harvard Law School and founder and director of the Harvard Negotiation Project, Roger has touched the lives of many thousands of students over the years. The coauthor of many books in addition to *Getting to Yes* (including *Beyond Reason: Using Emotions as You Negotiate, Getting It Done: How to Lead When You're Not in Charge, Coping with International Conflict: A Systematic Approach to Influence in International Negotiation, Getting Ready to Negotiate: The Getting to Yes Workbook, Beyond Machiavelli: Tools for Coping with Conflict,* and *Getting Together: Building Relationships as We Negotiate*), Roger has helped millions of practitioners think more clearly about their assumptions regarding negotiation and conflict resolution.

In his varied career as army officer, government official, international lawyer, scholar, educator, author, television producer, consultant, mediator, creative problem solver, and self-starting intervenor, Roger has dedicated himself to resolving international and domestic conflicts. He has worked tirelessly for more than fifty years to help people deal with their differences more productively and to inculcate a collaborative approach to negotiation into our culture.

Roger has had a deeply profound impact on us, and without his inspiration, we would not have chosen careers as professional negotiators. We owe him a great debt, and in a small gesture of our appreciation, we dedicate this book to him.

Contents

Preface   *xi*

Acknowledgments   *xv*

1 Introduction   1
What's the point?

2 The Deal-Making Mind-set   17
Why "yes" is often not enough

Part I **The Implementation Mind-set**

3 Treat the Deal as a Means to an End   35
What do you need beyond a "yes"?

4 Consult Broadly   49
Who do you need to get beyond "yes"?

5 Make History   67
How do you set the right precedent for implementation?

6 Air Your Nightmares   85
How do you discuss risk without risking the deal?

7   Don't Let Them Overcommit   99
    How do you help make sure your counterparts can deliver?

8   Run Past the Finish Line   111
    How do you stay focused on the real goal?

Part II   Negotiating and the Organization

9   Managing Negotiators   123
    How do you steer them toward deals worth doing?

10 Building an Organization That Does
    Deals Worth Doing   145
    How so many smart companies get it wrong

Part III   Critical Deals in Which Implementation Matters

11 Bet-the-Company Deals   183
    Mergers, alliances, and outsourcing

12 Bread-and-Butter Deals   215
    Customers and suppliers

13 Conclusion   231
    When "yes" is not enough

    Notes   239
    Analytical Table of Contents   245
    Index   255
    About the Authors   263

Preface

Yet another book about negotiation?

What would possess us to think we have something new to say? In part, the sheer volume of books out there that in our view focus on the wrong thing: *doing deals.* Unless nothing else matters once you sign the deal, treating the negotiation as if it were only about "doing a deal" may be setting yourself up for failure.

When actually implementing—not just signing—the deal matters, then a lot of the usual debates over whether to be a collaborative negotiator or a "power" negotiator, whether to "start with no" or "get to yes," whether to create value or claim value, pale in comparison to making sure that the deal you negotiate can actually accomplish what you intend. Otherwise, what's the point?

It is true that in some deals implementation is wholly irrelevant—for example, in day trading. But if you negotiate deals where implementation is key—they're pointless unless the parties *do* something together *after* the agreement is signed—then this book is for you.

It is also true that, all other things being equal, if you could get a little more rather than a little less in a deal, you would seem to be better off. Over the years, however, we have found that when negotiators focus their attention on getting a better deal, they sometimes lose sight of something more important: the point of the deal itself. It's not that trying to do a little better *has* to mean that you damage your ability to implement. You could certainly do not just a little but a *lot* better *and* have a deal that can be implemented effectively. But when your energy and attention are focused on the deal rather than what will happen as a consequence of the deal, you will inevitably reap less value and more frustration.

The other thing that has stood out for us over the years is how little advice is available to those who are concerned about not only how to negotiate personally, but also *how to manage other negotiators* and *how their organization as a whole negotiates*. Negotiation is at the heart of how most organizations relate to the outside world—for example, through sales, procurement, partnerships, alliances, and compliance—as well as how things get done between and among different departments. If you cannot be everywhere and do everything yourself, but you care about how well those negotiations are conducted, then read on.

We didn't start out intending to write a book. We are not academics. In our professional lives, we get our greatest joy from working hands-on with our clients, helping them negotiate and manage their most important relationships—with customers, suppliers, and business partners. At our firm, Vantage Partners, we roll up our sleeves every day and work with talented negotiators at very well-managed organizations around the globe. We have worked with clients on every continent except Antarctica (where we have yet to find a paying client), and we have found that our analytical approach to negotiation seems to resonate with clients in every culture. Even world-class professional negotiators find it helpful to think more systematically about how they prepare, how they build alignment internally, what they do at the table as well as away from it, and how they keep learning. We not only help create new strategic relationships and remediate troubled ones, but also help organizations begin to treat negotiation and relationship management as business processes rather than as an art.

Even though working with practitioners is what gets us on airplanes most weeks, we do like to take time to share ideas and lessons learned. Both of us, like our partners at Vantage, got our start in thinking about negotiation as a business process at the Harvard Negotiation Project (HNP). HNP is a multidisciplinary think tank at Harvard Law School that was started on the premise that there are useful things that diplomats can learn from labor negotiators, that labor negotiators can learn from lawyers, that lawyers can learn from entrepreneurs, and so forth. We have been involved since 1979 with the growth and maturity of negotiation as a discipline, cutting across specific kinds of negotiations and turning the process into something teachable and replicable, rather than something you pick up only through trial and error and experience.

We got so much positive feedback and encouragement after the *Harvard Business Review* article, "Getting Past Yes: Negotiating As If Implementation Mattered," that it seemed worthwhile to expand on those ideas. We want to go beyond simply advocating the idea that implementation matters even during the negotiation itself, and really explain how to negotiate when getting the other side to agree is not enough. When you need more than the other party's signature on the page to actually accomplish something, what should you do differently? How do you prepare differently? How do you behave differently at the table? How do managers of individual negotiators support and coach those people so they keep their eyes on the point of the deal? And how do organizations create the conditions in which negotiators can do deals that can then be implemented effectively?

We hope that those of you who find these ideas interesting will engage with us and other readers as we continue to apply and build on them. Have some anecdotes to share? Have a suggestion for how to improve on what's here? We have set up a discussion blog at www.pointofthedeal.com. Come visit and share your thoughts. We welcome your ideas about how to ensure that more deals have a point.

Acknowledgments

Many of our friends and colleagues were instrumental in helping us improve and sharpen both the concepts in this book and the prose that sets them forth.

Our partners at Vantage all contributed to the ideas in the book and were useful sounding boards throughout the writing and editing process. Jon Hughes, Stuart Kliman, Bruce Patton, Larraine Segil, and Jeff Weiss are wonderful, supportive colleagues, and we very much value their colleagueship and assistance in making the ideas in this book come alive. In particular, we appreciate the many hours Jeff and Jon spent going over early drafts of the manuscript.

As the dedication so clearly states, were it not for Roger Fisher, this book would not be. Aside from being a mentor and inspiration to both of us, Roger actually took the time to review an early draft of the book and provide feedback. One might think that, at age eighty-five, Roger would have earned the right to just relax on Martha's Vineyard, rest on his laurels content with the tremendous impact he has had on the field of negotiation and conflict resolution. But no—he still gets up early each morning to write, teach, send unsolicited advice to world leaders (which, more often than not, actually gets to the intended recipient), and give feedback to former students building on his legacy.

Throughout the process of writing and editing this book, we have relied heavily on Christine Kim to be our project manager and taskmaster. Christine was an analyst at Vantage when she started this project with us, and as we finish she is now a consultant—her promotion coming in spite of (and a little bit due to) the countless hours she spent researching, cite checking, editing, and brainstorming with us on *The Point of the Deal* content.

We owe a debt of gratitude to our agent, Rafe Sagalyn, for helping us get to yes with Harvard Business School Press two years ago when *The Point of the Deal* was just a concept, and for being an avid supporter throughout. We had invaluable assistance from myriad professionals, but we have to call out the early input from Jeff Kehoe that was instrumental in reconceptualizing and sharpening the organization and several constructs in the book. We are also exceedingly grateful to Jane Gebhart and Sarah Weaver for the patient and careful editing that has made your reading our words that much easier.

In the course of researching and writing, we had valuable input from many friends and clients. They were very generous in giving their time to share stories and insights, enriching the book with what they have learned from disasters and triumphs over the course of their careers. At great risk of omitting some from the list of people who added value, we want to thank:

- Ken Wolf for sharing stories of how Confluence effectively focuses on implementation as it sells financial services software

- Art Wilson for regaling us with tales of his many years at IBM, and also for giving us lots of examples from the oil and gas industry based on his current sales consulting practice leading Critical Path Strategies

- Paul Cramer, our former partner at Conflict Management, Inc., for filling us in on what he is now doing at Accenture in coleading their Negotiations Center of Excellence

- Dave Zechnich, the Contract Risk and Compliance Services leader and deputy managing partner for Internal Audit Services with Deloitte & Touche LLP, for sharing Deloitte's work on managing risk in the extended business enterprise

We save the loudest note of appreciation for our spouses, Sarah Reynolds and Nancy Gordon. In addition to being great sounding boards and forcing us to articulate nascent ideas more clearly, they endured writing schedules that often involved coming home from trips abroad and spending already-truncated weekends pounding on keyboards. Without the understanding and support of Sarah and Nancy, there would be no *Point of the Deal*.

1

Introduction

What's the point?

Why do so many deals look good on paper but end up in tatters? It turns out that for most deals, simply getting to "yes" is not enough. The parties find that after signing, there is a lot of work to do before they actually achieve anything worthwhile, but that how they negotiated the deal gets in the way. Often, the root cause of the problem is the deal-maker mind-set that leads negotiators to see the deal itself as their goal. They see the signed contract as the final destination rather than the start of something. They see the point of negotiating as getting a "yes."

There is another way of looking at negotiation and at the role of the negotiator that can cut through some of the noise about when to collaborate and how to win, and provide negotiators with a clear beacon. It starts not by looking at what happens during the negotiation, but what happens afterward.

Every day people negotiate all kinds of deals. For many of these individuals, implementation is the furthest thing from their minds. They are wholly and completely focused on getting the deal done, and when they do so, they will declare victory and go off to celebrate.

But should they?

The answer to that depends on what should happen next. When the deal is the only goal—for example, if the negotiation is purely over the price of something that is literally a commodity, like pork belly futures; if all important aspects of the deal are effectively consummated by the transfer of a few electronic bits flying over a wire; or if the environment in which they negotiated is so strictly regulated by law or tradition that the parties' obligations are crystal clear—then implementation truly doesn't matter, and you don't need the advice in this book.

On the other hand, if the purpose is to create a strategic partnership, most people would agree that getting the signature on the page is probably not the most important aspect of the negotiation. If the parties haven't established an effective governance mechanism, put the tough issues on the table, paid attention to how they are going to work together, clarified their commitments to ensure that they are mutually understood, and prepared to deal with the inevitable surprises they will face, they are doomed to failure. If they haven't taken the time to get the right stakeholders on board and to make sure they have the ability to contribute what the partnership needs, they will fail almost as quickly as the champagne will go flat after they finish toasting to their future success. Unfortunately, although most people nod knowingly when we make this point, few partnership negotiations actually take implementation into account, leading to outrageously high failure rates among alliances, as high as 70 percent by some measures.

In between those two extremes are the vast majority of negotiations, where implementation matters a bit more or a bit less. We've advised thousands of negotiators across all walks of life—from diplomats, entrepreneurs, and labor leaders to lawyers, salespeople, consultants, and *Fortune* 500 CEOs and board members—and in our experience most negotiators *underestimate* the importance of implementation to the success of whatever it is they are negotiating about. The result: they fail to do some critically important things during the negotiation, thereby undermining the value of the very deal they are trying to consummate.

If the negotiation is not the end, but the beginning of a process of realizing value for both parties, then the question of whether to try to win or collaborate, to create or to claim, becomes much less important. You can't "win" implementation. Outsmarting or outmaneuvering your counterparts at the table could well be pointless if in order to benefit, you have to work together after the deal is signed.

To be clear, we're not talking here about giving or getting a slightly higher discount or about which side gets more value. You can get more than the other party does and still feel like you didn't do as well as you should have; just as you can do a lot better than you expected and still get less than they did. To be worthwhile, deals do not have to be equal. When we say that "winning" the negotiation is not as important as making sure the deal can be implemented well, we mean that there is no point to "outnegotiating" your counterparts if what that means is producing terms so lopsided or silly or wrong that *you* would not have agreed to them. We're talking about the salesperson who gets a customer to buy more than she can really use, the buyer who squeezes the supplier to where it *really* hurts, the manufacturer who manages to pay so little to license an innovation that its original developer has little incentive to help get it to market.

There is no point to negotiation "victories" that cannot be implemented. Why get someone to agree to a deal on which they cannot deliver? Of what real value are customers who have overbought and therefore don't need to buy again for a long time (or perhaps even sour on a product they've had to store far beyond its normal shelf life)? As many high-tech manufacturers learned during the dot-com bubble and burst, overstuffing your distribution chain with product, though attractive at the time of the signature (and the booking of the revenue), comes back to bite you when the products are inevitably returned or your clogged distribution channels become unwilling to take your newer technology until they have disposed of the old models.

When any of these deals goes from contract to reality, the parties begin to experience the challenges of deals that essentially have no point, because they cannot be effectively implemented.

How the point of the deal gets lost

There is a fundamental difference between "doing deals" and negotiating for implementation. To understand what it takes to negotiate deals that actually have a point and can be implemented successfully, it may be useful to look at some of the reasons why deal makers get into trouble during implementation.

Your counterparts never intended to perform

Some implementation problems arise because one of the parties enters into the deal in bad faith, never really intending to do what is required of them during implementation. (This is sometimes called fraud, and legal remedies are often available to the injured party.)

Both sides intended to perform, but had different interpretations of what that meant

A more common problem is that the two sides have a different understanding of what they are agreeing to, or what their obligations are under certain circumstances. The dispute, when it arises, often turns into an argument about whose interpretation is the more reasonable one. Regardless of the eventual outcome, by then time has been wasted, value has been destroyed, and trust has been undermined.

The fear that the negotiating parties may misunderstand each other is one of the contributing causes to the lengthy legal documents that get churned out by the negotiators and their lawyers. Unfortunately, most of those pages, instead of being designed to help prevent misunderstandings, are in fact filled with language intended to help one side or the other prevail in court. Those are very different goals. When parties to a negotiation run into trouble during implementation because they had different expectations about how the deal would work in practice, or who was going to do what, or how, there's often little to guide them in the many formulaic recitations in the contract.

Everything was clear, but one party couldn't follow through

This is also, sadly, a common type of implementation problem whose roots lie squarely in the negotiation. Because of the focus on getting the deal signed, rather than on what will be required to implement it, many negotiations produce outcomes that one side or the other will be unable to live up to because they lack the resources, capabilities, or internal alignment necessary to implement the deal.

During the rush to get a deal done, negotiators often ignore "naysayers" who raise concerns about whether the parties can really do what they promise. Too many "what ifs" about possible scenarios can get those people disinvited to critical meetings because "their negativity is undermining the deal." Similarly, deal makers tend to want to limit negotiations to a small group of participants. They like to point out that "too many cooks spoil the broth." But if they are allowed to keep stakeholders in the dark until after the deal is done, they run the risk that one or more of those stakeholders will outright refuse to cooperate with implementation, or will participate only half-heartedly. In some cases, they will find that a stakeholder had information that would have changed the negotiator's thinking about the deal itself.

Everything was clear, but the circumstances changed

Perhaps the most common type of implementation problem in longer-term deals comes from the simple fact that the world is a dynamic environment. It is both true and trite to state that the only constant in the business environment is change—yet many deals are struck with the assumption that the future will always be the same as the present. Because of the focus on getting the deal signed, negotiators often don't take into account that many changes in people, markets, business conditions, laws, politics, the environment, and myriad other factors are likely to occur over the life of the implementation cycle.

Contemplating every possible contingency is both impossible and wasteful. Investing too much time on remote contingencies is inefficient and would surely kill many deals with a high likelihood of success that should be struck, notwithstanding some uncertainty about the future. However, too much focus on just getting the deal done may be putting your head in the sand and setting yourself up for disappointment later on.

Everything was clear, but the contract requirements were not enough

Attitude matters. The willingness of the parties to go above and beyond the letter of the contract often makes or breaks implementation. That, of course, is virtually impossible to *require* in a deal. You may not even be able to list in the contract all the things that might be necessary to success. That kind of implementation effort (doing things that can't even be named at the time the deal is done) flows in large part from the relationship the parties build during the negotiation.

Very few deal negotiators think of themselves as setting the precedent for how the parties will work together after the deal is signed. Yet, our experience tells us that when the two sides distrust and dislike each other at the end of the negotiation, the chances of successful implementation are necessarily lower. If the way the parties negotiate damages working relationships, then the likelihood of one or both sides going above and beyond what the contract requires is remote indeed.

Why negotiators often get themselves in trouble

Our assertion that many negotiators end up with deals that don't deliver the value they promise does not start from the premise that those negotiators are either dullards or neophytes. There are plenty of smart and experienced negotiators. Why do so many of them get it wrong?

The answer is that lots of the "conventional wisdom" serves them badly. The often-repeated sound bites have some merit, as you would expect, and are based on small grains of truth. But sometimes they are misapplied because they derive from a "close it at any cost" mentality or are based on some misguided assumptions about the best way to get deals done. Those assumptions, in turn, produce behaviors that have led many negotiators to get to "yes" only to find themselves unable to achieve the value they bargained for.

Chapter 2 lays out in some detail why seemingly sound, time-tested wisdom on getting good deals sometimes leads negotiators astray causing them to lose the point of the deal. We will look at how apparently sensible advice, at least in some contexts, can get negotiators in trouble. Examples include these familiar tenets:

- Avoid disclosing information when you don't have to.

- Keep them off balance.

- Keep a poker face.

- Treat the negotiation process as distinct and separate from implementation.

- Limit the number of people in the loop.

- If you don't have something nice to say, don't say anything at all.

- Lock them in early and often.

- Always be closing.

- Create strong sanctions to ensure they will perform.

The problem with a lot of the conventional wisdom is that it focuses on what may give you some temporary advantage in the negotiation itself. From our perspective, however, those conventional pieces of advice all focus on the wrong thing: the deal. When implementation matters, you have to look beyond the deal. And when you do, most of those conventions don't look so wise. The way you prepare, your behavior at the table, the role your stakeholders should play, the need to look out for the other side even if they aren't looking out for themselves—all these factors change dramatically when the point of negotiating is not simply to reach an agreement, but to actually *do* something with your counterpart.

In chapters 3 through 8 we provide the details of our advice intended for individual negotiators—those people who are literally at the table working out the deal with the other side. Negotiating as if implementation matters is quite different from just "doing deals" for the sake of reaching agreements. It means doing some things that go against common wisdom:

- Recognizing that the real purpose of the negotiation is not to sign a deal, but to *accomplish* something

- Making sure stakeholders (yours and theirs) are aligned so that implementation can proceed smoothly

- Recognizing that the way you deal with each other during the negotiation will impact how you work together during implementation

- Confronting the hard issues instead of repressing or minimizing them to get the deal signed

- Making sure your counterparts understand what they are agreeing to, and can actually deliver, rather than treating any ambiguity or potential difficulty in performing as "their problem"

- Paying attention to the transition from the negotiating table to execution

Doing these things is hard. It runs counter to a lot of incentives that have been built into the jobs of negotiators. It flies in the face of many things our culture teaches us about deal making. It requires some different skills, and it may cost you some deals that you might have closed if you had disregarded our advice. But we believe that if you have something worth negotiating, and if implementation matters, then doing deals any other way is just plain irresponsible and foolish.

Why managers don't steer negotiators in the right direction

If negotiators often miss the point of the deal, one would think that their managers would help steer them right. In many of our client organizations, we see some managers do a great job at helping, but an even greater number of them actually make the problem worse. Why do well-meaning managers take actions that will likely lead to deals that will fail?

Because managers tend to view the purpose of negotiation as "getting the deal done," they focus almost entirely on the results. Some managers give their negotiators a target, define how much they can deviate from it, and otherwise get out of the way. Those people tend to ignore the whole question of *how* the deal is reached. Others micromanage the negotiation, essentially turning the negotiators into messengers. In both cases, managers are acting on the assumption that what matters is the deal, and they want to either control it or abdicate any responsibility for it.

Negotiators don't make it easy on their managers. Having experienced both types of attempts to be "helpful," negotiators prefer being left alone, and they generally try to avoid being managed.

Some managers end up treating the problem of managing negotiators as a compensation problem. They try to figure out what they want the negotiator to accomplish, and then pay them for doing so. Unfortunately, this often leads to "incenting the close," which again reinforces that just doing the deal is what counts. How the negotiator gets to the finish line is usually ignored, so the incentives serve to reinforce the notion that getting the other party to "yes" is what wins the race. But in most complex organizations today, when implementation matters, we need to care not only about *what* the negotiators accomplish, but also *how* they accomplish it. And that requires a richer and broader set of management tools than incentives alone.

In chapter 9 we shift our focus from the front-line negotiator to the manager. We will discuss four common reasons why managers fail to deal with the challenge adequately and suggest better ways for how managers might help their negotiators be more effective at getting to deals with a point.

Why smart organizations fail to get it right

One would think that if individual negotiators are on the wrong path, and if their direct managers don't set them straight, then surely successful organizations would build mechanisms to ensure that deals deliver the anticipated value. Surprisingly, some of the systems, structures, and incentives that organizations put in place don't really solve the problem; often they make it worse.

In our experience working with companies large and small, we have noticed a series of errors that executives make about how they structure the negotiation function, how they employ and organize negotiators, and how they handle decision-making authority, especially with regard to the kind of significant deals where implementation matters. Given good intentions, how can smart organizations get it so wrong? We've seen six common errors.

Creating a separate "deal department"

Many organizations marshal their negotiating power by concentrating authority and expertise in a small group of people, setting up a specialized department or function. While the rationale for this is certainly understandable, it creates an organizational gap between negotiating and implementing. A group whose entire mandate is "doing deals" tends to be populated by deal makers who are divorced from the business areas on whose behalf they are negotiating. To excel, they have to do deals. It's up to someone else to do something with them.

Relying on third parties to do your deals

Other organizations hire third parties—like lawyers, investment bankers, advisers, and consultants—to negotiate key deals on their behalf. They bring in outside help for any number of good reasons, including lack of specialized expertise regarding a kind of transaction they don't often negotiate. At the end of the day, however, these intermediaries are usually compensated for "getting the deal done," and they act accordingly. Organizations go along, on the misguided notion that you can use these deal doers as your hatchet men and women, relying on the most aggressive techniques available to get favorable terms, and then patch up any relationship damage later by blaming the "hired guns" who have long since left town. Of course, that rarely works in practice.

Using deal-making metrics

Another common mistake organizations make, often in conjunction with creating a deal department, is to try to monitor and compensate the performance of negotiators by measuring their productivity as deal makers. Most commonly these metrics and incentives look to the number or size of deals, to discounts or other concessions obtained, or to things like "time to close," number of concurrent deals in progress, and frequency of escalations. But these metrics usually miss the point of achieving deals that can be implemented.

Allowing negotiators to "protect the deal"

Whether there is an organizational unit dedicated to deal making or not, in many organizations a small group is encouraged to maintain control over the deal process, and to avoid undermining that control by involving other stakeholders. Of course, there are many sensible reasons to limit information about a negotiation to a select group of individuals. Excluding people who are knowledgeable about what it will take to implement a deal and who are responsible for doing so may, in fact, close more deals. It will also inevitably close more deals that people will regret. If the deal is one where implementation matters, then the resulting agreement needs to hold up well when looked at closely by those who have to live with it.

Making it difficult for the negotiator to say "yes"

Of course, it is essential that any well-managed organization have constraints on what an individual is authorized to commit to. However, a problem with focusing on the negotiator's authority to say "yes" is that almost by definition, any arbitrary threshold will be wrong a lot of the time. Some deals shouldn't be done even when they are within the negotiator's limits, and others would be unnecessarily delayed or even lost because they are outside those limits.

Making it difficult for the negotiator to say "no"

Some organizations have developed norms that make it very difficult for a negotiator to think that he can ever walk away from a deal, even a bad one, without facing criticism internally for "losing the deal." A negotiator who is led to believe that not reaching agreement is a "failure" is less likely to devote any time or energy to reasons for not doing a deal, or to issues that might slow down or interfere with reaching an agreement. Whether it is a customer service mentality that leads to "the customer is always right" or a quota system that measures performance for closing sales, any organizational constraint that implies that walking away is "failure" is likely to result in a lot of deals that are not worth doing.

In chapter 10 we continue to expand the aperture of our lens, moving on to the organizations in which negotiators operate. We discuss these six common errors and suggest better approaches to treating negotiation as a business process, alongside its peers like sales, procurement, quality, R&D, and logistics.

Applying an implementation mind-set

You may be thinking this all sounds sensible, but what does this approach look like in the kinds of deals that you do? Is implementation important only for large, complex deals? What about the advice for managing negotiators: is that only for managers of sales reps?

Bet-the-company deals

There are certainly large deals that come around only once in a while. These include mergers, joint ventures, strategic alliances, and large outsourcing contracts. They usually involve large teams, including lawyers, bankers, and other specialized professionals. Surely those negotiators don't need to be reminded to look beyond the signing? Would that it were so. Success rates for many of those complex deals are dismal, and in our experience the seeds of the eventual problems are sown in the negotiation.

Large, complex deals tend to be unique, at least in their details. But they also have many things in common, especially in terms of how they are put together and by whom. Some of the ways things are "usually done" or the organizational context in which the deals are negotiated are actually part of the problem and act as blinders on the negotiators. The culture of the deal hits hard in these "bet-the-company" negotiations—but if you don't think about how the deal will actually be implemented, the bet often turns out to be a bad one.

Bread-and-butter deals

Most of us negotiate every day, whether we realize it or not. We negotiate when we work with our customers, our suppliers, even our colleagues down the hall. We may not be surrounded by lawyers and stacks of documents, but we are trying to influence others to do, or not do, something. When those agreements, whether formal or informal, require that we do something afterward, then they really should be looked at as negotiations where implementation matters.

Some buyers think they hold all the cards and can take advantage of sellers. Some suppliers think their job is to convince buyers to buy, whether they need to or not. Many individuals hardly think of their daily series of interactions as real negotiations. However, they have real consequences. How should the importance of implementation influence their thinking about their role in the negotiation and how they should prepare? If it doesn't, they are in for a series of disappointments.

In chapters 11 and 12 we apply all of the advice about negotiating when implementation matters—to individual negotiators, their managers, and their organizations—in the context of the many types of negotiations faced by businesses of all sizes. We consider the large, "strategic" type of negotiations like mergers, alliances, and outsourcing deals as well as the "bread-and-butter" smaller, everyday negotiations like buying and selling.

Finally, in the conclusion, we recap some of the big messages to take away from this book and answer the key questions you might have about how to improve as an individual negotiator and what to do if your organization is making it hard for you to negotiate deals worth doing.

Before we go on—meet our cast of characters

In the course of talking about how individuals and organizations should negotiate when implementation matters, we will offer lots of examples. Some will be real companies you have heard about. Others will be composites, built from our experience and intended to illustrate a broad range of situations and dynamics. We hope you will find some of them familiar and directly relevant. Before we go any further, let's meet the players in three typical negotiation contexts that we will use in the first half of this book to illustrate our points.

Resolving a conflict—buyer and seller

We'll start with an example where the purpose of the deal is the resolution of a conflict, and at first glance, the parties may not think they need to care a lot about implementation.

Our first situation involves a dispute between a buyer, Bill, and his supplier, Sue. Bill is a senior procurement officer for a high-tech company who buys very complex assemblies from Sue. Bill's manufacturing businesses integrate Sue's assemblies into their microchip manufacturing equipment. The components Sue sells range from $100,000 to over $500,000, and have to be crafted to incredibly exact specifications. The testing and acceptance criteria for Sue's parts are extremely rigorous. Last year one shipment with three assemblies had a hidden defect that neither Sue's manufacturing people nor Bill's fabrication teams discovered until after they had been integrated into machines sold by Bill's company. The parts have failed, and the cost to replace the parts along with damages owed to the owner of the microchip manufacturing equipment amounts to over $5 million.

Creating economic value—alliance partners

We'll then look at an example where the purpose of the deal is to work together to create economic value over time. In this example it is pretty obvious to the parties that they ought to care about implementation, since the value of their deal is created over time and not simply exchanged at the outset.

This example is an alliance between PharmCo, a large pharmaceutical company, and BiTech, a much smaller biotech company, jointly developing several molecules and compounds. Both PharmCo and BiTech know that many such development projects fizzle when the product turns out not to be as good as it looked originally. Negotiators for each side usually try to make sure that the product gets a fair shot and has all the resources it needs, and that they will be able to cease joint activity (and joint investment) as early as possible once it is determined that going forward does not make sense. The negotiators also know that these codevelopment deals compete for resources with other internal projects at each company, so they try to get the deal done and approved quickly, before too much resistance builds up at either company.

Working together—internal negotiations

Finally, we'll look at an example where the purpose of the deal is to make arrangements for working together. All of you who say "I don't negotiate *deals*" may find this one especially interesting.

We'll consider a fairly common situation—Manny, the project manager for HugeCo, runs a team that has gotten behind on a major project. Manny is under enormous pressure to finish the project on time, and he has gone to Jerr, one of his peers, to get some help. Though they aren't hiring lawyers or writing up a contract, they are certainly negotiating a "deal" for how Jerr's team will pitch in and help Manny's group. Internal negotiations—whether we treat them as such or not—are often even more challenging than external ones. The reason may be that as a rule, internal negotiations are more likely to require ongoing collaboration between the parties, both as part of implementation and beyond it. When you are negotiating an agreement for how you are going to work together, it's not just whether the other side says yes that matters.

As we focus on individual behavior and managers' actions, we will refer to these three scenarios for examples of what actual dialogues might sound like.

2

The Deal-Making Mind-set

Why "yes" is often not enough

The advice in this book is designed to help individuals and organizations in negotiations where "yes" is not enough. We will fess up at the outset, however, that implementation does not *always* matter. It matters whenever there is something that one, both, or all parties must do (or refrain from doing) after the deal is signed. That means, of course, that implementation does *not* matter whenever the parties have no further interactions, and either the full value of the deal passes at signing or the exchange of value is fully automatic and outside the control of the parties.

We have found that a handful of key indicators can typically determine whether implementation matters and how much. We have also found that parties often proceed as if implementation does not matter, although their interests would be better served if they considered implementation. Let's take a look.

Calculating the importance of implementation

At first glance, calculating the importance of implementation might seem like the Supreme Court's assessment of whether something is pornography: "you know it when you see it." Attempting to articulate a standard or test could, at first, seem somewhere between elusive and impossible. On the other hand, it's quite easy to spot deals where implementation falls at the extremes on the spectrum of importance, without the need to articulate the rationale that places them at either end.

You might consider implementation absolutely critical for deals like the following:

- Global outsourcing transactions

- Mergers

- Long-term supply agreements

- Contracts between unions and management

- Strategic alliances between pharmaceutical companies for co-development of new drugs or compounds

At the other extreme, where implementation is automatic, insignificant, or even irrelevant, you might put deals like these:

- Leasing a car

- Buying/selling stock of a publicly traded corporation

- Buying/selling virtually anything from a retail store

In between these extremes lies the vast gray area of deals where implementation matters, but without closer examination, it is not entirely clear why or how much it matters.

To go beyond the simple gut check of "Do I care about implementation?" we need a more systematic way to think about this topic. Figure 2-1 shows five key variables to consider in weighing the importance of implementation.[1] For any given deal, each variable can be evaluated on a scale where implementation matters strongly at one end and not at all at the other. If you feel that two or more variables are on the right half of the scale, which shows increasing importance of implementation, it is useful to proceed on the assumption that implementation matters to some extent. If, for any deal, you feel that most of the variables are on the right side of the scale, or that one or more variables are

FIGURE 2-1

Calculating the importance of implementation

1. Time to implement

| None | Days | Weeks | Months | Years |

2. Number of people who will be involved after the deal is signed

| None | One or two | A handful | Dozens | Hundreds |

3. Salient differences between the parties

| None | Small differences | Significant differences | Huge differences |

4. Interaction required/useful after the deal is signed

| None | Some | Lots | Constant |

5. Interaction likely outside of deal context

| None | Some | Lots | Constant |

on the *far* right side of the scale, proceed on the assumption that implementation matters *a lot.*

When you have determined that implementation does matter, you don't want just any deal—you want a deal worth doing. Before we jump to offering advice about what to do during the negotiation, let's spend a little time thinking about how so many negotiators miss the point.

Conventional wisdom, assumptions, and behaviors

There is a fundamental difference between doing deals and negotiating for implementation. To understand what it takes to negotiate deals that actually have a point and can be implemented successfully, we need to look more closely at some of the conventional wisdom embraced by those individuals who have lived by the "close at any cost" mentality. The conventional wisdom is based on a bundle of assumptions about how to negotiate deals, and those assumptions drive a set of behaviors that have gotten many negotiators to "yes" only to leave them unable to achieve the value they had bargained for.

The following list of assumptions is not comprehensive, but simply illustrates how pervasive the deal-making mind-set is and how much trouble it can get us into.

"Avoid disclosing information when you don't have to"

Traditionally, negotiators have treated information as a precious commodity, to be preserved and protected and not given away freely. Sharing more information than is strictly required has not been seen as very smart. The "wisdom" of keeping information to yourself comes in part from the notion that if the other side makes a mistake, you win. Therefore, unless the law requires that you "fess up" (as is the case in some real estate transactions, for example), some negotiators believe it is OK (and legal and even ethical) to do anything short of outright lying that may trip up your counterpart. Withholding information is one of the easiest of those things.

We have all heard that "knowledge is power." If that is so, why on earth would you educate your counterparts and make them more powerful? Many negotiators assume that the more information they disclose, the weaker they become; that it is up to the other side to do their due diligence and discover whatever information they need in order to proceed (or decide not to). In this view, it is not part of the negotiator's role to equip the other party with relevant information or to correct misperceptions. Indeed, many negotiators believe it is somewhat clever to let your counterparts make a series of mistakes—after all, the more they think you can deliver, the more they might be willing to offer. Or if they believe what they are agreeing to undertake is easier than you know it to be, they might ask for less in return.

This bundle of assumptions leads many negotiators to withhold information, play their cards close to the vest, try to catch their counterparts looking the wrong way, and fail to correct mistaken impressions. Good deal makers are expected to have "poker faces." When such behavior doesn't damage trust so much as prevent the deal, it still tends to lead to lots of surprises when the parties turn to implementation.

"Limit the number of people in the loop"

Negotiators focused on the deal tend to keep extraneous individuals (like operational people who might raise a lot of questions about how to implement the deal) from participating in the negotiation. In particular, such deal makers strive to keep naysayers from one or both organizations out of the loop until it is too late for them to interfere. We have all heard the maxim "Too many cooks spoil the broth."

We think this instinct to limit the number of people in the loop comes from the growing sense that negotiation is a specialized activity, and deal makers are professionals who have a particular job to do. That job means getting deals signed, and therefore negotiators have demanded some latitude to reduce or eliminate obstacles to the deal.

Many negotiators assume that they will be better off keeping anyone who might raise objections or concerns out of the conversation, lest they derail the deal. In addition to any stakeholders who might be adversely impacted by the deal, negotiators also tend to try to keep implementers out of the conversation. Even if the implementers don't object to the deal in principle, negotiators often fear that their operational concerns might prevent the deal from closing. Besides, "everyone knows" that getting too many actors involved makes negotiations overly complex. Each side is expected to keep its own constituents in line.

This bundle of assumptions leads negotiators to keep "outsiders" in the dark, keep deal implementers away from deal makers, and avoid discussing operational details during the negotiation. It keeps negotiators from asking too many questions about who from the other side should be in the room. These tactics often result in deals that generate strong opposition as soon as they are signed, full of commitments that are difficult, if not downright impossible, to implement.

Let's look at how that plays out in a situation like the one in which PharmCo is negotiating with BiTech to license a promising new compound and develop it into a marketable drug. Phoebe, the PharmCo negotiator, is trying to wrap things up with Bernie, the BiTech representative. (See "Dialogue Between Phoebe and Bernie.")

DIALOGUE BETWEEN PHOEBE AND BERNIE

What **Phoebe** is **thinking** but not saying	**Their actual dialogue**	What **Bernie** is **thinking** but not saying
This has been pretty smooth sailing so far. I was worried we were going to get more bogged down than we did. Good thing we kept the team small.	**Bernie:** Well, Phoebe, it took awhile, but I think we've made some good progress. I think we have a good set of terms here.	*This has been difficult and drawn out. How do they get anything done at all?*
	Phoebe: I agree. You understand, of course, Bernie, that this is all *preliminary* and subject to review by our Deal Committee.	*Don't tell me we're going to have to jump through a lot more hoops and committees!*
It's a good thing I resisted the pressure to put someone from the Labs on the negotiation team. If Phil had been involved, we'd still be debating the agenda!	**Bernie:** Sure, but that's just a formality, right? Your CEO wants this compound. And you have the budget and resources to do this deal, right?	*Still with the "once this is approved" thing—what else is it going to take? How can I get this deal signed up soon?*
Silly man. Of course we have the resources. We could buy your entire company with just one quarter's earnings!	**Phoebe:** Sure, sure. We're PharmCo, after all. We wouldn't be having this conversation if we weren't interested and if we couldn't afford it.	
	Bernie: I've just been a little surprised we haven't met anyone who's actually going to work on this drug.	
Oh, I can't wait for you to meet Phil.	**Phoebe:** Not to worry. It's just been premature. I'm sure that once this is approved, our VP of R&D will assign one of the Lab Directors, probably Phil, to run this from our side.	*Well, by then, it will be someone else's problem to deal with you guys. I'll be working on trying to structure that new licensing agreement with FarmaLtd.*

But at least the deal got signed, right? (What do you think will happen when the operational people first come together?)

"Treat the negotiation process as distinct and separate from implementation"

The traditional wisdom treats the negotiation as separate from the implementation. Deal makers assume these are two distinct sets of activities, to be carried out by different people. Implementation begins when the negotiation ends. Indeed, deal makers seem to have stolen a line from the Las Vegas marketing campaign—"What happens in the negotiation, stays in the negotiation."

There are good reasons to have different people take the lead while the deal is being put together and when it comes time to implement. After all, people have different skills. But we think that to some extent, this "wisdom" may have developed as a corruption of the advice in *Getting to Yes*, to "separate the people from the problem." The best way to do so, many negotiators assume, is to separate the negotiators from the implementers. The negotiators can then be as tough (or difficult, or dirty) as they think they need to be, and the implementers can start the relationship fresh.

This often leads negotiators to act as if there are no consequences to *how* they negotiate, so long as they get the deal. Any behavior that helps reach this goal (including coercion, threats, time pressure, parsimony with the truth, avoiding difficult or unpleasant topics, and glossing over issues that seem intractable) is fair game. The fact that the negotiators work independently of the implementers also tends to free them from real-world constraints—what will it actually take to get this done, how quickly can we do it, and so forth. The implementers (who might have known some of those things) are only brought in when the deal is done, and part of their mandate is to distance themselves from the negotiation team and disavow the tactics that got them there.

Sound familiar?

Still sound "wise"?

"Lock them in early and often" (a.k.a. "Always be closing" or "Time kills deals")

In the eyes of many, a great negotiator is one who can gain as many commitments from her counterpart as possible, while giving away as little as possible. This usually means moving to "yes" as quickly as possible, before the other party can "wriggle off the hook."

There is certainly some truth to the argument that the sooner a counterpart picks up a pen, the more likely the deal will be signed. That may well be the case in some hot real estate deals (remember the sleazy salesman in David Mamet's *Glengarry Glen Ross*?), used-car sales, "end of the quarter" specials on software or hardware, or just about any situation where once both parties sign, the deal is done. The notion that "time kills deals" comes, in part, from the fear that if the other side pauses to understand fully the value of the deal or what implementation will actually involve, they may back out. If you conceive of negotiations as mesmerizing your counterparts into committing to something unwise, the last thing you want is to give them enough time to discover their mistake.

"Fast closers" assume that the more quickly they can lock in the other side, the better off they will be. If the counterpart commits prematurely, these deal makers assume this will likely inure to their benefit. And if the other side has to renege or default on commitments, they can extract value from that party in exchange for going back on a prior commitment. These negotiators don't expect that it is part of *their* role to keep the other side from making mistakes. (Indeed, they are more likely to believe that it is part of the clever negotiator's role to try to entice them into making blunders through carefully laid traps.)

This leads negotiators to seek incremental commitments without knowing how the whole deal fits together, to take informal suggestions by the other side as hard commitments, to withhold their own commitments for as long as possible, and to allow the other side to commit to things the negotiators suspect or believe they cannot deliver. When it comes time to implement such an agreement, what actually happens is anybody's guess.

Consider, for example, what happens when Manny, the project manager in trouble, pushes hard for a commitment from his colleague Jerr to "close the deal" for more resources. Note how Manny avoids being too explicit about how much time will be required, and Jerr avoids being too specific about the constraints he faces. This is clearly a recipe for failure. (See "Dialogue Between Manny and Jerr.")

The "always be closing" philosophy may be useful in getting commitments more quickly, but it is a disaster when it comes to getting meaningful commitments in deals where implementation matters. If the other side really does not understand what "yes" means, it should be no surprise if you get commitments now, but little compliance later.

"If you don't have something nice to say, don't say anything at all" (a.k.a. "Silence is golden")

Many negotiators are taught to avoid saying negative things, particularly statements critical of the other side that could damage the working relationship. These negotiators prefer to avoid difficult issues that are likely to be contentious and to leave the "elephant in the room" unrecognized and undiscussed. Add a little bit of "What they don't know won't hurt them," and it's easy to see why many negotiators avoid tough subjects if they can.

Some of the literature on negotiation counsels that negotiators avoid potential deal breakers until later in the conversation. This bit of wisdom probably comes from the fact that parties to a negotiation are sometimes better able to grapple with difficult issues after they have built a bit of momentum toward a deal. If you tackle a tough and contentious topic before you have made some progress, sometimes one side or the other decides it is going to be "too difficult" or "not worth it" and gives up. On the other hand, if you are getting so close to a deal that you can almost taste it, the parties are more likely to work hard to get a tough issue behind them. Unfortunately, in practice, at that point negotiators are also more likely to ignore or bury that tough issue than to deal with it.

Many negotiators assume that refraining from tough conversations about negative perceptions and fears will prevent rifts in relationships.

DIALOGUE BETWEEN MANNY AND JERR

What **Manny** is **thinking** but not saying	**Their actual dialogue**	What **Jerr** is **thinking** but not saying
My team can't possibly get this done on time. I need more bodies—and someone else to blame if we are late.	**Manny:** Hey Jerr, my people could really use some help on the Huge2 beta version. **Jerr:** Well, my team is pretty swamped already.	*Why is Manny coming to me with this—he should be using his own people to get this done.*
Better start small—he's going to resist a bigger ask.	**Manny:** Yup, I appreciate that. But the CEO has made this project one of our top three strategic initiatives, and it takes priority. Can we at least get one of your guys on it right away, so we can hit the deliverable date for the beta version?	*Nice one—pulling out the CEO. This is just another strategic objective du jour. If we keep our heads down and ignore it, it will move to the back burner.*
We actually need three or four more people to get this done, but there's no way Jerr will agree to that now.	**Jerr:** Are you sure one person will really make the difference?	*Better watch out for creeping commitment of one person now, and then more over the coming weeks . . .*
If I get one of his people, and he has skin in the game, it will be easier to get more people later.	**Manny:** Absolutely. **Jerr:** Well, can he be on Huge2 just part-time until he can clear other projects?	*I have to keep the resource commitment down if I am going to hit all my goals for the year. If I can get away with a part-time resource, I can probably make this work.*
As soon as we get him in, we'll dump so much stuff on him, he will be 150 percent utilized.	**Manny:** We'll do our best to let him have time to handle other work as well. **Jerr:** I'll have to talk with my team and figure out who can most easily do this.	
Gotta get him to "yes" now. If he ducks this now, it's gonna be harder to close later.	**Manny:** I really need someone to start before the end of the week. **Jerr:** I'll see what I can do.	*Maybe I can duck this if I take long enough . . . Manny is probably making the rounds to grab the first person he can find.* *Don't call me, I'll call you.*
Got him!	**Manny:** Great, I really appreciate your being a team player! I'll call you tomorrow to find out who you're adding to the team!	*Darn!*

They worry that speaking openly and honestly about fears and doubts might open a can of worms better left untouched. Articulating negative perceptions about the other side, or concerns about how they would behave (or misbehave) during implementation, might indeed sour the relationship and make it harder to close the deal. *How* you raise these issues does matter, but not raising them at all is usually a bad idea.

Few negotiators consider it part of their role to articulate concerns about the other side that could cause the deal to blow up. However, this assumption leads negotiators to avoid discussing their concerns, to defer difficult conversations, and to hope that the problems won't materialize (or that if they do, they will be someone else's problems to deal with).

"Keep them off balance"

If negotiation is a battle of wits, then the more surprises built into the negotiator's strategy, the more the other side can be kept off balance. Surprises might be about who is at the table, what is on the agenda, what specific demands are made, or what information is requested or disclosed and when. There seems to be a traditional assumption that keeping the other side off balance is somehow an advantage.

We think this assumption comes from a tradition of viewing negotiation as one in which each side tries to get the other to commit to things that are not necessarily in their best interest. In this view, negotiation is a technique for getting people to give away things that, but for the skill of their counterparts, they would never agree to concede. A skilled negotiator, under that view, is someone who can almost cast a spell over the other participants, getting them to do things they normally would not.

Many negotiators assume that the more surprises they build into their approach, the stronger they will be. They believe that the other side is more likely to commit to something unwise if shocked and caught unawares. At the negotiating table, as in military confrontation, "shock and awe" is something many negotiators expect will work to their advantage. These deal makers don't view it as part of their role to make the process easy for their counterparts.

Putting them on the defensive by taking an aggressive stance in a blaming game is another favorite way of keeping counterparts off balance.

When people are trying to fend off blame, they are not necessarily focusing on the big picture or what they are going to do next.

Assumptions about the benefits of "winning" at the table, regardless of what might happen next, have led negotiators to blame the other party, withhold information, conceal their real agendas, play their cards close to the vest, raise surprise issues late in the game, and fail to correct mistaken impressions by the counterpart. Combined with other tactics that increase the pressure to close quickly, these behaviors tend to produce deals where one side or the other was just plain wrong about what would happen after signing.

Sounds like a good way to start working together, right?

"Create strong sanctions to ensure they will perform"

Many negotiators rely on tough lawyers to build strong sanctions into deals while they "papered the deal" at the end. In the absence of trust in dealing with counterparts, every commitment needs to be documented and penalties for nonperformance must be as stringent as possible.

Negotiators who go for the quick close, or withhold information, or try to surprise their counterparts at the last minute generally assume that they can rely on clear and enforceable contract terms, and that the more sanctions they can build into the deal, the better off they will be. They hope that onerous penalties, broad indemnities, strong default clauses, and liquidated damages provisions will incent scrupulous performance—and if they don't, then at least the penalties will make the defaulters suffer. These negotiators figure it is not their job to prevent the other party from making unwise commitments. They'll try to get their counterparts to commit to as much as possible, even to something they probably cannot deliver, hoping the penalties are so great that their counterparts will eventually find some way to deliver or, if they can't, will come crawling back offering huge concessions in order to avoid the penalties.

In our consulting practice, we have been surprised at how many customers believe that aggressive service level agreements (SLAs) coupled with tough penalties for missing SLAs will ensure that their interests are protected. Imagine the case of an auto manufacturer who outsources most of its information technology needs and application development tasks to a large service provider. Imagine further very stringent SLAs and very costly penalties for missing any SLA target.

On the one hand, the penalties built into the outsourcing agreement, however onerous, are not really enough to compensate the automotive company if its IT needs are not met. An automotive company whose IT function is not performing well gets itself into trouble fairly rapidly with its manufacturing teams, its dealers, its customers, its employees, its partners, and even the government. It doesn't take a lot of even modest failures to upset a dealer network, lose time in getting new models to market, or fail to achieve operational efficiencies on the plant floor. No matter what penalties the provider may have agreed to, they won't make up for those kinds of missteps.

On the other hand, strong sanctions *will* make the service provider focus its available resources and attention on meeting the SLAs—whether those are the most important things to do or not. And because the provider would never agree to be penalized for failing to meet intangible or subjective targets like "improved marketing insight" or "innovative supply chain enhancements," the SLAs will be certain to focus on less important technical measures of IT performance like router response time. This is a case where strong sanctions might make for good "by the book" performance but certainly not for good partners.

To be clear, we are not saying that SLAs are a bad idea or that you shouldn't have any sanctions built into your contract. Having clear metrics for success and an operational plan are very important, and specifying the consequences for nonperformance can be helpful. Incenting parties to implement is definitely a good thing—but it may not always be enough to ensure that you get the benefit of your bargain. You may have to go beyond the conventional wisdom to get unconventional value.

Less convention, more wisdom

If we told you we had some great techniques to share that would give you a temporary advantage in the negotiation, but that you could not keep that advantage through to signing, you might well ask, "Well, what is the point of those techniques? If I can't sustain the advantage until the end, I may not get any benefit from them." You would be right, of course, and that is our point. Achieving some advantage during negotiation is pointless if you can't sustain it through implementation.

So, let's talk about what negotiation success looks like when implementation matters. A good outcome in any deal in which implementation matters has the following characteristics:

1. The deal actually helps the parties achieve their purposes.

2. The people necessary to achieve those purposes are supportive and engaged.

3. The negotiation provides a history parties can turn to for guidance when implementation turns rocky.

4. The parties know how they will jointly manage the risks they face.

5. The deal is based on realistic commitments.

6. The deal transitions smoothly from the negotiation table to implementation.

To get to a deal that meets those standards, a negotiator needs a different set of operating principles than the conventional wisdom. We call this the *implementation mind-set,* and it needs to be driven by the following broad principles:

1. The deal is a means to an end.

2. Broader consultation means better implementation.

3. Negotiation is the first best example of how you deal with each other.

4. Airing your nightmares can strengthen relationships.

5. Getting the other side to overcommit doesn't serve your interests.

6. Running past the finish line gets you to the end.

FIGURE 2-2

Questions that illustrate an implementation mind-set

Implementation mind-set	Question
The deal is a means to an end.	What do you need beyond a "yes"?
Broader consultation means better implementation.	Who needs to get beyond "yes"?
Negotiation is the first best example of how you deal with each other.	What precedent do you want for how you will work together after the "yes"?
Airing your nightmares can strengthen relationships.	How will you deal with things you cannot predict or control after the "yes"?
Getting the other side to overcommit doesn't serve your interests.	Have you made it likely that all parties can deliver on their "yes"?
Running past the finish line gets you to the end.	How do you get from "yes" to your destination?

Figure 2-2 pairs each of these principles with the key question negotiators need to ask in order to get beyond "yes" and achieve the value of their deal.

The next six chapters dig into how you can shift into the implementation mind-set. For starters, try answering the six key questions in the context of an upcoming negotiation and start treating the six principles like a personal action plan.

PART I

The Implementation Mind-set

3

Treat the Deal as a Means to an End

What do you need beyond a "yes"?

We begin with a relatively simple, although not always obvious, principle: if implementation matters, then the deal itself cannot be the end goal.

The deal is a *means* to something else. When you have shaken hands, signed the papers, and raised a toast, what else do you need in order to achieve something valuable and meaningful? If the answer is "nothing," then implementation clearly isn't very important. But if the answer is anything else, then you must approach the negotiation as a *way* to achieve your purpose, rather than as if the deal were the destination.

Alice's Adventures in Wonderland is a wonderful story, full of all sorts of insights for living in the world above the rabbit hole. One of our favorites is Alice's encounter with the Cheshire Cat, whom she asks for directions:

> "Would you tell me, please, which way I ought to go from here?"
>
> "That depends a good deal on where you want to get to," said the Cat.
>
> "I don't much care where—," said Alice.

"Then it doesn't matter which way you go," said the Cat.

"—so long as I get *somewhere*," Alice added as an explanation.

"Oh, you're sure to do that," said the Cat, "if you only walk long enough."[1]

Just like your intended destination should define which path you take, your purposes for a deal should guide what you do at the table. Only when the deal itself is the only goal can you say that how you negotiate doesn't matter, as long as you reach agreement.

It may be useful to share a simple but illuminating story a client told us. We have no clue whether the story is true or apocryphal, but it is a wonderful story either way.

Picture the American Airlines claims desk at the chaotic baggage claim area at Terminal B in Boston's Logan Airport. Picture a very large man leaning over the claims desk and, at maximum volume and with uncivil language, screaming at the petite agent on the other side of the desk, saying things like:

> Listen here little missy. I have a $2,000 custom-made suit in my bag and you lost it. I have a business meeting at nine tomorrow and I need my suit. What the [expletive] am I supposed to wear to see my biggest client? I have over five million miles on your [expletive] airline. I spend hundreds of thousands of dollars a year to fly with you. How hard is it to get a bag on the right plane from DFW to here? What kind of incompetent morons work for your airline anyway? I want a [expletive] apology letter from the president of American Airlines. I have been Executive Platinum since before you were born. I demand better treatment than this.

When he paused from his tirade for a breath, the diminutive claims agent said: "Sir, there are really only two people on Earth who care where your bag is now, and one of them is rapidly losing interest."

Sometimes how we behave in a negotiation makes it harder, not easier, to achieve our ultimate purpose. Getting the baggage claims agent to do her best to find the bag, enlisting her friends in Dallas to search for and rush the bag to Boston when they find it is probably more in the irate customer's interest than simply venting his spleen and having her agree to accept the claims form, with no intention to do anything more than let the process run its course. The bag might turn up a day later, or not at all, without the agent doing her utmost to try to expedite its recovery.

When you focus on closing the deal and getting it signed, your attention, your planning, and your behavior tend to be aimed at doing those things that get you to an agreement. But as we've seen, there are lots of situations where "yes" is just not enough. The value of the deal is often not achieved when the parties say yes, but when they actually implement their agreement. Our irate traveler was not clear on his purposes: Did he want his bag back in time for his meeting? Money for a new suit? An apology? Or did he just want to vent? We're not suggesting that you just be nice and hope that others will be nice in return. However, if by focusing on getting an agreement you do some things (or ignore some issues) that will hinder implementation, then the deal does not really achieve your purposes.

If we think about it for a moment, most of us recognize that good ideas alone don't solve problems or create value. It usually requires hard work to translate them from wishful to realistic thinking, then into something that others will agree to do or support or finance, and finally into action. Some variation of this continuum is the norm for any activity that involves one or more other parties, whether we are talking about building a house, starting a business, launching a new product, or entering into a partnership, not to mention resolving a conflict or putting together any kind of coalition of actors on an international scale. (See figure 3-1.)

Many experienced negotiators intuitively grasp this. When someone buys or sells a home, the realtors rarely declare the deal done until after the home has passed inspection and the buyer has gotten financing. Why? Because they know the transaction won't go through until those two things happen. The buyer will never move in and the seller will never get paid, even though they both shook hands and signed a contract; by itself, the piece of paper doesn't accomplish anything. It is a means for getting to the end of the transaction. Even at Enron International, where negotiators were quite evidently just deal makers

FIGURE 3-1

Continuum from idea to achievement of purpose

Conceive	Explore	Negotiate	Commit	Achieve purpose
Idea, thought, or concept	Initial exploration, development, or discussion	Term sheet, LOI, or MOU	Contract, agreement, or "deal"	Implementation, action, or change

who thought someone else should worry about implementation (more on how that worked and what problems it caused in chapter 10), they knew that simply signing a deal was not enough; they had to have financing in place, or they would not be compensated for the deal. Why? Because they recognized it was not really a done deal if it could not be financed.

The same reasoning should have you asking yourself in every negotiation: "What is the purpose of this deal?" If it is not *just* to get to "yes," but to accomplish something, then the agreement is one of the necessary, but not sufficient, steps to accomplishing your purpose. What else does it take to achieve your real purpose?

What is the point of your deal?

In our experience, the purposes of most negotiations tend to fall into three broad categories: resolving a conflict; purchasing, exchanging, or creating economic value; or making organizational or interpersonal arrangements for working together. While all of these can be done more or less well, each tends to have some particular implementation challenges that can be anticipated and minimized during the negotiation.

Resolving a conflict

When the point of negotiation is to resolve a conflict, the parties must find a mechanism for adequately settling their differences. The last thing you want is to reach an agreement that only replaces one conflict with a new one. Getting the other side to agree to something that you know won't hold up once the parties leave the room is pointless. If implementation requires good faith and cooperation, then the way you reach such a deal must also address and resolve some of the underlying hurt or distrust that produced the original conflict. If implementation just seems to require that the two sides stay out of each other's way, perhaps such deeper resolution is not necessary, but then the agreement must also include mechanisms for addressing possible changes or complications without requiring real collaboration.

Purchasing, exchanging, or creating economic value

When the purpose of a deal is to purchase, exchange, or create economic value, it must enable the parties to do what is required to actually create that value after they reach agreement. Just how robust and comprehensive the deal must be depends on the nature of the transaction, the nature of the relationship (past and future) of the parties, and how closely the parties have to work together to achieve the deal's purpose. Keep in mind, however, that negotiating tactics that assume the deal is done once it is signed tend to backfire during implementation when you need the other party to do something (or refrain from doing something) that is not spelled out in detail in the contract.

We have seen myriad examples of clever procurement people losing sight of the real purpose in negotiating deals with a supplier, striking deals that looked good at the outset, but failing to accomplish what they needed. In the wake of several mergers between large petroleum companies, cost cutting became imperative to meet Wall Street's expectations for the synergies that would come from combination. In some cases, the procurement teams found they could save money by shifting well services away from the traditional players like Schlumberger and Halliburton to smaller players that offered a 20 percent discount. In some cases, this led to a savings of some $20,000 per well. Sounds like a nice win, right? Not once you learn that many of these players failed to provide the services in the same way the ousted incumbents did, leading to well failures and production stoppages. With an individual well producing as much as $200,000 a day in revenue, there didn't need to be too many failures before paying less was costing the oil companies a bundle. A better purchase price at the cost of hugely expensive downtime does not achieve the purpose the oil companies actually had.[2]

Making organizational or interpersonal arrangements for working together

To make arrangements for working together, a deal must obviously involve the right individuals. But long-lasting success requires more than that. For the parties to achieve their purpose, they must negotiate the deal in the same way they expect to work together. The precedent they set and the history they create together will impact how they collaborate after the deal is done. Simply signing a "teaming arrangement" with another organization, or writing a memo about how a department will be reorganized, does not, by itself, produce the desired behaviors.

Deals can also have multiple purposes, and complex ones often do. You may want to make arrangements for working together *and* to create value in the process. Or you may be trying to resolve a dispute within the context of an ongoing relationship where both parties intend to continue buying from and selling to each other. Recognizing those as the purposes of the negotiation, beyond simply reaching agreement, will have everything to do with the ability to achieve them.

Remember the case of Bill, the buyer from the high-tech company that produces microchip manufacturing equipment, who seeks to settle his dispute with seller Sue? At one level, their purpose is to resolve their dispute over who will bear what share of the $5 million liability. But if they are going to continue to work together, they must also sort out how they will prevent recurrence of this expensive problem. Bill thinks the root cause of the problem was the failure of Sue's manufacturing team to produce, and then test, the parts to the specifications. Sue thinks the real cause of the problem was that Bill's testing and acceptance teams mistakenly approved the parts, his fabrication teams did not spot the defect and used the bad parts, and his quality-control people OK'd the now-defective machines that went out to the end customer. Regardless of how they ultimately decide to divide the $5 million in damages and whether Sue actually pays cash for the damages or simply compensates via discounts, services, or other noncash benefits, the more important (and more economically valuable) issue for each of them is how to avoid bad parts and defective end products in the future. That doesn't mean they don't care about what the current dispute costs them; it just means that there is *even more* at stake in preventing future problems.

How they implement their agreed resolution of this dispute could have significant consequences on their ability to work well together in the future in a relationship that is critical to both of them, where they have to collaborate closely to engineer new parts, where they have to share proprietary technology, and where neither can afford to walk away from the other without adverse consequences. For this conflict to be truly resolved, the parties have to agree on more than who pays how much of the current $5 million liability—they have to know how to prevent bad parts from being produced, delivered, and installed as well as what they will do if, despite their best efforts, the problem recurs. They will also need to be able to look back on this negotiation and feel fairly treated by a counterpart who brought both creativity and a positive problem-solving attitude to the situation.

How do you ensure your deal has a point?

Most books about negotiation tend to focus on what the parties should do at the table, when they are sitting face to face. While there are important and valuable things to talk about in that setting, there is also a great deal that negotiators need to do before they ever walk into the room. Effective negotiation begins with effective preparation and internal discussion. It's also important to recognize that deal makers don't do deals in a vacuum; numerous factors might influence their behavior. These might include their compensation system, the fact that they belong to a "deal-making department," or the way they and their manager interact. While we focus here on what deal makers can and should do to make sure their deals have a point, we'll take a look at the organizational context and the role of managers in chapters 9 and 10.

Ask in advance: what will be different "the day after"?

When implementation matters, then usually the day after the deal is signed something is different. A conflict is resolved and there is—sometimes literally—a "cessation of hostilities." Or the parties have begun to design, build, or operate something that they are buying from or selling to each other or collaborating to create. Or the parties have started to work together to get things done more effectively. Whatever you are trying to achieve, if you really want to be well prepared for a negotiation in which what happens after the deal is signed is important, then "what will be different?" is a critical question to ask early and often.

It is hard to just happen upon the point of a deal without some advance focus or discussion. And deals can take on a life of their own, with deal makers convinced they have to get them done, because, well, that's what they do. But when deals don't actually help the negotiators or their organizations achieve their purposes, then what was the point?

Confluence is a Pittsburgh-based, privately held software developer in the financial services sector that understands the difference between closing deals and implementing them. Its software automates hundreds of different kinds of reports that mutual fund companies issue to their customers. Unlike some others in their industry, they have aligned around a view of success that focuses on the customer's ability to use and benefit from their product; they describe their approach to negotiations with their customers as being almost like negotiations with a channel partner, where "we cannot be successful unless they are too." What this means is that Confluence resists simply doing deals when it feels implementation is at risk. The company has made an explicit choice to extend its sales cycles and even lose some deals rather than let customers buy its software without understanding what it takes for them to be successful. The vice president of sales requires salespeople to take the time to educate their customers and to insist that Confluence staff be involved during the installation and deployment to make sure it's done right.

Ken Wolf's business card may say "vice president of sales," but, as he puts it, he's really "VP of Promises—promises that have to be kept by others in our organization." Ken is quite certain that, at least for them, getting a contract signed is not the goal: "The contract is more like the fifty-yard line," he explains. "We have to get the customer all the way through implementation to feel we have succeeded." It's not always easy, in the heat of the moment, to stay focused on the point of the deal. "It sometimes feels like I have a little angel on one shoulder and a little devil on the other. The devil says 'Make the sale. Get it signed.' The angel, on the other hand, says, 'Wait. Make sure they understand, otherwise we will both fail.'" To help make sure everyone in the organization is aligned, Ken's sales teams are commissioned on the size of the deal, but their payment is aligned with the timing of the business result.[3]

Challenge your team: what kind of relationship do you need to implement well?

This is the other critical preparation question that will help you and your team get and stay aligned around your ultimate purpose. If the parties have signed a deal that looks great on paper but now can't stand each other because of how they negotiated, they won't accomplish much. Too many negotiators believe that negotiating the deal and living with it are two different things. In too many organizations, these are activities carried out by two different sets of people, out of the mistaken conviction that by changing the players you can leave behind all the nastiness of the negotiation and start with a clean slate during implementation.

More than twenty-five years ago, our colleagues wrote in *Getting to Yes* that negotiators should "separate the people from the problem," and we couldn't agree more. You need not treat people badly to get a good deal, and you need not be "soft" on the merits of the negotiation in order to have a good working relationship after the deal is signed. We think that point bears elaboration in this context, because some have misread that statement and interpreted it to mean that they should separate those tough, nasty deal makers who can bash each other about from the nice, collaborative implementers who can take it from there.

If you don't want the point of your deal to get lost, you have to do more than just change players once the deal is signed. Replacing the negotiators doesn't build the kind of relationship you need for implementation. At best, it means trying (and often failing) to mitigate the damage you may have done. If your purpose is to *do* something with the other participants after you sign, then thinking about how you need to work with them is part and parcel of defining your purpose for the negotiation. If implementation is the point, and not just an afterthought, then it's not enough to plan on how to undo the damage: you have to define and build the right kind of relationship from the start.

We're not saying that you have to be "nice" or make lots of concessions during negotiation to be likable during implementation. Neither are we saying that the individuals leading your negotiations must have skills focused primarily on managing implementation projects. What we are stressing here is that if implementation matters, it implies a need for some kind of working relationship postsigning, and preparing for that relationship cannot wait until negotiations are over. Building that partnership must be part of your definition of the end you want to achieve, and your means must be consistent with that end.

Although just signing a complex deal might feel like an accomplishment, it is usually not enough to reap the intended value: the parties have to be well positioned to work together. For example, the ultimate purpose of the alliance between the global giant PharmCo and BiTech, a smaller biotech company, is to develop jointly several molecules and compounds. Such collaborations typically take years. If they are to be successful, their negotiations must address how they will work together over the life of the joint venture. A wise deal maker putting together the PharmCo–BiTech joint venture will think hard about what it will take to maximize the venture's chance for success. Signing the contract is not a success—getting new compounds and molecules into development is success (or deciding this was not a fruitful scientific venture and shutting it down as soon as possible). If the purpose is to create something of economic (and social) value, and joint activities are necessary to create that value, then the negotiator has to ensure that the way the deal is negotiated enables the parties to achieve that purpose. If PharmCo sends in the deal makers just to bash on BiTech's negotiators and get them to agree to a bunch of onerous terms in the hope that when the heavyweights leave the picture, the scientists will get along, they are in for a big surprise.

This is not at all about holding back from difficult conversations and playing nicely together. The negotiators must engage in a discussion regarding the risks their venture must manage and how they will mitigate the impacts if those risks come to pass. They must consider the likely changes in circumstances (competitors' products, regulatory developments) and figure out how to respond. They must also make sure that as they negotiate, they create a precedent for working through challenges jointly and with an open mind, instead of having each side try to come up with the "right" answer and then push the other side to accept it. The trick is to do all of the foregoing in a way that builds the kind of relationship the parties will need when they face those challenges and have difficult decisions to make together.

How do you make sure the point is clear to your counterpart too?

Figuring out what the point of your deal is should not be a solitary endeavor. After all, there will be (at least) two parties to this deal. If the parties are going to work together after the deal is signed, you want to be certain they are not working at cross purposes. Here are some tips for ensuring that everyone gets the point of the deal.

Engage others in the purpose discussion early on

Making sure that you and your counterpart agree on the point of the deal does not mean that you both have to want the same things. Indeed, many negotiations create lots of value precisely because the parties want *different* things. You have a plot of land and money with which to build a house. I have expertise as a home builder and a set of resources I can bring to get the house built. You want my skills and I want the compensation you can provide. We have different interests, but our purpose—to build the house—is clear.

In order to get to "yes" in a negotiation, you need to understand the interests on each side, so you can be creative about ways to meet them. But to get past that "yes" and make sure you have something you can implement, both of you, early and often, must discuss goals to be served by this deal. What is the end toward which you both are working? What will it take from each of you to get there?

To be sure, you don't need to agree on everything about the purpose of the deal. You may have differing views about how things will turn out (e.g., how competitors will react, what regulators will say, how large the market will be). You might be more focused on the long-term view (how implementing this deal leads to future deals) and your counterpart might be more interested in short-term results (simply implementing this agreement). What is critical is that you both understand what, beyond signing, is required for success.

Genpact is a spin-off (still partially owned) from General Electric that delivers business and technology services to firms around the world. Genpact executives have built their brand around helping global organizations improve their revenue, cash, costs, margins, speed, and customer relationships through operational excellence. They cannot deliver those benefits, however, without a close working relationship, access to senior executives, and the ability to influence business processes outside the scope of their own services. When they negotiate a deal with a potential new customer, they have learned to ensure the client sees the point of the deal the same way they do. Otherwise, they fail.

V. N. Tyagarajan, executive vice president for business development (who goes by the name "Tiger"), stresses to his teams the importance of engaging the customer early in a dialogue about the point of the deal. "We try to understand what the customer is trying to accomplish in terms of growth, acquisitions, back-office integration of dispersed business units, etc. We invest a lot of time speaking with the customer about what we think it will take to achieve significant business improvements. But if we cannot get the access we need to have these conversations, we conclude we will not be successful implementing for them and there is no point in trying to do a deal."[4]

Try a little "backwards thinking"

Part of bringing an implementation mind-set to your negotiations is to keep your focus on the end goal and all the things (including, but not limited to, an agreement) that are required to get there. Our best advice is not to be quiet and circumspect regarding implementation, but to be unabashedly explicit about your goals and concerns for that phase. Wear your "day after" thinking on your sleeve and wear it proudly.

When we encourage you to try some "backwards thinking," we mean putting into practice the notion that the negotiation is a means to an end, by talking explicitly about the end goal and working backwards from there. We find it useful to take a blank sheet of paper, turn it sideways ("landscape" format), and write your end goal at the far right-hand side. Describe in a few words what that goal looks like when it is achieved. Then ask yourself, "What needs to happen the day before, for that goal to be achieved?" This often leads to an interesting conversation that unearths all sorts of unstated assumptions about the point of the negotiation. It also often helps identify issues that did not seem necessary to cover just to sign the deal, but clearly need some discussion.

After you clarify what needs to happen right before you accomplish your goal, then ask, "What must happen before *those* things can occur?" Usually, yet more interesting discussions ensue, and more useful topics come up.

Continue to repeat the above step until you work your way backwards to the negotiation itself. When you can truly say that the only thing required is the agreement of the parties, you know that you are on the same page regarding the point of the deal. That doesn't mean you don't still have a lot to do to make sure you can reach a workable agreement. But it does mean that if you get to "yes," you will also be on the path that will get you "beyond yes" to your real goal.

In our experience, the more often you engage your counterpart in a discussion about what it will look like, and what it will really take, to achieve your purpose, the more likely you will be successful. Whether it is a conflict you are trying to resolve, a value exchange you want to create, an arrangement for working together you hope to establish, or some combination of these, the sooner you start working backwards from that future outcome to where you are today, the more effective you are likely to be.

Once you and your counterpart are clear on what you are trying to achieve, it is important to focus on who needs to be involved, in what ways, to make sure you can accomplish your purposes. That is the subject of the next chapter.

4

Consult Broadly

Who do you need to get beyond "yes"?

When a negotiator views his objective as getting the deal done, every instinct in his body tells him to limit participation. More people at the table means it takes longer to reach agreement. More people who have to approve what happens in the negotiation also increases the time it takes to close and probably also increases the risk that someone will raise an objection that will kill the deal. More people means more hands to hold, more concerns to be addressed, and more interests to be accommodated. More people almost always means more headaches for the negotiator. There's a reason why people worry about "too many cooks in the kitchen," and deal makers know it well. However, if the deal is a means to an end, then the thinking about who must participate has to change.

When implementation matters, usually so do the goodwill and active participation of key individuals who can make better or worse choices about how they implement the contract. Getting buy-in from the right people doesn't just magically happen after the deal is signed. Indeed, there are lots of things negotiators do, or fail to do, that can doom implementation by creating enemies, dismissing potential supporters, or failing to take into account issues or information that might turn out to be critical.

Surely this is obvious, you say. Everyone knows that after the deal is done, people who were not involved in the negotiation will have to get together and do some things that they didn't know about, wouldn't have agreed to if asked, and for which they might have had better alternatives. But that's just how it works, isn't it? You can't expect the negotiators, with all the other things they have to worry about, to think about who they need to involve in the discussions, other than those who can say yes or no to the deal.

We think the answer is that it *doesn't* work that way. Not that negotiators don't do it that way, but that it *doesn't work*, at least not when implementation matters.

We all know why deal makers tend to be underinclusive in their zeal to get a deal done quickly. But let's spend a moment looking at all the reasons why in doing so, they miss the point.

1. Leaving people out cuts off your access to their knowledge and information.

2. Leaving people out often has the perverse effect of encouraging them to try to knock down the walls to get in—and when they do, they are mad, suspicious of why you were keeping them out, and not very open to whatever it was you were talking about behind closed doors.

3. Leaving people out of the negotiation often costs you their buy-in and personal commitment for implementation.

4. Leaving people out risks damaging relationships and trust.

Yes, there are risks to being overinclusive as well, including the possibility that someone may try to sabotage the deal or that more people will think they get to vote on whether your deal gets done. But if some people are so opposed to the deal that they may try to keep it from happening, chances are they will interfere with it during implementation, too. Sure, some people who are left out might dislike some of the potential deal terms—but they are likely to both dislike the terms and *hate* being surprised and excluded. If they are really in a position to hamper implementation, then you want to know and understand their perspective sooner rather than later, and see what you can do about it.

There is no point to doing a deal if you're not able to implement it. But if implementation requires goodwill, creativity, the exercise of judgment or discretion, or anything more than checking off items on a list, then you need some degree of buy-in from those who will have to follow through. In chapter 10 we look at this challenge through the lens of the organization, and how some well-meaning practices, like creating a separate "deal department" or promoting a culture of letting deal makers "protect the deal," contribute to this problem. But here we'll focus our advice on the negotiators themselves. How do they get themselves in trouble and how can they do better?

You probably already ask yourself whether there are individuals who may not be part of the negotiation but who will have the right to approve or disapprove the deal. If so, you know you need to find out what they expect the deal to accomplish and what they consider a good (or not-so-good) outcome. We would add that if there are better or worse ways to do a deal (*a quick hint*: there usually are), the difference often depends on information held by individuals who are not at the table. That means you need to find some way of getting access to them or to that information.

In cases where a single individual can act unilaterally and related parties have no say in going forward, are not impacted by the deal, and are not required for implementation, gaining broad buy-in is clearly irrelevant and may not be a good use of time and effort. In business, governmental, organizational, and even family contexts where multiple parties are involved, however, it is imperative to think through which stakeholders ought to be involved in what ways before the deal is done. In working with our clients, we often see deals fail not because they were bad deals, but rather because they lacked adequate buy-in from key stakeholders before being finalized.

Our colleagues, David Lax and Jim Sebenius, have very useful insights into what they call "deal setup" in *3-D Negotiation: Powerful Tools to Change the Game in Your Most Important Deals*. Their third dimension is setting the table to ensure "that the *right parties* have been approached, in the *right sequence*, to deal with the *right issues* that engage the *right set of interests*, at the *right table or tables*, at the *right time*, under the *right expectations*, and facing the *right consequences of walking away if there is no deal.*[1] Lax and Sebenius are very clear that an effective "all-party map" would consider potentially influential players, potential allies and blockers, and those who must implement the agreement once it is done. They share the story of Matsushita Electric buying MCA (the owner of Universal pictures, record companies, and theme parks) for $6.59 billion in a transaction where Michael Ovitz kept the parties apart for as long as possible and implementers were excluded from the deal. Had implementers been more directly involved, the transaction would not have to have been unwound a few years later at a huge financial loss to Matsushita as well as significant loss of face.[2]

Let's return to the deal between PharmCo and BiTech as another case in point. Business development negotiators from both sides are generally tempted to limit the participation of stakeholders because it slows them down. They also often try to limit access to information about the deal because it can be sensitive and impact the stock price of one or both companies. But at what cost? Let's see what happens when some of the operational people first come together.

Phil is the lab director at PharmCo who will have to manage the new project on the PharmCo side. Bjorn is the senior scientist at BiTech who led the initial discovery team. Both will need to work together to drive this project. Neither was directly involved in the negotiation. (See "Dialogue Between Phil and Bjorn.")

No matter how good the deal looks on paper, neither PharmCo nor BiTech will actually reap any rewards from it unless they can work together to get this drug all the way through the process and to the market. If the people who have to collaborate most closely, apply their best judgment and insight, and be creative start out thinking, "Not with my resources!" or "Why would we partner with these people?" then implementation is at the very least at risk, and perhaps doomed from the start.

How do you line up the right people for the negotiation?

Getting the right people involved the right way requires clear thinking about more than just how many people are too many or too few, or about their formal place in the hierarchy. You also need to think more

DIALOGUE BETWEEN PHIL AND BJORN

What **Phil** is **thinking** but not saying	Their actual dialogue	What **Bjorn** is **thinking** but not saying
	Bjorn: Hi, Phil. I just wanted to review the project plan for our joint team.	*I wonder what it will be like to work with this big bureaucracy.*
Oy! Another project, and my team is already overstretched. I don't think I have budget for this.	Phil: Yes, well, you have to understand that this was dropped on my head by the business development guys, and I don't have anyone just hanging around with nothing better to do.	
		Actually, if you guys had a lot of worthwhile projects, your CEO wouldn't have paid us a bunch of money for our little compound, would he?
	Bjorn: Well, I have to admit I was a bit surprised too. I had expected a deal to come later, after we had processed the compound a bit further.	
Say what? Is this another wild-goose chase courtesy of those deal guys? I'm going to have to escalate this. We can't have another half-baked idea taking up valuable resources and making my lab look bad.	Phil: Oh, so, it's not really ready for us to work on it? I'll have to let our people know. You know we follow some strict protocols around here.	*I heard your guys waved so much money in front of us that we jumped. I would have preferred to let my team take this to the next stage.*
		Oh, kill me now!

broadly than just about who should participate directly at the table. To set yourself up well for implementation, first identify the different types of stakeholders, then set and manage the expectations for each person's role.

Identify different types of stakeholders

Choosing the right people must lie in striking the proper balance, right? If you are underinclusive, you put implementation at risk. But if you are overinclusive, you put the deal at risk. Although there is no easy answer to this question, we think a couple of principles can help.

First, if you have to be wrong, it is better to be wrong by including too many, rather than too few. After all, too many people may keep you from doing a deal, but not all deals are worth doing. Too few participants, however, may keep you from getting any value out of the deal after you have invested a lot of time and money as well as your reputation. Second, if you think systematically about the different kinds of people who can affect whether the deal gets done and whether there is any point in doing it, you can dramatically reduce your chances of erring either way.

As we noted earlier, involving the necessary stakeholders does not mean involving everyone. Who should be involved and what level of buy-in you need from them will vary according to the individual's (or group's) role in decision making and their criticality to implementation—in some cases, what's needed is merely passive acquiescence. In other cases, unless you get their active, enthusiastic participation, your deal will not be implemented effectively.

When trying to identify stakeholders and determine who is necessary to a deal, we find figure 4-1 useful. It helps us understand the different types of stakeholders and the level and type of buy-in required of each. It is worth noting that some stakeholders will not be so easy to categorize and will cluster in the ill-defined middle of this matrix. For the sake of clarity, however, let's look at each box in turn, and think of the characteristics of a pure stakeholder of each type.

Bystanders

Bystanders play no role in decision making and no role in implementation. Clearly, investing a lot of resources in lining up bystanders and getting their buy-in will yield a poor return on investment. One can understand that some deal makers enjoy getting applause from the bystanders, and having their buy-in may be gratifying. However, unless their influence on blockers will make approval more likely, or their support will motivate enablers to get the job done, or their buy-in will help with broader corporate change initiatives or other deals, investing much time in getting bystanders' buy-in may be misguided.

In the PharmCo–BiTech deal, at least at this stage of the game, sales, procurement, manufacturing, and operations are all bystanders.

FIGURE 4-1

Decision-making/implementing matrix

High

Role in decision making

Blockers	Essentials
These are usually individuals with some ability to stop the deal or some aspect of it. Because they are in a position to insist on particular terms before they accept a deal, they may need to be educated about implications for implementation.	These individuals are most closely aligned with doing the deals, and only those deals, that can be implemented. Even if they are not themselves at the table, they can be the strongest advocates for making sure there is a point to the deal.
Bystanders	**Enablers**
Bystanders are necessary neither to the deal nor to its implementation. Yet they are often engaged when they really ought to be left on the sidelines.	Without their support, implementation may fail. But because they are not strictly needed to get to "yes," they are often ignored.

Low   High

Criticality to implementation

Eventually, they may have a role to play, but for a deal that is about working together to determine whether there is a product worth making, the connection of these functions is too remote, and little input will be needed from these groups for months, if not years.

Blockers

Blockers play a critical role in the decision to do the deal, but have little involvement in implementation. Most experienced deal makers know to take blockers into account and try to satisfy them. To be most effective, however, this consultation should be a two-way street. In addition to obtaining sufficient authority to negotiate and an understanding of what kind of deal is likely to be approved, it is critical that negotiators educate blockers well about what is required for implementation. In the absence of such understanding, the blockers' instructions to the negotiator and their threats to veto terms they do not like may get the negotiator to "yes" but not much beyond it.

Sticking with our pharmaceutical alliance example, the PharmCo CFO may well be a blocker. She is not going to be very involved during implementation, but the deal probably cannot get done without her approval. The negotiators will need to help the CFO develop a realistic picture of what implementation will entail, so that her approval is not based on mistaken assumptions—for example, of how the R&D budget might be impacted under different scenarios. They don't want the CFO to set conditions for the deal that create disincentives for BiTech's active participation or that starve the project by denying it critical resources.

Enablers

Enablers are not important to approving the deal, but are critical to implementing it. Even if key individuals can't veto the deal, they can be its undoing by failing to act on their implementation responsibilities. When the deal maker is counting on others to do (or not do) certain things to effect the deal, those people must be aligned in their expectations and understanding of their role and responsibilities. The kind of buy-in you need from enablers is their personal commitment to devote their attention, time, energy, and resources to implementation activities, as appropriate to their role and responsibilities. Therefore, enablers need to understand the purpose of the deal so they can act consistently with that purpose and, when required, go above and beyond the formal terms of the deal to accomplish the ultimate goal.

In the PharmCo example, a lab director on each side is clearly an enabler, and the negotiators ignore them at their peril. For their deal to be successful, these lab directors must buy into the collaboration and make sure that the joint projects are prioritized appropriately and receive the necessary resources and support. Neither Phil, PharmCo's lab director, nor Bjorn, his counterpart at BiTech, are senior enough in their respective organizations to be key decision makers when it comes to establishing codevelopment alliances worth hundreds of millions of dollars. Thus, they are neither blockers nor essentials; they are enablers. In many traditional organizations, they would not be brought into the conversation until after the deal was signed and the alliance fully negotiated—and as good soldiers, they would be expected to do their best to make the alliance work, whether they had bought in or not. This, however, is part of the reason why, among traditional organizations, more than half the alliances formed fail to meet their stated objectives. If the critical enablers are unconvinced that they need to form a partnership at all, or one with this particular partner, or with this particular scope, then the chances for its success are much lower. If commitments are made on behalf of the organization that these enablers feel they cannot (or should not, to be true to their other obligations) meet, the chances of underperformance or outright failure are much higher. In the PharmCo case, obtaining input and some degree of buy-in from the key lab directors somewhere along the negotiation process will promote, rather than hinder, the point of the deal.

It is important to remember that there are usually enablers on both sides of the deal. While most experienced negotiators try to learn about the other side's blockers (because in some ways that is really who they are negotiating with, even if those people are not in the room), few keep in mind the other team's enablers. A wise negotiator does not assume it's "the other side's problem" to deal with its own enablers. If they fail, so do you. Engage your counterparts in a conversation about what their stakeholder matrix looks like and explore ways that you can help each other. Remember, there are individuals necessary to implementation on both sides of the negotiation, or even external to it.

Essentials

Essentials are just that—people who are essential to deciding to do the deal as well as implementing it. Essentials are the linchpin to both getting a deal and achieving its benefit. The kind of buy-in you need from essentials is the sum of the buy-in you need from both blockers and enablers. That may sound like a tall order. But in reality, essentials are the best friends of a negotiator who cares about the point of the deal. Their perspectives are well aligned with yours, even if you disagree about fairly fundamental things in the negotiation. They want a deal worth doing, or none at all. They understand that signing the deal is not the end, but merely a milestone on the way to achieving its purpose. In the case of a pharmaceutical development alliance, essentials are typically the heads of the relevant business units who will both benefit from the success of the drug and bear the cost and risk of the failure of the collaboration.

Set and manage expectations about roles

The deal makers are right. Involving too many people who can say no or set conditions is a recipe for never closing the deal. To think broadly and inclusively about who should participate in the negotiation, you have to define how different individuals will participate, and at what points in time.

There are likely as many ways to manage expectations with a group of stakeholders as there are negotiators, and you will have to adopt something that fits your style. In looking across varied management styles, however, we do see a pattern: many negotiators make the same erroneous assumptions about the roles various stakeholders can play. We urge you to question these assumptions when you find yourself falling into them.

One assumption is that a stakeholder either is a decision maker—with a seat at the table and possibly veto power over the whole deal—or is excluded entirely. Faced with that choice, most of the stakeholders we just encouraged you to include would want a seat at the table and the right to say no. But if you allow that, you have just complicated your life and likely doomed your deal, because you may never fully satisfy them all.

The second faulty assumption both negotiators and stakeholders make is that, whatever a person's role or rights with respect to the decisions in a negotiation, they are the same for all the decisions in the negotiation. Most people confuse their decision-making powers in a negotiation with their own status or importance, and therefore conclude that it must be the same for all the different issues that will need to be resolved. If you set both of those assumptions aside, you can come up with a relatively clever way to let different stakeholders participate in different ways on different issues.

Delineate roles for decision making

First, delineate the roles that different individuals can play on any given decision: make decisions, drive, inform, consult, and negotiate (see figure 4-2). Instead of giving someone veto power or none at all, consider

FIGURE 4-2

Decision roles

Issue for

Decision	Drive	Inform	Consult	Negotiate

the range of decision-making powers you could assign: who should be informed of a decision before it is broadly announced, so they are not surprised or embarrassed by learning of the decision in the local paper or from a competitor; who should be consulted before a decision is made, so that they may provide input or share relevant information or expertise; and who must be part of negotiations before a decision can be made. Members of the negotiation team will typically (but not always) drive the process, framing decisions as they need to be made and perhaps formulating recommendations, about which they might consult with some, negotiate with others, and eventually simply inform the rest.

Each of these roles not only implies a right—to be consulted, to be informed, and so on—but it also has a corresponding obligation, or responsibility. If you are in the consultation role for a particular decision, for example, that means the driver has to get your input and take it into account before a decision is made. It also means, however, that you have an obligation to provide the driver with timely and informed feedback when consulted. Similarly, if your role entitles you to be informed and you will have privileged access to information, you might reasonably be expected to maintain that information in confidence for some period of time.

Assign different roles for different decisions

Next, separate out the decisions that need to be made and recognize that different individuals can play different roles for different decisions. Someone doesn't have to be in the "consultation" category for every issue. Participants' roles should depend on their knowledge and expertise, on how they will be affected by the decision, and on the role you need them to play in the deal and its implementation. The more you unbundle decisions, the easier it gets to assign roles, because people become comfortable with playing a less involved role on some issues if they see that they can be substantially involved in those things that really matter to them. Figure 4-2 shows what it might look like to lay out the different roles that people can play across different issues, in a single table.

Most skilled negotiators intuitively have a table like this in their heads, but very few have a systematic framework to ensure that the right people are involved in decision making along the way. We have seen this tool (or variants thereof) put to great use by a range of organizations, from the Chilean postmaster general working with the postal workers' unions to the governance teams managing DuPont's outsourcing deals with Convergys, CSC, and Accenture.[3] We have seen it used internally and between partners in numerous alliances and preferred-vendor agreements. We have seen boards of directors and corporate officers use it to define their decision-making processes. And it is something we use regularly to facilitate and expedite decision making in our own firm.

We think Brett Pauly, a Cisco alliance director, probably put it best when he described his own experience: "I had thirty-one different stakeholders in eleven different [internal] groups to keep happy." By clarifying the different roles individuals would play, "we significantly shortened the internal cycle times for approval of nonstandard terms; improved our speed of getting contracts done; reduced the number of instances where a stakeholder has complained that they are 'out of the loop' or 'bypassed in the approval process'; and reduced the occurrences of the negotiation team being overruled on an escalation."[4]

How do you get sufficient buy-in?

Ground rules that clarify the role that different stakeholders will play in a negotiation are very useful when it comes to getting buy-in for implementation. But to be effective, you need some buy-in to the ground rules themselves. Keep a few simple rules in mind to help you get the right roles and responsibilities in place: define a process and set expectations early, consult with critical stakeholders early and often, and help your counterparts make sure their own stakeholders are on board.

Set expectations early

The more complex the negotiation and the more critical the implementation, the more likely that your negotiation will take some time, and that you will need to consult repeatedly with your stakeholders between negotiating sessions with your counterpart.

It's not always easy to get the right people engaged in deal discussions in the right way, and to do so not only on your side, but on the other team as well. How you ask does make a difference. The decision roles framework outlined above, for example, can seem very bureaucratic and complicated if you focus on all the details when you first describe it. If you are indelicate in how you proceed, it might be seen as a power grab or invasion of others' turf, and elicit hostile or defensive reactions. Your putting it forward might seem autocratic and presumptuous if your message appears to impose limitations on people and assign them roles. But it doesn't have to be any of those things. Consider the following simple e-mail and how it describes a framework and its purposes.

Dear Colleagues:

I, like many of you, have experienced some difficult negotiations involving many different parts of the organization, where your choices were either to participate in every conference and every meeting, or fear that your point of view would be ignored. But few of us can make a commitment to be at every meeting, and frankly, if we all did that, it would be a recipe for gridlock. Also, we cannot expect that when we are not there decisions are on hold, and that nothing can be agreed to until everyone signs off. That's a recipe for not being taken very seriously by our negotiating partners.

Please let me know what would be wrong with agreeing that:

1. Joe, Sally, and I will help clarify issues and frame decisions that need to be made, and we will be at the table with our counterparts.

2. *On matters of finance, we will consult Steve and Mary, but Sarah will have a veto right over anything that changes the net present value of the deal more than 5 percent.*

3. *On matters related to marketing, we will consult Steve and Rosemary, but Gary will have final word.*

4. *On matters of production schedules, we will consult Jean, but Juan Carlos and Jerry will have the final say, and we won't proceed without both of them on board. We will also make sure you are all informed before the schedule is published, so you can be prepared to discuss it with your teams.*

5. *Drafts and meeting minutes will be placed on the shared drive so you can all access them as you like, but to keep e-mail clutter to a minimum, they will not circulated regularly.*

   I am happy to chat with any of you over the next three days if you have any questions or suggestions for improving this process. Please let me know by COB Friday your concerns about proceeding in this fashion. If I do not hear from you in this time frame, I will understand that to be a "thumbs up" from you.

Applying a simple framework like this one need not take a lot of time or overhead. In some cases it can be established through a simple exchange of e-mails. The payoff, in terms of time saved later and quality of the deals achieved, is hard to beat.

Consult early and often

It is not enough to think ahead of time about who your critical stakeholders are and to set expectations for their roles. You then have to actually do it. And do it again. And again.

If you have done your homework and set some expectations about when, how, and why you will be communicating with these stakeholders during the negotiation, then actually doing so can be fairly efficient. Picture the PharmCo negotiator Phoebe's call to Phil, the PharmCo lab director.

Phoebe: Hi Phil, I just wanted to check in. As you know, we're having highly confidential exploratory conversations with BiTech about their new compound, and I wanted to get your thoughts on a couple of things. Do you have a few minutes?

Phil: Well, yes, and I have some very strong views about that. I am not sure that we should be buying someone else's compound at all. We have some promising things in our pipeline—

Phoebe: I'm sure that's true, Phil. And as you know, Frank, the head of the division, green-lighted the negotiations, so the question is really what kind of a deal would or would not make sense, rather than whether we should be considering doing it at all. Let me test some things with you though. What kind of lead time do you think you would need to staff up a codevelopment effort with BiTech if the decision were made to go ahead?

Phil: Well, that's going to depend on how far along they are. From what I have heard, they have only made lab-scale batches. We'll need to move to the pilot plant to make enough bulk drug to support the animal safety and early Phase I clinical studies. I need lots more information on the status of their synthesis.

This will be a back-and-forth conversation between Phoebe and Phil that will help them figure out what each of them needs to know to determine how to get ready for a smooth implementation. But by consulting Phil on critical implementation factors, and giving him some notice of what may be required of him, Phoebe does not have to give Phil veto power over the deal. This is a "consultation" based on Phil's expertise and his role managing critical implementation resources. It is not an invitation to decide whether or not to do the deal.

If they are to be successful not only in signing the deal, but in making it work, it is likely that Phoebe and Phil will need to have several more such conversations, which will in turn enable Phoebe to negotiate more confidently and more effectively.

Help your counterparts make sure their stakeholders are on board

The alignment of participants on the other side may be as much your concern as theirs. This advice is startling to some negotiators. Unlike the traditional assumption that disarray in the "opposing" camp will inevitably accrue to your benefit, in deals with a point, you have an interest in the other party's ability to deliver what their negotiator is promising. If your counterparts fail to line up their stakeholders, then the likelihood that you will *both* fail in implementation increases dramatically.

Trying to help them get the alignment they need to negotiate a deal with a point may take some delicacy. If their assumptions are more traditional, they may not like the idea of having to involve a lot of individuals, and they may like even less that you have suggested it. They may wonder whether it means that you don't trust them, or don't think them competent enough to rein in their side.

There are no magic bullets when it comes to raising the topic with your counterpart, but the following are a few things that have proven useful.

Ask about their enablers and essentials as well as their blockers

Most negotiators already make a habit of trying to find out who will have the ultimate say in whether a deal goes through or not. But you would be well served to add to your repertoire a set of questions about other key stakeholders. If nothing else, such questions will help your counterpart think about it and be better prepared.

Ask about the time and place for some joint meetings among key implementers

This can be a delicate question, but if framed as simply being about when and how such meetings should take place, it will feel less confrontational. It should be noncontroversial that *at some point* the implementers will have to meet. By raising the question relatively early, and as a process question, you help your counterpart begin to think beyond closing the deal to the kinds of things that need to happen early to lay the groundwork for effective collaboration later.

Describe your own consultation process

Volunteer some information about how you view the different stakeholders on your side who are important to the deal *and* to its implementation, and about how you intend to engage them during the process. This will go a long way toward letting your counterpart see that you are willing to share with them the same kind of information that you are asking for, and that you consider it important enough to have given it some thought.

Consider a joint effort to build the necessary alignment

Not every deal needs a concerted effort to communicate with stakeholders on both sides. But when the deal requires it, there is tremendous power in having both negotiators reach out together to each other's stakeholders to describe the deal, its context, and what it requires from the stakeholder.

Once you and your counterpart know which stakeholders will be involved in what ways, it is important to focus on what kind of precedents you need to ensure you will work well together during implementation.

5

Make History

How do you set the right precedent for implementation?

By the time most negotiators wrap up a complicated deal, they tend to feel they know everything they need to about the players on the other side and what it's like to deal with them.

- Are they trustworthy, or do you need to double-check every word of every document they send you? Do they do what they say, or do you have to worry that they will come up with some excuse and fail to honor their commitments?

- Are they creative and good at problem solving, or do you expect that every little problem will require lots of formalistic posturing and threatening before they back down and do the reasonable thing? Do they escalate to get issues resolved or try to settle them at the lowest reasonable level in the organization?

- Do they share information, or is getting input more like pulling teeth? How do you make sure you know what you need to know to make implementation work?

We could go on, but you get the idea. You learn a lot about your counterparts during the negotiation that affects what you think about them as you head past the signing and into implementation.

Of course, they also learn something about you.

If implementation matters, the time to begin figuring how you are going to work together is not the day after the deal is signed. By then it is simply too late.

"Oh wait," you may say. "Those things are not really true about us. What happened before, that was just how we negotiated the deal. Now we get to work together to do something positive."

Sadly, much as you may want it to, real life hardly ever works that way. First impressions are very hard to change. Much as you might hope that "what happens in the negotiation stays in the negotiation," the reality is that those things spill over into implementation. As soon as a challenge arises during implementation, large or small, the parties are likely to recall their negotiation experience and act accordingly. To make sure that the behaviors they default to are ones likely to help, rather than hinder, implementation, negotiators need to recognize the role they play in creating history, both good and bad.

Let's return to one of the examples we introduced in chapter 1, the dispute over the chip assemblies that Sue's company supplies to Bill's firm for use in making sophisticated manufacturing equipment. Bill and Sue have approached their negotiation as if the only purpose were to reach agreement over who is to blame for the bad parts. In doing so, they both prepared arguments about what the other one did wrong; they asked their lawyers to come up with arguments about what the contract meant. During the negotiation they each tried to shift responsibility away from themselves and intimidate the other into accepting blame. They may have reached a compromise to split the costs, but in doing so, they have likely left each other feeling somewhat abused. The lesson each has learned is that they had better protect themselves in the future from what the other might try to do to them. On the advice of their lawyers, as part of their deal, they have put in place procedures to avoid this problem in the future.

Let's listen in to what happens three months later (see "Dialogue Between Bill and Sue").

DIALOGUE BETWEEN BILL AND SUE

What **Bill** is **thinking** but not saying	**Their actual dialogue**	What **Sue** is **thinking** but not saying
I'm concerned we haven't heard anything for two weeks. Time is ticking away.	**Bill:** Sue, can you update me on the schedule for the new assemblies?	*I hate this new process, but it's what we agreed to when we settled the last problem.*
How can they be waiting!? These assemblies are critical to our launch timetable.	**Sue:** We're waiting on your guys to sign off on the latest revision to the specs. **Bill:** But we told you to go ahead two weeks ago!	
Oh, for heaven's sake!	**Sue:** We still don't have written confirmation about those changes or a new version of our acceptance protocol.	*No, no, no. The clock doesn't start running until we get the sign-off. You're not sticking me with the consequences of your lack of discipline again.*
I can't believe she's gotten all "by the book" on us. We were so reasonable sharing in the cost of their mess last time—we took $3 million of the $5 million liability.	**Bill:** Sue, we need to get these assemblies. Our product launch depends on them. **Sue:** We can't be held responsible for due dates for components that are not even fully defined.	*You taught us an expensive lesson last time. We have to protect ourselves against your changing things constantly.*
How can they be so rigid when we were so flexible with them?	**Bill:** But we have signed orders from our customers—these tools cost $25 million each, and we have six of them on order. We need to ship by year-end to hit our targets!	*I learned my lesson last time—we can't go out on a limb to help you out, because you will turn around and blame us if anything goes wrong. If you lose $150 million in sales, it's simply not my problem. I'm not going to risk another $2 million hit to my bottom line.*
Having a single source supplier is a total disaster. We need to get one of Sue's competitors in here so we get some leverage!	**Sue:** As soon as you follow the new protocol, we can get going.	

If Bill and Sue had thought that the first negotiation was going to set a precedent for how they would deal with each other in the future, they undoubtedly would have approached the negotiation differently. They would have recognized that they would both be better off if they could collaborate more, rather than less, closely in the design and engineering of new parts. Moreover, they would have seen that the purpose of their negotiation was not just to reach an agreement about who would pay how much, but to change how they work together in order to minimize the chances this problem would repeat itself. How do they reduce the likelihood of these problems in the future? How do they identify them earlier in the process, so that they cause less damage? That would require a very different approach to the negotiation: if achieving Bill and Sue's main purpose (to reduce costly mistakes) requires increasing the flow of timely information, they need this negotiation to create the appropriate conditions for that information flow.

How do you anticipate the history you need?

It may sound odd to be encouraged to "create your own history." Most of us assume that history is immutable, save for the occasional science fiction story where you get to go back in time and change things (and then you invariably set off some wholly unpredictable chain of events). Yet it is only true that history is unchangeable once it has already happened. Today, we cannot change what we did yesterday. But because today will inevitably become tomorrow's yesterday, there is often a lot we can do to affect how the negotiation will be remembered—to create the history we want.

The way we negotiate any deal will inevitably have consequences on how it will, or will not, be implemented. Everyone can recognize that *how* we get to "yes" has a significant impact on how happy we are with the outcome, how enthusiastic we are about going forward, how we manage the continuing relationship with the counterpart, and our appetite for doing more with them in the future. The precedents we set during negotiation about how forthcoming we are, how well we listen, whether we can be empathetic, the respect we accord each other, how we work out disagreements, whether we give each other the benefit of the doubt—all are likely to affect how we work together as we move into implementation.

It is easier than you might expect to "create history." In fact, you can hardly help doing so. The trick is to understand what kind of history will be most helpful during implementation, and what kind of history you may come to regret. If during implementation of a deal you have experienced problems with counterparts who withhold information or seek to twist your arm when they have the upper hand, or who seem unable or unwilling to apply any creativity when things don't turn out exactly as expected, then you know exactly what we are talking about.

Let the point of the deal define the precedents you need

One useful place to start anticipating the kind of history you might wish to create is to think about the purposes of the deal. What are you trying to accomplish, ultimately, and what kinds of precedent are likely to help if you get stuck? Different negotiation purposes are likely to produce different implementation challenges, and therefore require different kinds of precedent. For example, when the purpose of a negotiation is to resolve a conflict or settle a dispute, it is likely that the parties will distrust one another. It is also likely that unless the parties have figured out how to work well together, the agreement itself may give rise to new disputes. If, however, they have created a useful set of precedents during the negotiation, they may be able to look back on that shared history and see both sides treating commitments carefully, making them only after appropriate consideration, and then keeping them. Moreover, if they have treated each other with respect during the negotiation, they may have created a foundation for dealing with each other respectfully as new problems arise.

When the purpose of the negotiation is purchasing, exchanging, or otherwise creating value, during implementation the parties often have to deal with changes in circumstances or assumptions that turn out to be incorrect. Under those circumstances, the parties who have created useful precedents for sharing information and applying creativity to problem solving are more likely to do well than those who lack such a history. A corollary is that when circumstances change, bargaining leverage can also change. Those parties who have a history of not relying solely on leverage or coercion, but of looking to objective standards and of using persuasion in their relationships, may be better able to benefit from such a precedent when the shoe is on the other foot. Those who exploit whatever leverage they had for however fleeting a moment they had it may regret it when bargaining power shifts.

Finally, there are those negotiations whose purpose is to create arrangements for working together. As those deals move into implementation, and more people become involved, the challenge is usually one of preserving the "spirit" of the arrangement—in other words, to collaborate as if both sides really want to work together and not just because a contract says they have to. It can be very difficult to capture the fruits of an arrangement to collaborate unless the individuals involved feel respected and motivated, and unless there is an adequate flow of information. In our experience, these collaborations are more likely to succeed when the parties have made sure that during the negotiation they set constructive precedents for how they treat one another and how they share information.

In table 5-1 we show some basic categories and leading questions that may help you create useful precedents. This is by no means a complete list; you should certainly tinker with it, adding your own items or modifying those here as appropriate.

This list includes the kinds of things we have often found you wish were working for you, instead of against you, when problems come up. If you have ever negotiated a deal that required working closely during implementation, then you are probably familiar with moments when you encounter a problem and wish you could say, "Remember when during the negotiation . . ." and get a morale boost that sends you toward some resolution. Unfortunately, more often than not, looking back on the negotiation is not so helpful.

If you didn't have to worry about how you use leverage or creativity or information sharing during the negotiation, and you could just pick the kind of history you would like to have going into implementation, the answers are pretty obvious. You would rather have a precedent for not trying to take advantage of each other, for sharing information, for giving and getting the benefit of the doubt, and for solving problems

TABLE 5-1

Precedents and related questions to consider during negotiations

Type of precedent	Question
Use of power/leverage	How much do the parties rely on (often temporary) advantages in bargaining power to get their way, as opposed to looking for objective criteria, standards, industry practice, and benchmarks?
Information sharing	How open are the parties in sharing what kinds of information?
Commitments	Do the parties make commitments carefully, and do they take them seriously?
Creativity	Do the parties look for solutions that help both of them achieve their objectives, even if it requires breaking new ground?
Respect/dealing with differences	Do the parties treat each other courteously even when they disagree, and do they behave in a way that appropriately recognizes differences in perceptions or culture?
Benefit of the doubt	Do the parties leap to the worst assumption about what might explain the other's behavior, or do they give each other the benefit of the doubt and ask questions before jumping to conclusions?

creatively. You would rather have a reputation for sticking to your commitments and for being easy to work with.

But some deal makers would argue that it's not so simple. They believe that you need to be tough and aggressive in the negotiation, which includes using whatever leverage you can obtain (and temporary advantage is just fine, so long as it gets you what you want at the time). They think that interim commitments during the negotiation are just ways of getting the other side to go along with something, rather than being truly binding agreements. They find that while creativity is nice, it's better coming from the other side, while they stick to their guns and insist on what they want.

So, to have the best of both worlds, many organizations conclude that they should have one team to negotiate the deal, and a different one to implement it. That way they can put in an aggressive deal team who will push every way they can for the best possible terms, and then appoint an implementation team to clean up the relationship mess caused by the negotiators. Unfortunately, the assumption that you can savage your counterparts in the negotiations, but expect them to be splendid partners during implementation, is foolish and arrogant in the extreme.

This approach is quite prevalent in many corporations using procurement professionals to negotiate with suppliers. Many sourcing and procurement teams squeeze suppliers hard on price (which is not surprising given that many such teams are evaluated based on savings). Though they are often successful at getting better prices initially, they frequently find that they don't get the value they expected. Their "total cost of ownership" (what it costs not just to buy something, but to use it) does not actually decrease nearly as much as the apparent price reduction once suppliers start finding ways to grab back some margin (by offering less robust warranties, charging separately for service and maintenance, charging huge fees for "change orders," unbundling some items that had formerly been thrown in "for free," and the like).

Even more devastating to the buyer is experiencing a shortage of the commodity for which the supplier got squeezed. It should not be a big surprise if the supplier first fulfills orders for the buyer's competitors (who weren't as aggressive during procurement), and fulfills orders for the buyer only if there is enough of the commodity left. Buyers who beat up suppliers when there is excess supply in a competitive market should not expect anything other than reciprocal treatment when demand outstrips supply.

It rarely matters that it was procurement that bullied the seller and a different part of the business that needs the cooperation later. Most people assume that when procurement or other deal makers take a tough and aggressive stance it is not some random event: they believe that those negotiators are behaving as expected, as part of a deliberate strategy by the other side to gain as much advantage in the negotiation as possible. It seems perfectly justified to them, then, to return the favor when the tables are turned, even if they are dealing with different individuals.

Instead of assuming that negotiation is a process separate and distinct from implementation, it is more useful to conceptualize the two as different stages in a continuum of contacts between the parties. (That continuum might even be a circle, or a Möbius strip looping back on itself for future negotiations, instead of a straight line. See figure 5-1.)

FIGURE 5-1

The negotiation–implementation continuum

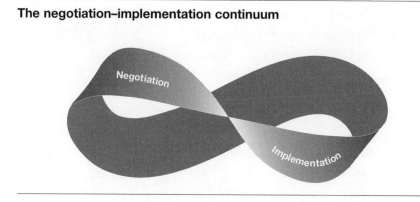

We find that the most successful negotiators treat all interactions with their counterparts as possible precedents for how they will work together during implementation. In effect, implementation often starts during, not after, the negotiation, and certainly during implementation there are many additional negotiations.

Align your team on the precedents you want to create

Whether you are talking about the tough deal makers who create problems for the "kindler, gentler" implementers, or just a single, difficult member of a negotiating team who undermines efforts to set the right tone, a lack of alignment and coordination can kill even the best-meaning effort to create a constructive history. Unfortunately, even one "bad apple" can create a history. But in most organizations, when a negotiator takes an aggressive stance and does things that leave a bad taste in everyone's mouth, that person hasn't acted out of spite or evil intent. Lots of negotiators genuinely believe that those tactics are necessary to achieve the best results possible in the real world. Under pressure to produce results, they will do what they believe will pay off.

To improve your team's alignment on key issues, let's take another look at table 5-1, introduced earlier. Which of these precedents—benefit of the doubt, respect, creativity, commitments, information sharing, and leverage—require (or might benefit from) a different stance during the negotiation in order to get a good deal? Are there any where a tough and aggressive negotiating team would likely get better results than a team focused on building precedents designed to smooth implementation? Are there any where you can reasonably expect the other side will forget how they were treated by a tough and aggressive negotiator when they get to implementation?

Benefit of the doubt

Let's start from the bottom of the list, benefit of the doubt. There is no particular negotiation advantage in leaping to assumptions about what your counterpart has done and making unfounded accusations about their intent. It's possible there may be a very limited set of circumstances where an unsophisticated and insecure team might be bullied into making concessions because the other side was furious at them for something they did not do. But this can hardly be the norm. In most cases, you would expect your counterpart to bristle at being accused of acting in bad faith if they had not done so and thereafter to become much tougher with you for not giving them the courtesy of asking before accusing. If, for some reason, you do not want to give them the benefit of the doubt during negotiations, it is unlikely they will soon forget about it as you move into implementation.

Respect

Now let's move up to respect, which is slightly more nuanced. Being respectful does not detract from your ability to be firm about ensuring your interests are met or about applying appropriate benchmarks or market standards. You can disagree without being disagreeable. Being respectful in the relationship does not mean you concede any substantive points at all. We have heard some negotiators worry that by being seen as respectful and mild-mannered, they might sacrifice the leverage they could gain by threatening to walk away from the deal. And yes, you ought to avoid moves that seem so deferential as to undercut the message that your alternatives are real, viable, and attractive. However, preserving a viable walk-away alternative is a far cry from being deliberately disrespectful to the counterpart during negotiation. Just because you might choose to walk out the metaphorical door does not mean you have an interest in slamming the door behind you. Behaviors that are disrespectful tend to give rise to strong emotions in the other party, and they are likely to linger long after the negotiation team has been swapped for the implementation team.

Creativity

When considering creativity, another important kind of precedent, some negotiators feel that they can extract some value by being absolutely rigid and unwilling to invent new possibilities during the negotiation. While we understand that perspective, and certainly see value in taking strong, principled stands on some issues, we see no particular advantage to fielding a tough and aggressive negotiation team that will refuse to be open to inventing even better options than the position it came in with. Being creative about possible solutions does not mean you have to accept a less desirable one. Rigidity for the sake of firmness is cutting off your nose to spite your face. Keeping an open mind about what you *might* agree to, while being fairly careful about what you *commit* to, is a powerful combination. On the other hand, if in your attempt to win some advantage at the table you are closed-minded, there is little reason to assume that the implementation team can credibly change its stripes or successfully erase the impressions created by negotiators.

Commitments

There might be a perceived advantage during the negotiation to making commitments and then not keeping them. Some negotiators believe they can gain more concessions from their counterparts if they appear to give something away and then take it back, claiming they misunderstood or lacked authority and were overruled. Some organizations believe that those tactics work to their benefit, so they send in a negotiation team to use them, and then remove the "tough guys" from the picture so the implementation team can start to rebuild trust on its own.

Experience shows that both premises are badly flawed. Deliberately making commitments you can't keep typically doesn't get you anything that can't just as easily be taken back by the other side. If you won't live up to your commitments, you have limited ability to insist that your counterparts live up to theirs. You do, however, create an impression that your organization is sloppy or just plain untrustworthy, which, like it or not, will tar your implementation team with the same brush, even if those individuals were not part of the negotiation. You are far better off making commitments carefully, recognizing that you are creating a shared history about the reliability of those commitments.

Information sharing

Information sharing is a somewhat more subtle type of precedent. There are differences in the level and nature of information sharing that we would recommend during negotiation and during implementation. During the negotiation, it is likely you'll want to withhold some limited kinds of information from your counterpart. Some such withholding of information is tactically or strategically advantageous and perfectly legitimate. For example, there is usually very little reason to answer questions like "What is the most you are willing to pay?" or "What is the least you will take?" Under most circumstances, the person asking won't really believe your answer. And if she did, she would be encouraging you to be misleading. It's just a silly topic for discussion, and you should label it as such. Full and complete disclosure is simply an unrealistic expectation.

Other questions may concern the urgency of your need for the deal or the viability of your walk-away alternative. Whether asked directly or indirectly, you might reasonably prefer not to answer such questions. Doing so might render you vulnerable. Talking about what you'll do if you don't sign a deal may occasionally be necessary, particularly when your counterparts underestimate your walk-away alternative and may not realize they are about to blow the deal. But generally, when you're talking about such things you are not talking about how to work together—the issue then is not so much what kind of precedent sharing the information sets as whether it is a useful topic for the negotiation.

On the other hand, more productive discussions—for example, about your interests with regard to a particular issue, about ideas you might have (without committing to them) for solving a particular problem, or about relevant comparables that might help you zero in on reasonable valuations—all seem like fair game. As you think about what kind of precedent you want to create for how you share such information, fast forward to implementation and consider what kind of information flow will be required for success. The more closely aligned the negotiators are with postdeal expectations, the better they will be able to create the kind of history that will come in handy later.

Use of power or leverage

A wholly unsubtle aspect of precedent setting concerns the use of power or leverage. There are certainly situations where one side has, and can effectively use, significant leverage in the negotiation. This tends to occur most frequently when one side needs the deal more urgently than the other, or one side faces time pressure and the other does not. We have seen some negotiators who are quite skilled at understanding such power imbalances and at doing their best to create or exaggerate them. There is nothing inappropriate, in and of itself, in letting the other side know that you have a pretty good set of alternatives, and that if they want a deal, they need to propose something better than those alternatives. Just remember that when implementation matters, there is at least the possibility, if not the likelihood, that the balance of power may shift over time. If the precedent you set holds that "whoever has the club wields it," you may not much like that model when that club is coming back at you.

While there are no guarantees that precedent, good or bad, is going to reassert itself during the implementation phase, it is safer to assume that "what goes around, comes around" rather than the opposite. The more you can create positive, useful precedents during the negotiation and preserve some continuity in the relationships between the individuals involved, the more likely you will be able to benefit from them. Experience suggests that while you cannot bank on positive precedents getting you out of difficulty later in the relationship, you can almost certainly count on negative ones getting you into it.

Keep in mind that even one bad apple on the negotiation team can sabotage your attempts to create the kind of history you want. For whatever reason, human beings tend to focus more on negative behaviors or events and remember them more distinctly. Positive actions are often harder to notice because to some extent they are "expected," whereas negative ones always strike us as more unfair and unwarranted. By way of example, consider how many of us take for granted the many wonderful things our significant others do, and spend a disproportionate amount of time griping (or arguing) about some smallish issue that annoys us. We know it's not a balanced view, but we do it anyway.

Your chances of creating the kind of history you want are much greater if you do so deliberately and if your team is aligned around the importance of setting useful precedents. When a negotiation team recognizes that doing a deal is not worth much if you can't implement it, and shares a picture about how the team's behavior during the negotiation can make it easier (or harder) to implement the deal, participants will be much more in control of their collective fate.

Consider the assumptions and behaviors in table 5-2. There is a real difference between the assumptions that deal makers bring to the negotiation and those shared by negotiators focused on implementation. Those assumptions translate directly into behaviors at the negotiation table. While you cannot script a negotiation, we find that when team members are aligned around some critical assumptions, they are more likely to behave accordingly, even when they have to improvise.

Of course, this table does not cover every assumption that might drive the behavior of a particular negotiator, and you cannot account for every eventuality. As with many things, the specifics are somewhat less important than the core principle: are you creating a helpful history or not?

To determine whether the negotiation process is setting the right kind of precedent for an implementable deal, ask yourself some commonsense questions:

- "If the process we are using now is the same process we use to resolve differences we may have during implementation, will I be unhappy with that result?"

- "If I am pushing hard now, using the leverage I have before we close the deal, might that leverage shift to my detriment after the deal is done?"

TABLE 5-2

Deal-maker assumptions versus implementation-minded assumptions

Negotiation tactics	DEAL MAKER		IMPLEMENTATION-MINDED	
	Assumptions	Behaviors	Assumptions	Behaviors
Creativity	"It's not my job to solve their problems."	• Sit back • Wait for their proposals and poke holes in them	"How I help resolve negotiation issues today may set the stage for how we will deal with implementation issues tomorrow. I'd want their goodwill and creativity then, so I'd better put some forward now."	• Explicitly suspend evaluation and criticism during brainstorming • Suggest possible solutions that are good for both of us, rather than just the ones that are best for me
Information sharing	"It's not my role to equip them with relevant information or to correct their misperceptions."	• Withhold information • Fail to correct misimpressions	"I don't want them entering this deal feeling duped. I want their goodwill during implementation, not their grudging compliance."	• Create a joint fact-gathering group • Commission third-party research and analysis • Question everyone's assumptions openly
Grabbing value wherever and whenever you can	"Get while the getting is good. Keeping them from making a bad deal is their job, not mine."	• Ask for it all; start "high" • Use their need to force concessions	"If we take advantage now, just because we can, they are likely to try to return the favor if they ever get the chance."	• Ask yourself: "How would I feel if the situation were reversed? How would it impact our attitude toward implementation?" • Name the precedent: "This feels like a tough issue; I wonder if we can solve it by looking beyond what each of us is willing to do to what makes the most sense for our ultimate goals during implementation?"

Source: Reprinted by permission of *Harvard Business Review*. From "Getting Past Yes," by Danny Ertel, November 2004. Copyright 2004 by the Harvard Business School Publishing Corporation; all rights reserved.

- "If I were in their shoes, would what we are doing now create a desire for revenge or payback later on?"

- "If the way we are interacting now is exactly the same as the way we interact the week after we sign the deal, will I be concerned about getting the benefit of the deal?"

If the answer to any of the foregoing questions is "yes," then you ought to think about how you might change how you are negotiating, so that it can serve as a useful precedent for working together toward implementation.

How do you get others to see your view of history?

Wars have been fought because two sides had a very different view of history. In our work with Israeli and Palestinian negotiators, the narratives we hear from each side have few points of overlap. Human beings are very good at selectively recalling what happened in the past. Those of you familiar with Akira Kurosawa's film *Rashomon*, where the same events are recounted by four different characters in very different ways, know that the way a story is told depends entirely on who is telling it and from what point of view they experienced it.

You may want to follow much of the advice we've been giving just for its own sake. For example, sharing information about your interests or being creative in how you solve problems is good for you, good for the deal, and good for implementation, whether it creates precedent or not. However, if you want some aspect of how you negotiated a deal to become the default way of approaching problems during implementation, simply relying on having behaved that way once isn't enough. You need to make it clear that you acted in a certain way, and that it was a *deliberate* choice and a *model* for how you hope both sides will behave in the future.

If you haven't established precedents explicitly, your history still might be able to bail you out of a problem during implementation. You might turn to your counterpart and say, for example, "Remember when we put this deal together and we shared with you a lot of information we didn't have to?" or "Let's try something that helped us do this deal in the first place; let's do some joint root cause analysis before we start making demands of each other."

But you would be on safer ground if during the negotiation you had shot off fireworks and put up a big neon sign over the information sharing or the joint problem solving when it happened, rather than long after the fact. The reality is that while you might be very conscious of your own feelings, perceptions, and intentions during a negotiation, they are likely opaque, if not downright invisible, to your counterpart. People filter all kinds of information and apply their own interpretations to it. We make attributions all the time, often negative ones, about why someone is doing what they are doing, especially if the context feels even a little adversarial. It's all too easy for others to miss some of your brilliant moves, or even if they notice them, they may think you made them inadvertently rather than deliberately. So a little spotlight on precedent-setting moves can be helpful.

If during the negotiation you say something like, "I think it's important that we start by getting some key information out on the table, and that we take some time to figure out what we each need to know in order to make a good decision," you have at least called attention to the fact that you are proposing to go a little beyond the usual guarded, cards-close-to-the-vest approach seen in many negotiations. If you follow through by actually defining the information that is needed and establishing a collaborative process for gathering and exchanging it, you have a better chance of being able to refer back to that event later on.

Next time you find yourself trying to resolve a dispute, especially if you are the aggrieved party, consider naming the kind of approach you *don't* want to take: "Let's not jump right into a blaming game; there's plenty of time for that later. How about we start by first trying to understand the underlying causes of the problem and the ways that different things we did or didn't do may have contributed to the current situation? They might provide us with some good clues about how to remedy it." Whether it works or not to help you come up with a good answer, you have at least called out that you and your counterpart have choices you can make about *how* you work together. Doing so during

the negotiation may help you later, when you might be in a more difficult position with regard to some problem.

As we've said before, there are no silver bullets. Negotiating deals
that work well during implementation is hard work. Similarly, there are
no guarantees that if you try to create a positive history and set constructive precedents during the negotiation, others will follow your
lead when problems surface during implementation. They may not
have found the precedent persuasive or applicable to the new problem.
The actors may have changed and the new ones may not care about
who did what back then. They may just not be capable of being constructive under the current circumstances.

But one thing we and our partners have learned over the course of
working with literally thousands of negotiators over twenty-five years:
while there is no guarantee that your counterparts will follow a positive
and constructive precedent, you can be fairly certain that they will
embrace and react to a bad one every chance they get. It is a bet worth
making.

Air Your Nightmares

How do you discuss risk without risking the deal?

Every negotiator, in every deal that requires implementation, at some point wonders what might go wrong.

It is certainly possible to be too concerned about risk, even paralyzed with fear. On the other hand, it is also possible to be reckless and overly cavalier. The difference between the two extremes is sometimes just a matter of opinion, or perhaps depends on how you assess the risk of doing nothing at all. We have no way of knowing how risk-averse you may be, or should be, given what you negotiate. We won't urge you to take more or less risk than you consider appropriate.

What we do know is that most negotiators don't have the risk conversation with their counterparts often enough, and when they do, they don't do it well enough. Some of that reluctance to engage in discussion seems driven by organizational issues, like corporate metrics or compensation systems that reward getting deals done, rather than walking away when the implementation risks seem too high. We'll talk a bit about those in chapter 10. In other cases, the reluctance is more personal, tied to an individual's discomfort with difficult conversations.

Are there risks to avoiding risk discussions?

From what we have seen, there are a couple of different philosophies about raising concerns during a negotiation. One is reasonably characterized as "if you don't have something nice to say, don't say anything at all." Negotiators who fall into this camp usually worry that raising concerns will be taken badly by their counterparts—as an accusation that they are not capable or not acting in good faith. The result is that they suppress legitimate fears, and in doing so, lose an opportunity to discuss them collaboratively in the negotiation. Sometimes those fears are so significant that they end up killing the deal without even being voiced, as when one side concludes that the other likely won't be able to deliver and walks away.

The other prevailing attitude encourages negotiators to provide for every possible contingency in the contract, requiring redundant capabilities, insurance bonds, and/or steep penalties if something goes wrong. Interestingly, we sometimes see the first attitude morph into the second: the parties are unwilling or unable to discuss their fears in a constructive way, so they leave it to their lawyers to create a "bullet-proof contract" that will protect them if any of their unstated fears come about.

As you can probably tell from our characterization of these two approaches, we think they get negotiators in trouble, and unnecessarily so. When the parties fail to discuss a concern that one of them has, or when they deal with it through contractual penalty provisions, they buy themselves a fairly adversarial and contentious climate in which to work.

Put yourself at the negotiating table: as you sit across from your counterparts, you worry that they might not be able to deliver, or that some external event is going to come along and keep you both from achieving your goals. But you don't hear them worrying about anything, so you get frustrated. You want to figure out what to do about the problem, but you don't want to raise it because it might offend them or lead to a difficult conversation. But not raising the issue doesn't make your concern go away. If anything, it just makes you increasingly unhappy and feeling somewhat powerless. So you continue to worry, and continue avoiding the issue—sound like a vicious cycle you have been caught in at times?

When you try to protect yourself with appropriate contractual provisions, you end up doing so from the premise that if something goes wrong, your counterparts have to make it up to you. Of course, they are not particularly pleased with the demand, or with the implicit accusation that they may fail to live up to their commitments. And they don't want to carry all the risk of what might go wrong. So they tend to minimize your concerns, defend themselves, and limit their exposure. Maybe they even do get offended by proposed contract terms that feel one-sided.

Of course, their resistance to your request for such contingencies in the contract or their reaction to the proposed language only serves to confirm both of your fears: that the negotiation was going to become adversarial, and that you were right to push for these protections in the first place. The result is a new set of barriers to working together as you go forward—some suspicion or distrust, by one or both of you, about the other's abilities, good faith, or willingness to work collaboratively when trouble does strike.

This painful cycle is avoidable, and the best evidence of that is to consider how you would approach it if this were *not* a negotiation where you're trying to convince the other side of something. If this were just a private conversation among your closest and most trusted friends, about something that concerned all of you equally, how would you go about discussing potential risks?

To start, you would be clear that talking about a risk does not make it more likely, so you would not worry that by "focusing on the negative" you might lead the group to fail.

Next, you would be relatively confident that talking about a risk would not offend your friends—they would not think you were raising it as a tactic. Whether they agreed with you about the risk or not, they would assume you were just being careful and trying to anticipate what might go wrong so you could all do something about it. Indeed, they would take it as a sign that you were trying to help and actually being a good friend by raising the issue.

Finally, you would find that by raising the issue and getting your friends to help you think about what might go wrong, you were better prepared to prevent the possible problems, or to mitigate their impact if they proved unavoidable.

So, how do you have that kind of a conversation in the middle of a negotiation, with a counterpart who may or may not give you the benefit of the doubt when you raise it? Sadly, we cannot eliminate all the risks involved in such conversations, but we can make a few suggestions that will help.

How do you decide which risks to raise?

The result of a negotiation ideally ought to be one where neither side has significant *unarticulated* concerns about the possible risks and challenges in implementation, and where both sides have a clear sense of how the major risks will be managed. The simple answer to the question of when you should air a potential nightmare is to do so when the potential benefit is greater than the likely cost.

The benefits are generally quite straightforward. Identifying and discussing risks and challenges in advance can enable the parties to develop early warning systems, contingency plans, and support mechanisms for coping with various concerns, or possibly have a useful conversation about risk allocation (so there is a clear understanding of who takes a hit if things go badly). At the very least, each side can make a more informed judgment about the likelihood of success and the consequences of failure before saying yes to the deal. Nightmares based on changes in the market, in the economy, in national security, in the physical environment, and the like seem quite sensible to contemplate as part of a negotiation where implementation matters. When Manny and Jerr talk about having Jerr's team help on Manny's project, it would be a mistake to skip over a conversation about how they would handle a further delay of Manny's project or a sudden crisis on Jerr's team.

On the other hand, to many negotiators, discussing concerns about your own or the other side's ability to perform sounds quite risky. More than risky. Possibly suicidal. Indeed, it's your acute awareness of those costs that keeps you from raising them in the first place.

Raising concerns about *your* organization's ability to follow through might raise red flags for your counterparts, create doubts they didn't yet have, and unduly alarm them about remote contingencies that are unlikely to happen. Or scare them away entirely. Why tell them that you might do something "wrong" when you have no intention of failing to live up to your responsibilities? In particular, why give them something that might turn up as evidence against you in litigation years from now, when you are sued for breach of contract after your worst nightmare comes to pass?

Raising concerns about *their* ability to follow through might annoy your potential partners, lead them to think you are untrusting, cause them, in retaliation, to push harder on *your* capacity to perform, or drive them to walk away because you showed them how difficult their tasks really might be. Why tell them you fear they might fail to implement effectively when they seem to be honorable people who have every intention of performing their part of the bargain?

The balance, therefore, is very dependent on the context of your deal and the nature of the risk. Figure 6-1 summarizes some of the costs and benefits of airing potential nightmares. If those are the main risks and benefits of talking about risk during the negotiation, then it's easy to come up with a relatively simple equation for when to raise a particular nightmare and when not to. It basically comes down to applying some well-proven risk management thinking to the risk of talking about risk.

Start with the magnitude of the potential problem: how bad would it be if it happened? Then discount it by the likelihood that it might occur. In other words, if you can quantify the risk, multiply the potential damage by the probability of its happening. If you don't do anything—if you don't raise the issue with your counterpart—that's the "expected value" of your nightmares.

Expected value = Probability of risk × Magnitude of risk

If the expected value of the risk is fairly small, you may conclude that the cost of raising the risk isn't worth the possible minor benefit. This will be the case for many things that you might imagine could go

FIGURE 6-1

Costs and benefits of raising potential nightmares

Benefits of raising nightmares during negotiation	Risks of talking about risks
• The other side might persuade you that there is no problem, and you won't lose sleep worrying needlessly.	• You might offend your counterparts.
• You might jointly find a plan to mitigate the risk or ease the challenge, so that effective implementation is much more likely.	• You might point them to a potential problem they had not thought about, which might keep them from doing the deal.
• You might change your deal to explicitly address risk allocation issues; then if your nightmare does come to pass, at least each side knows what happens next and who bears the consequences.	• You might give away some bargaining power (for example, if the risk you talk about is your own ability to deliver, or if your concern implies some weakness in your walk-away alternative).
• You might decide to walk away from a deal that was a disaster waiting to happen.	• You might end up with a more complicated deal with lots of penalty provisions (and a larger legal bill for creating the more complex contract).

wrong, but are really unlikely to happen, or for problems whose cost would be fairly trivial. In the case of our friends at PharmCo and BiTech, for example, such risks might include a meteor striking the physical plant at BiTech, a strike by the food service staff, or an accounting scandal involving the CEO.

If the risk still feels material and worrisome, however, you need to look at two different ways you might try to deal with the risk: unilaterally, or jointly with your counterpart. In other words, how much better will you and your counterpart together be able to manage the risk if you raise it than if you do not? If you are relatively well positioned on your own to prevent the problem from happening or to deal with the consequences if it were to occur, you might not get enough benefit from raising the issue. If your counterpart cannot really add much to what you can do to prevent or manage the problem, there is no reason to incur the risk of raising it. Suppose PharmCo is worried about a regulatory problem with the new compound. If PharmCo believes that it has a lot more experience dealing with the FDA, and the BiTech staff can't really help, then PharmCo may conclude that this is also a risk not worth raising.

If you have gotten past both of these filters and are still considering whether to raise a problem that feels material and probably can be better managed by working with your counterpart, then the question becomes how best to raise the topic.

How do you minimize the risk of talking about risk?

In our experience, most negotiators are overly risk averse about raising doubts or concerns. In other words, even when they recognize that the other side could help them prevent or minimize a problem, they fear that the benefit of that potential collaboration is outweighed by the danger of broaching the issue. While we cannot say that negotiators who believe that are universally wrong, we can say that a little care in how you raise these issues goes a long way to mitigate the risk of doing so. If you can reduce the risk of raising the issue, you can tip the scales so that such a discussion becomes worthwhile.

Make joint risk management a natural part of the conversation

One way to "de-risk" the conversation about risk is to treat it as an ordinary, yet necessary, part of the negotiation. Don't spring it on your counterparts as a big, scary problem or as a direct consequence of something they said. (Them: "We're going to have Jean run implementation." [pause] You: "Oh, let's talk about risks and nightmares.") Do put risks on the agenda early as something that you will eventually need to talk about. Manny might say to Jerr: "I really appreciate your willingness to see if you can help us out. Maybe it would be useful if at some point we talked through some of the risks, like our project dragging on too long or your team suddenly getting crunched with other work? If we understood how likely something like that was to happen, or what we might do about it, we might both feel better about taking on some level of risk."

Precisely where and when you should talk about risk and nightmares depends on the nature of the deal you are working on. But if you will be working together in some way after the deal is signed, then there are always things that might go wrong—things you can likely antici-pate, and thus manage better. What would be wrong with putting the issue on the agenda that way, as something that you will need to talk about before you consider the deal "done"?

Putting risk on the agenda doesn't mean you have to get into a detailed exploration of all the risks before you have even figured out the deal's basic contours or whether it makes sense. But you may want to make sure that everyone expects you to discuss risk at some point, so that when you do, no one feels blindsided or fears that you are raising the topic because you suddenly found some reason to worry or to dis-trust them.

Another useful way to "de-risk" the risk conversation is to lead with some ground rules for the conversation. For example, we have seen some negotiators do a very nice job of breaking down the risk man-agement part of the agenda into component parts, to make it clear that the topic is really not that different from other things they have dis-cussed. Each part of the agenda in turn applies some familiar ground rules as well as additional ones intended to make the risk conversation feel safer. Figure 6-2 shows an example of an agenda for a "nightmares" conversation. Of course, this particular agenda will not fit all negotia-tions and all circumstances. Consider it only as illustrative of how you might organize this part of your "nightmares" discussion.

Be a little humble about risk management

The risk management or "nightmares" part of the negotiation is a dif-ficult one for most people. Other parts of the negotiation, where you are focused on how you are going to create something valuable, resolve some dispute, or develop plans for working together are all about look-ing forward, typically with some air of optimism. Risk management starts and ends with things going wrong.

It is easier to talk about what might go well, and how you each can contribute to it, than the opposite. A tone and manner of speaking that comes across as confident and assertive when talking about the positive can sound threatening and accusatory when focused on the negative. Taking the lead in exploring interests and developing options during deal discussions may feel welcome and highly collaborative, whereas

FIGURE 6-2

Sample agenda for a "nightmares" conversation

1. Brainstorm possible risks we might face during implementation.
   Purpose: To explore things that might go wrong, so we can jointly figure out how to manage the risks
   Products: A set of risk categories we should manage (e.g., market, resources, regulatory, natural disasters) and possible risks in each category

   Ground rules:
   • Brainstorming only.
   • No evaluation or criticism of ideas.
   • No attribution to individuals—not "Joe's nightmare" but rather "the possible problem with X."
   • "Don't worry about it" is not an answer.

2. Prioritize risks to be managed.
   Purpose: To help us focus and prioritize our joint risk-management efforts
   Products: Shared view of the probability and magnitude of the risks we may face during implementation and of those we will seek to manage proactively

   Ground rules:
   • Ask questions for clarification before stating a contrary view.
   • Share your reasoning and any data behind it.
   • Differences in perception about risks are OK—we are looking for risk management plans, not absolute truths.

3. Develop risk management plans.
   Purpose: To develop plans for preventing some of the nightmares we have discussed, and/or for mitigating their impact should they occur
   Products: Specific action plans for further work to be done to better understand the risks and to refine plans for prevention and mitigation

   Ground rules:
   • No commitments to plans today; there is still more cost/benefit analysis to do.
   • Drive to specific possible actions: Who could do what, and when? What do we need to know to better understand the risk, its likelihood, or how to mitigate it?
   • Commitments around process are OK: Who will do what research, collect what views, share what information with the group, by when?
   • Ensure that any specific action steps have an owner and a time frame and are written down before we leave the room.

similar behaviors when talking about what might go wrong could feel manipulative or pushy.

There are, of course, entire books written just on the topic of how to prepare for and engage in a difficult conversation, and we won't try to reproduce that information here.[1] We do think, however, that you dramatically ease and improve this very important part of the negotiation if you keep a few things in mind. The first can be a real tough one, but in some ways that's what makes it all the more important and all the more powerful: be a little humble.

If you jump into the risk management conversation as if you are certain about everything and know what must be done, you are likely to do more damage than good. An effective risk management conversation is an exploration about what *might* go wrong, and what you *could* do, by working together, to prevent it, or to mitigate its impact. But neither side *knows* whether any of these nightmares will occur; each of you is likely to have fairly different views about what might make a problem more or less likely and which of those things can be influenced.

If Bill is worried that Sue's QA team may not get the job done, instead of just accusing them of incompetence or not caring, he might ask some questions: "We're all trying to avoid repeating what happened here, and we've talked about some new time lines and new procedures for documenting the specs. How will we know we have done enough, but not so much that we get bogged down? What could we do that would give you more confidence about what goes into QA? About what comes out of it?"

Be a little curious about how your counterparts are thinking about the situation. Don't assume that you know better and that your job is to persuade them to see it your way. We are talking about uncertainties, after all, and your approach to the conversation should reflect that. Your job *is* to get the issue on the table so that you both can examine it and figure out what additional information you both need to make a good decision. Your job is also to make sure that you don't just bury your head in the sand and hope the problem never happens. And finally, your job is to make sure that by talking about this, you are both better off and better able to work together when something unexpected happens.

With those as your central assumptions about your role in the "nightmares" conversation, try to build the following techniques into your repertoire.

Separate intent from impact

You know what you meant. But others at the table may not. All they know is how it came across and what impact it had on them. You, on the other hand, can't be certain of what impact your words or actions had, despite how you meant them.

The reverse is also true. While you know how they offended or hurt you, their actual intentions are invisible to you. When you raise these issues, be careful to speak about their possible impacts without attributing ill intent. Try to be clear about your own intent without being dismissive of how they may have interpreted it. Consider the different ways of talking about difficult issues contrasted in figure 6-3.

Help your counterparts understand your thinking

You may have quickly figured out what something means or where it is leading or what the consequences might be. But if you share only your conclusion, others may not understand how you got there. If you then argue about whether the conclusion is valid or not, you will never know whether the disagreement is because you are looking at different facts, have different prior experiences that lead you to interpret facts differently, or are simply thinking about the problem differently.[2]

Explaining how you each think and what assumptions you are each making will not only lead to more effective implementation plans, but will also let you get to know each other better, which will help you deal with those things you didn't anticipate.

When discussing things that might go wrong, it can be very helpful to describe how you got there—your thought process—especially if this helps others understand that your concerns weren't triggered by something they said or something about them that you distrust. For

FIGURE 6-3

Different ways to talk about nightmares

Overly certain about uncertain things	A little humble
"When we get down the road a bit and a supply shortage puts you in the driver's seat . . ."	"I'm not sure how things will play out, but we would be badly impacted if we could not rely on you for a steady supply, even if there is a shortage in the market."
"Don't take this the wrong way, but I know that after you've spent our money it's going to to be a lot harder to get your attention."	"We've never worked together before, so please don't hear this as a prediction of how you will act. I have seen other situations where regular access and communication gets harder after the initial disbursement of funds."
"How dare you accuse me of trying to take advantage, after all the concessions I've made and all the good faith I've shown you throughout the whole process."	"I'm not sure how you meant that. I should let you know that it made me feel distrusted despite all the good work we've done together so far. Help me understand what message you intended to convey to me."

example, you might point to some data, a prior event, or some example in the market that got you thinking. Next describe how you connected those dots into a picture—how you interpreted the possible implications for your deal. Finally, lay out your conclusion about the risk and why you think it's real and relevant. That is a very different approach from just jumping to the nightmare; it's easier for others to hear the story and your reasoning path instead of just sitting back, feeling accused, and thinking of how to defend themselves.

Express your concerns as hypotheses, to be tested jointly

When you are working together on an implementation plan and trying to decide how you would deal with potential problems, you don't need to convince anyone that the problem *will* happen. The point of having the conversation is for both sides to explore the issue and jointly assess how worrisome it is and how much effort to put into risk management.

If others disagree with you, don't fight back. Take the time to figure out what part of it they see differently and why. In the realm of risk management, there are at least three major reasons why people might think a risk is not worth doing anything about. They might not believe it's very likely. They might believe that even if it happened, it wouldn't have much of an impact. Or they might think that even if the risk is real, there are relatively painless ways of dealing with it later.

Any one of those might lead someone to say, "Don't worry about it" or "That's not a real problem." Aside from how dismissive those comments sound, they're also insufficient responses, because they don't tell you why the person thinks the risk doesn't need to be managed.

So ask.

Don't just get annoyed or insist that it does have to be addressed. Others may know something you don't about the probability, magnitude, or possible ways to mitigate the risk that might put your mind at ease. Or there may be something they don't understand about why the risk is more likely or more costly, or why the mitigation they had in mind doesn't solve some important aspect of the problem. Now *that's* a conversation worth having.

Acknowledge the difficulty of raising the topic

Recognize that putting some of these issues on the table may trigger strong emotions, for you or for the other side. Recognize that even mentioning problems may leave some people feeling unfairly scrutinized or attacked, and that their reaction may keep them from engaging in the discussion on a purely rational basis. Cut them, and yourself, some slack, and ask them to do the same for you as you undertake a difficult but valuable step in the negotiation.

Make it easier for others to raise their nightmares

Part of preparing for an effective risk management conversation is to recognize that you are not the only one with possible concerns. You, of course, are not responsible for other people's nightmares. It is not your job to uncover their misgivings, and indeed, doing so can be difficult and problematic. But it *is* your job to make it *easier* for them to air their concerns. So, how do you do that?

The first thing to remember (and to act on, which is harder than just remembering it) is not to take offense when your counterparts put something difficult or awkward on the table. Remember that it was probably difficult for them to do so, and they may not be particularly skilled at having this kind of conversation. Focus on the risk they are worried about, and not on how they raised it or what kind of assumptions or attributions they have made.

This is a part of the conversation when it can really help to be at least a little curious. It is likely that when they put a problem on the table, that little voice in your head will react by shouting, "How dare they" or "They must think we're evil!" If you allow that to go on for very long, you will likely miss some of what they are saying, as you go into hyperdefensive mode and start preparing all your arguments for why they are wrong to worry about *that*.

Instead, try to adopt a more curious stance. Direct that little voice in your head in a more useful direction. For example, "I wonder why they think that" is a great neutral way to enable you to listen to what's next. "What prior experiences have they had that leads them to worry about this?" and "What do they think would be the impact of that?" are also helpful questions. You need not actually say these things out loud. But if you can make yourself wonder what the answers are, you will listen in a different way than if you are just thinking up rebuttals.

Keep in mind that people tend to be pretty good at detecting fakery. If you just try to handle their concerns by offering some tired script like, "Oh, I feel your pain," they will recognize it and take offense. On the other hand, if you get truly curious about the risks that worry them, they will see it and appreciate that you really do want to examine and deal with their concerns.

The other useful thing to remember about making it easier for others to discuss their fears is to give them an opportunity to prepare for the risk conversation. If you just spring it on them, they may not be able to perform on the spot. This kind of conversation is not quite like brainstorming solutions, which sometimes thrives on spontaneity. Talking about risk management and worst-case scenarios is hard work, and it requires that both parties to a negotiation do some thinking in advance.

Consider the risks you are going to put on the table. You've had time to study them, evaluate how likely you think they are, how bad they could be, and how well you could address them on your own, and have concluded that it is worth raising them. Give others the same courtesy. Make sure they have an opportunity to think through what risks are worth talking about and which ones are not, as well as how to frame them as constructively as possible.

This suggests that the risk management conversation is one you want to broadcast in advance. Let your fellow negotiators know that at the next meeting, or at some future time, you want to talk through this issue. Share with them a draft agenda for the conversation. Give them an idea of how you are preparing for the conversation yourself. This shouldn't feel like you are dictating what they must do; you simply want to provide some transparency about what you are doing, so they can choose whether to follow your lead.

Having put risks on the table and made it easier for fellow negotiators to do so as well, you are likely moving toward closure. Ensuring that both sides are making realistic commitments is the subject of the next chapter.

Don't Let Them Overcommit

How do you help make sure your counterparts can deliver?

As a negotiator, your job is to get your counterparts to agree, isn't it? And getting them to agree isn't easy. That's why they pay you the big bucks.

You may be smiling right now because you are amused at the thought of "big bucks"—or maybe you have a somewhat different view of why you earn them. But "getting them to agree" is fundamental to the notion of what negotiators do, isn't it? Engineers design things. Doctors help us get healthy. Pilots fly airplanes. And negotiators reach agreements.

Yet when implementation matters, reaching agreement is only a necessary, but not sufficient, condition for a successful deal. Just having everyone at the table nodding does not mean that what you have agreed to is actually doable.

"Good negotiators are good closers," or so some people believe. We might believe it too, if "good closer" meant someone who closes deals *well*, as opposed to just closing lots of them. If there is a point to your deal, then you *and* your counterparts must be able to deliver. Simply getting them to agree to something, so you can later argue about why they failed, hardly seems worth the effort.

Closing quickly may get you more signed contracts. But what *they* don't know can hurt *you*. Even if you succeed in securing a really tight contract that locks them in to their commitments, if you do so before they know enough to be certain they can deliver, you may not have done yourself any favors. Strong sanctions in the contract may help *if* those sanctions can actually deter the other side from defaulting. But collecting on those sanctions when someone doesn't deliver is rarely the point of doing a deal.

Some of you may be wondering, but doesn't it depend? Aren't there some kinds of deals where it really *is* the other side's problem if they fail to deliver? The answer is that yes, in some cases that's probably true. Our claim is not that there are *no* conceivable situations where you might negotiate a deal and be wholly indifferent to whether the other side lives up to its end of the bargain or fails miserably trying. But most of the time, implementation teams want results, not disputes or the right to apply sanctions.

Overcommitment in different types of deals

Let's run this through the filter of the different kinds of deals that you may do and see if there are any significant differences. When the purpose is to resolve a conflict or settle a dispute, the parties tend to be fairly distrustful of one another and will often insist on some kind of verification of performance and some consequences if one side fails to deliver. They may even negotiate fairly draconian penalties. That said, if the purpose of the negotiation is to resolve the conflict, not just transform it into a different kind of dispute (over the penalties and whether or not they should be applied), then the parties generally want a deal that can work, rather than one that is likely to end up with one side failing to deliver.

When the deal is about buying, selling, or creating some kind of value, the parties certainly want the value they thought they were contracting for. Whether or not they have good liquidated damages provisions or an efficient arbitration clause, in most situations collecting on those provisions is not as attractive as actually getting the benefit of the original bargain, if only because of the cost and uncertainty of having to impose those consequences. There is no question that the defaulting party is unhappy about the penalty provisions. There is also no doubt that the injured party is better off having some kind of recourse—to penalties or some kind of insurance—than facing a situation without those provisions. But what we are saying here is that both parties would much prefer for the deal to work and for both sides to do what they committed to, rather than be forced to exercise these other rights.

Finally, when the point of the deal is to make arrangements for the parties to work together, if one side fails to live up to its commitments, it completely undermines the fundamental purpose of the deal. Not only do the two groups fail at something they both agreed to, but they make it that much harder for the parties to trust each other or work together in the future.

Stretch versus overcommitment

So, how do you know whether the other team is overcommitting and will fail to deliver? Boy, if we could answer that one, we could save a lot of people a lot of heartache. The reality is that you can't always tell. Tricksters and frauds aside, most negotiators working in good faith on commercial deals *intend* to live up to their commitments. Unless they are an extreme version of the "deal-minded cowboy" who just wants to sign the deal and move on and doesn't care what happens next, they probably don't deliberately make wholly unrealistic commitments.

In business today, lots of negotiators agree to things they feel may be a stretch, with every expectation that their implementation teams will rally and make them work. In the PharmCo–BiTech example, neither Phoebe nor Bjorn, the two deal makers, believe they are agreeing to things their organizations are incapable of doing. Phoebe may suspect that her lab director is pretty busy and that he may even get annoyed about a new project landing on his lap unexpectedly. But she doesn't expect that Phil is going to sabotage the project or refuse to assign people to it. She assumes that if Phil needs more budget or more staff, he'll just work something out internally. After all, PharmCo paid a lot of money for the new compound, and they'll want to do what it takes to develop it. Similarly, Bjorn doesn't believe that he's promoting snake oil. He and his organization really do have a lot of faith in the potential for the new drug, and he fully expects that their scientists will work hard to get it ready and make their milestones.

What we are concerned about is not that parties sometimes go out on a limb. "Stretch" targets encourage businesses to grow and reach new heights, and organizations often achieve more by "pushing the envelope." When working with your counterparts, you might want them to try hard, innovate, improve, and not just commit to what they can do with average effort. However, you also don't want them to over-commit and jeopardize the deal. Therein lies the dilemma for the implementation-minded negotiator. How do you walk the line between underambitious deals and unrealistic ones? Our advice is not to layer every deal process with expensive, slow, and cumbersome due diligence. In our experience, however, there are a couple of things you *should* do to make sure the deals you close are likely to achieve your ultimate purposes.

How do you keep the other side from overcommitting?

Getting the other party to overcommit in the negotiation doesn't serve your interests. After all, if they shouldn't have said yes, and can't come through on the deal, what have you actually accomplished? Let's look at what you should do about that.

Avoid extracting pointless overcommitments

The easiest part of the problem to fix is the one you have control over. With the exception of those negotiators who set out to misrepresent what they can do, most of the time, when a negotiator agrees to something he or she shouldn't have, it's because the other side did something to extract that commitment. Viewed this way, if you fail to achieve your purposes because you pressured the other party into commitments it could not keep, then your injuries are self-inflicted.

This advice, at the heart of it, is pretty simple. Remember that you are looking for the value of the deal, not just a big but empty commitment from the other side. Telling you, in effect, to "avoid making a mistake" may sound a bit thin as a piece of advice, especially since you probably were not intentionally making a mistake in the first place. Yet if it's rarely the intention to extract pointless commitments, then how does it happen so many negotiators behave as if it were? The problem may lie more in the mind-set that can lead someone to make such a mistake without realizing it. Perhaps our advice needs to be more nuanced and aimed at the assumptions behind some of those tactics.

Adopt an implementation mind-set

Why would anyone in his right mind try to extract commitments that won't be met? Generally, he wouldn't. What we find is that some negotiators are so focused on doing the deal—code for getting the other side to agree—that they don't pay enough attention to what will happen after the ink is dry and people have come to their senses. They employ more or less sophisticated versions of the car salesman's "this offer is good today only," but with self-destructive consequences—if the other side succumbs, there may not be any point to the deal. Take a look at table 7-1 for another version of the deal maker versus implementer mind-set chart we first encountered in chapter 5, this time focusing on some of the more egregious examples of extracting commitments.

If you can eliminate some of the behaviors listed under deal makers and replace them with those listed in the implementation-minded column, you are less likely to extract commitments that your counterparts simply cannot live up to (or will not, once they've had the opportunity to reflect a bit).

Recall our internal negotiation example between Manny and Jerr over whether Jerr might lend some help to Manny's team on a project that was behind schedule. Manny was very pleased with himself for trapping Jerr into a soft "I'll see what I can do" commitment. But what has he really accomplished if, upon reflection, Jerr decides he really cannot spare anyone, or not for long, or not anyone with the right set of skills? Well, you might argue that Manny now can blame Jerr for his troubles. But how helpful is that? If you were Manny's boss, how much slack would you cut him if he explained that the reason his team couldn't deliver a critical project was that a different team did not come through with additional resources? Manny would be better off with a truly

TABLE 7-1

Deal-maker assumptions versus implementation-minded assumptions

Negotiation tactics	DEAL MAKER		IMPLEMENTATION-MINDED	
	Assumptions	Behaviors	Assumptions	Behaviors
Surprise	"Surprising them helps me. They may commit to something they might not have otherwise, and we'll get a better deal."	• Introduce new actors or information at strategic points in the negotiation • Raise new issues at the end	"Surprising them puts us at risk. They may commit to something they cannot deliver or will regret."	• Propose agendas in advance so both can prepare • Suggest questions to be discussed and provide relevant data • Raise issues early
Closing techniques	"It's not my role to equip them with relevant information or to correct their misperceptions. It is in my interest to press for a close as quickly as possible."	• Create artificial deadlines • Threaten escalation • Make "this day only" offers	"My job is to create value by crafting a workable agreement. Investing a little extra time in making sure both sides are aligned is well worth the effort."	• Define interests that need to be met for the deal to be successful • Name it: Be explicit about the difference between closing the deal and being well-positioned to implement
Realistic commitments	"As long as they commit, that's all that matters. After that, it's their problem if they don't deliver."	• Focus on documenting commitments rather than on testing the practicality of those commitments • Rely on penalty clauses for protection	"If they fail to deliver, we don't get the value we expect. 'Will this really work?' is a legitimate question to ask."	• Ask tough questions about both parties' abilities to deliver • Make implementability a shared concern • Establish early warning systems and contingency plans

workable deal and a realistic commitment from Jerr (or someone else who really could help).

An effective negotiation should produce commitments that each side has carefully considered. Deals that are hastily made, without forethought and without sufficient alignment of internal stakeholders, are often prone to breach or breakdown during implementation. For many negotiators, it may seem counterintuitive that they actually have an interest in helping the other party think through the deal and its ramifications. In the heat of the negotiation, while trying to secure a deal with the best terms possible, they may prefer to let the other side make its own mistakes, and commit to things without weighing them carefully.

In *The Power of a Positive No: How to Say No and Still Get to Yes,* Bill Ury has many wonderful insights into why negotiators often get to a "yes" and commit to something when they ought to say no.[1] In his introduction, Ury refers to the "Three-A Trap" many of us fall into when we try to balance maintaining the relationship and exercising our power—we cycle between accommodating, attacking, and avoiding. Most relevant for us here are Bill's explanations of why we *accommodate,* saying yes when we want to say no (stressing the relationship even if it means sacrificing our key interests), and why we *avoid,* failing to say no (even when we strongly disagree). Whether we are getting an active or a passive "yes," it behooves us to ensure that our counterpart is truly committed.

In 2006, Accenture established a Negotiations Center of Excellence. The center is co-led by two senior executives at Accenture, Paul Cramer and William D. Perry. Part of the center's mission is to ensure that Accenture reaches deals that are implemented well by clarifying expectations before parties enter into a deal and making clear both sides' obligations and commitments. Cramer told us: "We ask people to be realistic and careful about the commitments they are making. We want to continue to deliver value for our clients by ensuring both parties are unified in their expectations, their commitments, and their obligations to make the relationship the success both parties envision. The setting of these expectations starts at the outset of the sales relationship, but requires reconfirmation throughout the negotiation process." Cramer went on to say: "For engagements to be successful, neither side should overpromise on what they can deliver. That is not a fair and responsible way to establish a trustworthy relationshop."[2]

Many lawyers believe that the best way to make sure that *yes* truly means "yes" and to incent performance of a contract is to build in strong sanctions. Thus, they focus on default provisions, liquidated damages, specific performance requirements, favorable choice of law provisions, and the like. Coming from that background ourselves, we believe that there is an important role for sanctions in many well-crafted contracts. But we have learned through experience that it is a mistake to rely on powerful sanctions for nonperformance as the primary driver of good performance. If your objective is successful implementation, a far better driver is having counterparts who understand what they have committed to and the implications for follow-through, who have gotten alignment of all stakeholders in their organization who need to have a role in implementation, and who still feel that they are getting good value from the deal.

There may be times when you don't want the other side to have the opportunity for sober reflection lest they realize how advantageous the deal is for you—and foolish for them. However, most such deals are simple purchase transactions where the seller has an interest in getting the buyer's money before the buyer realizes he paid too much, or cannot afford the item, or does not need the item, or discovers the item does not work as promised. And in many cases there are consumer protection or other laws designed specifically to protect buyers from ill-advised impulse purchases of this sort.

Take the 80/20 hindsight challenge

Create a plan that enables the parties to move to implementation. A negotiator who keeps this simple prescription in mind will think about not just what she is agreeing to do, but who, when, and how it will get done. The plan ought to offer a real road map for the (potentially tortuous) path to achieving the parties' ultimate purposes and for dealing with the likely twists and turns along the way.

In any deal where there are significant implementation tasks and the parties have to work together to achieve the purpose of the deal, ensuring conscientious closing, as opposed to a race to finish, is likely to meet both sides' interests. Take the "80/20 hindsight" challenge: ask yourself (and your counterpart) to imagine you have fast forwarded into implementation and to identify the 20 percent of decisions and commitments you now wish you had clarified further—the ones that will make you both 80 percent more confident that the deal delivers the value you are counting on.

It's easier than you think, and you have more access to the information you need than you might expect. First of all, simply asking the question gets you much more focused on the issue of implementability. Second, unless this is the first time you, or anyone in your organization, or anyone you know has ever done this type of deal, then you have access to experience that should tell you what kinds of issues and decisions tend to be badly underspecified in these deals. Make it a priority to benefit from the experience that is out there for the taking, and apply it to your deal. The resulting commitments you both make are more likely to be realistic.

Genpact, the business and technology services provider, makes a point of tapping into its knowledge of what kinds of commitments are realistic and bringing that to bear in negotiations. It starts with how Genpact develops its negotiators, making a point of moving people back and forth between operational and sales roles during their career. This allows negotiators to understand in a very practical way what it is like to try to live up to unrealistic commitments. Genpact also assigns operations staff to negotiation teams early in the process, helping make sure that commitments made in the negotiation are achievable and that the operations team understands the point of the deal and can start implementing right away.[3]

It's not necessarily your role during the negotiation to specify every detail of how implementation will work. We are not suggesting that you need to map out a detailed project plan with Gantt charts and timetables. That may well be a more appropriate task for the implementation teams as they get started. But it helps tremendously to talk through the key items that require some additional thought and discussion to make sure you and your counterpart have the same understanding. It helps to clarify who will be involved in making those key items work, and to make sure that you have indeed identified and engaged the key stakeholders critical to successful implementation.

If this advice feels a bit too simple, that's a good thing, because it should mean that you will have no trouble following it. Reflect for a moment on some of your recent negotiations, where implementation really did matter. What would have been wrong with adding to the negotiation agenda a specific item for developing an initial implementation plan? How would you and your counterpart have behaved differently if you had dedicated some time and attention to that question *as a part of the negotiation* rather than after the deal was done? What would you have changed about your deal?

If the answer is nothing would have changed, it probably means that you were already fairly careful and implementation-minded throughout the negotiation. Good for you.

If the answer is that you would have changed a few of the things you agreed to, then taking the "80/20 hindsight" challenge would have helped you and your counterpart reality-test your commitments and make them more implementation-ready. Would that have been worth the effort? The answer will vary from deal to deal, but the more things you wish you had done differently, the more worthwhile the exercise.

If the answer is that you wouldn't have done the deal at all, then we would argue that the 80/20 hindsight challenge was crucial, and omitting it was a really bad decision. Sure, you can probably think of some examples where with hindsight you would not have done the deal, but you are still glad you gave it a shot. "Better to have loved and lost," as they say, "than never to have loved at all." While that may often be true in the world of romance, and even occasionally in the world of complex commercial deals, we stand by our claim that deals that fall apart when tested against what it will take to implement them generally shouldn't be done. There's no point.

Engage with all the enablers and essentials

Finally, as one last mechanism to prevent others from overcommitting, make sure they have engaged with their stakeholders who will be directly involved in implementation. Beyond getting the other negotiator's assurances that enablers and essentials have been included in the process, it might be prudent to find a way to meet with them yourself (or, perhaps more appropriate, have the enablers and essentials on your side engage with their counterparts).

The purpose of finding a way to connect with these people is not to second-guess whether your negotiation counterpart has done an effective job at getting alignment. Rather, it is to see whether the implementers have the same degree of enthusiasm for the deal as the negotiator. It is not unusual for the negotiator to have a high degree of psychological investment in the deal and passion for getting to closure. The deal, after all, is his or her baby. If the enablers and essentials you meet are skeptical or negative about the deal, or voice concerns about how well it will work out, that may be a sign that the negotiator overcommitted them. Just because others have concerns or lack enthusiasm, you can't conclude that there necessarily is a problem of overcommitment. But there could be, and it might be worth checking out before the deal is done.

Having done everything you can to make sure commitments are realistic and the deal can be implemented, you are finally done and ready to rest, right? Not if you want the next stage of the deal to start off on the right foot. In chapter 8 we discuss how negotiators can help smooth the transition to implementation.

Run Past the Finish Line

How do you stay focused on the real goal?

If the point of the deal is not just to sign a contract, then it stands to reason that the negotiation isn't done when you reach agreement. Even a well-planned agreement that has involved all the right people and created the right kind of precedent will fall short of its ultimate purpose if the negotiators put down their pencils when they have concluded the deal.

Competitive runners say that in order to do your best, you have to look beyond the finish line, to propel yourself beyond it at your peak speed. If you think of yourself as being done when you cross the line, you will actually start decelerating prematurely so you can come to a stop. But to achieve your best time you don't want to slow down until you are well *past* the finish line.

Don't let up

The race is only a metaphor, and we are reluctant to stretch it too far, but we do think it offers some useful lessons for negotiators. The first is that if you let up before reaching agreement and lose your focus on those things that matter—the point of the deal—you are more likely to find yourself in trouble come implementation. Too many mistakes are made in the final moments of a negotiation because the parties have the end in sight and become somewhat distracted by it. As they get closer to being "done," negotiators find it increasingly tempting to defer details to be worked out later (during implementation).

While it would be unfair to say that there are never issues that can safely be deferred, in our experience the irresistible pull of closing the deal leads negotiators to *over*estimate how "done" they actually are, and to *under*estimate the risks they are imposing on implementation by leaving some issues unresolved. The natural tendency of deal makers to want to close one deal and move on to the next is often further reinforced by artificial deadlines imposed by bosses, the ending of fiscal years, and so on. Though important, these generally have very little to do with what will make implementation a success.

Let's recall the example of Bill and Sue, who were trying to resolve a dispute over the damage caused by the installation of faulty components, made by Sue's company, in equipment that Bill's company shipped to its customers. If they let up once they agree on how much of the $5 million in damages each of them will bear, they may fail to put as much energy into more important issues, like how to avoid this problem in the future. Many details of their new way of working together will get left to be resolved later, and they will miss an opportunity to create lasting value.

Pay attention to momentum and handoffs

The second lesson to be drawn from the race metaphor is that deals have a kind of momentum. If you fail to capitalize on the energy, creativity, and goodwill that propelled you to reach an agreement, you risk dissipating that momentum and having to start implementation from a standstill. That is what happens when negotiators sign the deal and move on, leaving a new team to start the transition and implementation work without a thorough understanding of the issues. They don't know why some matters were resolved the way they were or even what details were left for them to work out. Lacking a solid working relationship to help them sort it all out, the implementation teams are unlikely to do as good a job as the original negotiators would have.

This loss of momentum often dooms deals before implementation even starts. Instead of enjoying a "honeymoon" phase, implementers end up stumbling over misunderstandings and misinterpretations. The more uncertainty there is about what the deal makers meant or why they structured the deal a certain way, the more that others who were not part of the negotiation feel free to reach their own conclusions. When there is not a good mechanism to communicate the spirit and intent of the deal to the implementers, you end up with literally dozens if not hundreds of individuals who believe *they* should be interpreting the contract and acting as contract managers, which is a recipe for trouble.

A negotiation can be fast and sweet like a short sprint, or it can be lengthy and exhausting like a marathon. Regardless of which situation you find yourself in, if the negotiators target the finish line and fail to look beyond it, they stop short of the real goal, and they leave the implementers starting off on the wrong foot. Perhaps a better metaphor for the kind of negotiation where the value lies in actually implementing the deal might be a relay race. The job of the negotiator is not only to develop a good deal. It is also to hand it off effectively to the next member of the broader team that will solve a problem or produce value. If the negotiator fails to set up an effective handoff or, worse, if he drops the baton (see figure 8-1 for some examples of how such failed handoffs

FIGURE 8-1

Typical ways that negotiation handoffs are fumbled

- Negotiators fail to make clear to implementers the ultimate purpose(s) of the deal.

- Negotiators fail to share lessons learned about working and solving problems with the other side.

- Negotiators fail to tell the implementers about informal (i.e., unwritten) commitments they made during the negotiation (especially those made toward the end, when the parties were fatigued and trying to wrap up).

- Negotiators tell their respective sides different versions of what is in the deal and why.

- Negotiators fail to brief their implementers on implicit understandings and why some matters were resolved the way they were; then implementers do things inconsistent with the spirit of the deal.

- Negotiators rush off to the next deal, leaving the implementation team feeling abandoned and unsure of where to start.

occur), then what was the point of having run a fast first leg of the race? Not much.

How do you move from "yes" to implementation?

A deal is not really done when it is signed. Whether you personally will be accountable for implementation or not, if you have negotiated the deal you have a responsibility to make sure implementation gets started appropriately. If the purpose of a deal goes beyond the "yes," then the negotiator's job is not over until there has been an effective transition from those who crafted the deal to those who will implement it.

Make transition a part of the negotiator's role

There is simply no substitute for looking past the signing of the deal and considering what happens next to be an integral part of getting the deal done.

There are certainly many ways to handle transitions, and we are confident that the same kind of creativity and smarts that got you through the deal will help you plan for and execute an effective transition. How you take care of your transition obligations is, to some extent, less important than recognizing that you do have that responsibility. This is a significant change in mind-set for many negotiators.

Briefing the implementation team cannot be something a negotiator does only if he or she has time to spare or no other deal to pursue. Complex deals usually take longer to negotiate than anticipated, and the negotiators indeed have obligations to turn to other projects. But if they fail to help the implementation team hit the ground running, they have not really done their job. If they fail to articulate the trade-offs that were made, the things they set aside for lack of time, or the implicit understandings between parties, they will doom the implementation to one problem after another.

Consider a joint handoff meeting

An evolving best practice that we have seen at the most forward-thinking of organizations is not only to require that negotiators give the implementers a thorough contract briefing, but also to insist that such a briefing be conducted jointly by both negotiating teams, for both implementation teams. Where we have seen it done—and we're sorry to say it occurs somewhat sporadically at best—we have seen some wonderful consequences for the implementers and for the negotiation itself. The first benefit is that the two implementation teams get to hear, "straight from the horse's mouth," what the deal is intended to accomplish and why it was done the way it was. They get to ask questions about what things mean, how they are supposed to work, and what the negotiators' expectations were, and both teams get to hear the answers.

Doing this well takes some preparation. The last thing you want to happen during such a briefing is for the negotiators to give different answers to a question or deliver different messages about how things are supposed to work. That would be disconcerting, to say the least. That risk alone sometimes scares people off, and despite the best of intentions, they fail to hold the joint handoff. But pause for a moment before you flee. Other than causing the negotiators some temporary discomfort, what would it mean if the two sides gave different answers?

If what it means is that they have different perspectives about how the deal they just negotiated is supposed to work, then when would you want to realize that difference: at the handoff meeting, or several weeks or months into implementation? (If the negotiators get to ride off into the sunset, never to be bothered by the deal again, *they* might prefer that such gaps were realized later. But seriously, if your deal has a point and you care about how it's going to work, when would *you* want to realize the other side has a different understanding of what was agreed to?)

Painful as it might be, after all that work, to realize that there are some things you didn't fully resolve, it is generally far less damaging to the deal and to its ultimate goals to recognize that sooner rather than later. When you learn of it later, it usually comes with a lot of recriminations and ill feeling, expressed in sentiments like "they are not living up to their commitments" or "they are not trustworthy." It is also much harder to figure out later what you misunderstood or failed to resolve, because people's recollections are affected by the passage of time and by the need to defend their own interpretations of the agreement.

It is never fun to find that you have more work to do. But the joint handoff is a bit like a quality-assurance process for a negotiation. If there are problems, you want to catch them before the product leaves the factory and creates bigger and more expensive problems. It's like a fire drill: if the exits are blocked or if people may have trouble navigating a dark stairwell, you want to know that before there is an actual fire.

The joint handoff is more than just quality assurance. Its purpose is not to find where the negotiators disagreed. The principal benefit of the joint briefing is giving both sets of implementers a shared picture of the underlying purposes of the deal, what they should be doing together to achieve those goals, and why the negotiators structured the deal as they did.

The primary kind of discrepancies you want to head off are differences in how each side might *interpret* what the negotiators meant, simply because they weren't there and didn't have the benefit of the full discussion. The final agreement represents a set of conclusions the negotiators reached, but rarely does it articulate their reasoning or provide a rich understanding of the logic behind deal terms. In the realm of legislation, a legislative history provides additional information about lawmakers' intent and help in interpreting ambiguous provisions. Negotiators might usefully give implementers similar, if less formal, clues about how to proceed after the deal is done.

The other important benefit of a joint contract briefing is that the very fact that you plan to have a joint meeting at the end impacts the negotiator's behavior from the start. Imagine if, as lead negotiator, instead of just moving on to the next deal or (at best) pausing to brief your team on "what I got for you," you know you'll have to explain the deal to both sides, with your counterpart present to add his or her own perspective. If that were the case, then during the negotiation itself you might begin to think about and discuss the rationales for terms and why (or whether) they are appropriate.

"Those terms might be OK," you might say, "but how are we going to explain how we got to them?" A negotiation that proceeds on the basis that both negotiators will have to be able to articulate the rationales behind the deal to both sides' implementers is more likely to be defensible. It's also more likely to gain the kind of buy-in from the implementers that will be necessary if the original "yes" proves not to be enough. A negotiation that is supported by objective criteria, industry standards, best practices, or accepted precedents is more likely to be accepted by those who did not have the opportunity to participate in the negotiation. Implementers will also have those standards in mind as they move ahead and will be better able to make the next set of decisions or trade-offs in a manner consistent with how the deal was created.

How might Bill and Sue have benefited from a joint briefing or handoff? For starters, in explaining the deal to their respective implementation teams, they might have realized that a deal that only settled who had to pay how much of the $5 million didn't actually tell anyone how to avoid repeating the problem. As they described the new, somewhat cumbersome process for submitting and validating requests, they might have heard individuals in manufacturing or QA question whether that process would get in the way of sharing information and working more closely. Had they known in advance that they were going to have to explain the deal to others, they might also have worked harder to find a way to split the costs that felt legitimate, and thereby reduced ill will on both sides.

How do you maintain momentum to carry you through change?

When you negotiate a deal whose timetable for implementation is measured in months or years, it is a pretty fair bet that something will be different before you are done. Deals that do not account for changes or for discrepancies between expectations and reality are deals that at the least get slowed, and at worst are completely derailed when they move from theory into practice. Negotiators who want their deals to pay off must recognize that challenge and consider contingencies that are reasonably foreseeable.

One of the biggest problems that implementation teams face as they try to pick up where the negotiators left off is finding that things in the field are not what they seemed like at the table. When they encounter changes or differences in expectations, they tend to lose momentum, and can lose faith in the deal itself.

Planning for change goes beyond traditional "right to cure" clauses, which usually give one side an opportunity to "fix" their performance before the other side has the right to terminate. In our experience, by the time parties trigger "right to cure" clauses, they are often just laying a paper trail for possible litigation. Rather than waiting for these events to occur during implementation and starting then to figure out rights and responsibilities, who bears what risks, and how to deal with the changes anyone could have predicted, deal with them before you get to implementation.

Even if there will likely be changes whose details are impossible to forecast with any accuracy, there may be a procedural way to deal with them. Lenders can't predict exactly what will happen with interest rates, but they design into mortgages or credit facilities variable interest rates based on certain standards, like the London Interbank Offered Rate (LIBOR) or T-bill rates. IT outsourcing service providers can't predict the unit price for computing or storage resources or the state of the art in desktop hardware five years from now, but they can put benchmarking mechanisms into long-term contracts. These so called "second order" agreements are useful when you know there will be changes, but can't forecast them accurately and will need to realign to the market some time in the future. While you can't determine the actual answer, you can agree on a fair process to give an answer when needed in the future.

Let's return to PharmCo and BiTech for a moment. They know that as their codevelopment deal evolves, they will learn new things about the science of the products they are developing. They will also learn more about the behavior of the patients who might eventually use their drug. The competitive landscape will change. The FDA's processes or even their standards for approving new drugs will change. It would be foolhardy in the extreme for their deal not to include a plan for periodically considering how they are doing against their original purpose, whether their deal still has a point, and what they might jointly do to improve their odds of success.

In *3-D Negotiation*, David Lax and Jim Sebenius lay out some very useful suggestions for building a "social contract" into your negotiations to supplement the economic contract. Their vision for a social contract goes well beyond a good working relationship. They advocate for a social contract that governs the parties' expectations about the nature, extent, and duration of the venture, about the process that will be followed, and about the way that unforeseen events will be handled.[1] They urge negotiators to think about what they can do to make a deal stick and to craft a deal that adapts well to changes, especially reasonably predictable ones.[2]

Planning for change so that, when it inevitably comes, it doesn't kill your momentum doesn't have to involve complex financial instruments or third-party services. It can be as simple as recognizing that part of your agreement has to include a way to keep the deal current. Regular planning meetings, as part of an agreed-to governance process, are critical for complex medium- to long-term agreements. Are there better or worse ways to organize those meetings, determine who should participate, and decide what topics they should cover? Sure. But agreements that include *some* such mechanisms and negotiators who dedicate some time and energy to discussing how governance should work, instead of leaving that to the implementers, produce better and more lasting results.

PART II

Negotiating and the Organization

9

Managing Negotiators

How do you steer them toward deals worth doing?

Do you know many people who say that their job is managing negotiators?

Executives and managers in organizations tend to manage all kinds of staff, but very few conceive of their job as managing negotiators. You would never dream of having sales reps sell without sales management, or buyers buy without sourcing and procurement management. Yet very few managers would say that they really manage the negotiators who report to them *or that they could even articulate what that would mean*, other than to give them a target and a minimum position and constrain their authority within those bounds. Therein lies a tale of serious mistakes, unending frustration, and missed opportunities.

In prior chapters we described the changes in an individual negotiator's assumptions, behaviors, and habits that are necessary to negotiate deals with a point. Now consider what support the individual negotiator has for meeting that goal. In most organizations, the answer is: virtually none. Sure, most organizations have clearly delineated signing limits, and negotiators usually know the bounds of their own authority. But that's a far cry from really being managed.

When you "manage" negotiators by just giving them a target and a minimum position, you limit their ability to be creative and, even worse, to be persuasive. You also send some very clear messages about what you as their manager consider important, which is usually all about closing the deal above the minimum position. Unless your message also provides some strong guidance about the importance of a deal that can be implemented and how to achieve one, don't be surprised when your negotiators miss the point.

Why don't managers steer negotiators in the right direction?

Negotiation remains the last unmanageable frontier in business. Why do negotiations persist as either untouchable or, at the other extreme, undelegable? Why do managers of negotiators tend to either cede control entirely to the negotiator or refuse to give the negotiator any autonomy at all? The answers come down to just a few interrelated causes.

Oversteering: micromanaging the negotiator

Part of the problem is the prevailing belief that negotiation is all about art and skill, about the application of experience to make great judgments "in the moment," and therefore cannot be managed. Based on that belief, some managers conclude that they must either hire great negotiators and just stay out of their way, or they must be very hands-on and tell their negotiators exactly what to do and how.

But if you leave negotiations wholly in the hands of individual "star" negotiators and their impeccable judgment, timing, and experience, you will inevitably end up with deals you don't want or that sound good but can never deliver on their promise. Left entirely to their own devices, negotiators—who are effectively your agents—will make choices that are not necessarily what's best for their principals (i.e., the company). An all-too-familiar example is the sales rep who immediately offers customers the maximum discounts to close more deals by the end of the quarter. Forget precedent. Forget the fact that you are training your customers to wait until the end of the quarter and squeeze you for every concession. Deals closed this way also rarely have an adequate plan for implementation or the support of all the key people who are needed for success.

At the other end of the spectrum are the negotiators who lack "diva" status. Their managers don't believe that the front-line negotiator is better than the manager, but rather the other way around—that the manager would do a better job. They just can't be everywhere at once. When managers believe that results turn on the skill of the negotiator, and that they themselves are more skilled, they therefore conclude that for the negotiations to be successful, *they* have to drive the strategy; *they* have to make the tough decisions; *they* have to call the shots. In effect, the managers become the negotiators, and the folks at the table are merely messengers who leverage the time of the real decision makers. But messengers are wholly unable to persuade anyone or to create anything. Consider your own reaction to the car salesmen who always have to run back to their managers. Even if you recognize this as a tactic to get you to commit while they don't, it shows you why a negotiator who is perceived as just a messenger is completely unpersuasive.

Understeering: lacking a clear process for managing negotiators

The challenge faced by managers reminds us of the old Sidney Harris cartoon in which a couple of scientists are looking at a set of equations on a blackboard, with a notation right in the middle saying "a miracle happens here." Lots of organizations that think of themselves as well structured and managed and very process driven still tend to draw flowcharts for a business process that include a single box or step called "negotiation." Everything that happens within this "black box" remains opaque, untrackable, unmeasurable, and consequently unmanageable. Even those managers who want to manage negotiators lack any useful way of doing so. To be effective, managers need a well-defined process or set of activities to follow. But most negotiators tend to think of the steps in a negotiation as something like this: Run some numbers. Go in and pitch (or go see what they have to say). Make and get some concessions. Threaten to walk away. Make and get some more concessions. Close the deal (or fail to do so). No wonder managers don't manage negotiators. There's nothing there for a manager to do, other than get in the way.

This issue is even more acutely felt when implementation matters. For managers to play an effective role, they need to be able to do more than say, "Please get a better result." To get deals that are worth doing, managers must be able to lay out a definition of success that incorporates the purpose of the deal—what should happen *after* the deal is signed. Very few managers have a clear process for doing this.

Backseat driving: negotiators resist being managed

When pushed to explain themselves, negotiators often retort, "You had to be there." But we don't accept that from anyone else, so why from negotiators? At least a part of the answer is that managers themselves lack confidence in their ability to manage negotiators, and thus shy away from it. Negotiators don't make it easy for them, either.

We treat negotiation as being all about the outcome, and managers don't want to be responsible for an outcome they can't control. To avoid that, some are completely hands off (which just confirms for the negotiator that the manager has no value to add, and he is right to resist). Most others tend to micromanage (which also reinforces the negotiator's resistance, because he loses all control and meaningful role in the negotiation). In each case, the manager's behavior produces more resistance from the negotiator, which in turns makes the manager's job even harder. Have a look at a typical dialogue and what the manager and negotiator are probably thinking as they go through this all-too-familiar dance (see "Dialogue Between Negotiator and Manager").

The checkered flag: incentives make the problem worse

Some organizations treat the problem of managing negotiators as a compensation problem. They try to figure out what they want the negotiator to accomplish, and then pay them for doing so. Often that leads to "incenting the close." This again reinforces that "getting the deal done" is what counts, because that is what is counted. In many organizations, paying a salesperson to close the deal before the end of the quarter or fiscal year will indeed create a flurry of activity at the end of the period, because salespeople do their best to "make their numbers" and pocket their bonuses. Unfortunately, in deals where implementation matters, negotiated outcomes are usually complex and require attention to multiple dimensions; treating the close as the bonus-worthy event rewards the wrong goal.

DIALOGUE BETWEEN NEGOTIATOR AND MANAGER

What the **manager** is thinking but not saying	**Their actual dialogue**	What the **negotiator** is thinking but not saying
I need to know what's going on, in case anyone asks.	**Manager:** How's that negotiation coming? **Negotiator:** OK. As you would expect.	*Oh, please. Don't make me spend a bunch of time rehearsing every move.*
C'mon, give me something.	**Manager:** So, you think you're going to close it soon? **Negotiator:** Oh, I don't know about that. You know how these guys can get.	*Oh, no. I'm not going to forecast this yet. It's going to depend on whether we're willing to come up with what it's going to take.*
OK. Maybe he needs a little coaching on how to close this. I've done this before.	**Manager:** Sure, sure. Been there, believe me. How about you offer them another 1.5 percent? **Negotiator:** I can try that. But I'm not sure if that's going to be the end of it. How far can I go?	*Here we go; 1.5 percent is something, but probably not enough. Can't you just give me the bottom line so we can get this done?*
As I figured. He has no idea what it's going to take. If I give him more now, he'll just give it away prematurely and come back asking for more later.	**Manager:** Well, do your best. We want to put this one in the win column. But come back to me if you think you need some help.	*Gee, thanks, boss. Glad you could "help."*

While it is easy to see how incentives may make the problem worse in the case of sales and purchase negotiations, an even more complex and thorny example is found in licensing negotiations. We can recall a conversation with the CEO of a global pharmaceutical company who was trying to improve the firm's business development process. He wanted his team to negotiate better deals, sure. But his definition of "better" was somewhat elusive. It wasn't necessarily paying a little less for a new product, or having a little more control of marketing decisions downstream. In his mind, licensing was about managing strategy risks. He needed to fill gaps in a pipeline, where a very successful drug could represent $1 billion or more in revenue, but where expensive failures were more the norm. He wanted the team to move through the complex negotiation process faster, and he wanted to avoid big mistakes. And while he didn't particularly care to squeeze the licensees down to the lowest royalties they'd take, that didn't mean that he was willing to be careless with his stockholders' money and overpay for a compound. What incentives should he have used?

The more complexity you add to your definition of a successful negotiation, the harder it is to design an appropriate incentive plan. The more mechanistic the incentive, the easier to game and the more likely it is to produce unintended (and undesirable) consequences; however, the more subjective the incentive, the less likely it is to drive specific, compensable behaviors. Combined with the all-too-frequent disconnect between the company's interests and those of the individual negotiator, these "agency problems" lead salesmen to offer big discounts at the end of the quarter to make their quotas, or drive procurement negotiators to leave tremendous value on the table in improved service or access to innovation for the sake of a much smaller gain in a volume discount. The reality is that in most complex organizations today, we care not only about *what* the negotiator accomplishes, but also about *how* he or she accomplishes it. And that requires a richer and broader set of management tools than incentives alone.

The problem posed by ineffective metrics is further aggravated by the simple fact that first-line managers typically can't control the design of the incentive system. Even if they recognize that an incentive system rewards the wrong negotiation behavior, there's often little they can do about it. Faced with a blunt tool that doesn't help them accomplish what they need, they end up instead using information as proxy, holding back their real objectives or their real bottom lines so that negotiators won't jump directly to that outcome too early in the negotiation.

So . . . what's a manager to do?

The easiest answer to that question is that if you want your negotiators to come up with deals worth doing, you have to play an active role as a manager and a coach. You need to spell out the point of the deal and those activities that you think are critical to achieving it. Then, depending on what you perceive to be the strengths and gaps in a particular negotiator's repertoire, you will need to monitor, reward, and coach him or her accordingly.

But let us not leave it at "it depends." Recognizing that an effective manager will have to tailor management activities to suit the task and the negotiator charged with accomplishing it, there are still some general prescriptions worth putting into practice.

Use the implementation mind-set to define success

When implementation matters, it is not enough to send someone out to "do a deal." Success has to be well defined, and the guidelines we described in chapters 3 through 8 can serve as a useful road map for managers as well as for the negotiators themselves. It is your responsibility as a manager to define success for your negotiators in such a way that their victory dance is a well-deserved celebration, rather than a premature tribute to a deal that fails to deliver value. Here are some of the specific things a manager can do to help:

- *Clarify the purposes of the deal.* Make sure that you know why you are doing this deal, and that your negotiator understands the purpose as well. The purpose is not to sign the contract; it is to accomplish what the contract specifies. What goals is each party pursuing through the deal and what will it take to accomplish them?

- *Take a broad view of who the stakeholders are.* Does the negotiator understand that if he or she keeps naysayers out just long enough to sign the deal, "success" will not necessarily follow? Check in with your negotiator occasionally to review who has been in the loop and whether there are any parties on your side, or the counterpart's, who ought to be brought in before the deal is signed.

- *Require your negotiators to set useful precedents.* What challenges do you know from experience tend to beset the kind of deal in question, and what kind of precedent do you want to set during the negotiation for handling them? Give your negotiators the benefit of your managerial experience and your knowledge of deals worked on by other negotiators, so that they can apply "80/20 hindsight" to the new situation. Remind your negotiators that a deal's success is measured not only by what's on the paper, but by the parties' ability to implement it, and that, like it or not, the negotiation is the first example of what it is like to work together.

- *Coach them on how to air nightmares and discuss obstacles to implementation.* Many negotiators will be hesitant to discuss the "elephant in the room"—what might go wrong during implementation. Give your negotiators a clear vision for how to put these "undiscussables" on the table in a useful way—not as confrontational accusations, but rather as shared problems to be dealt with during the negotiation so that both sides can implement the deal well.

- *Demand nothing less than crystal clarity on commitments given and received.* Exhort your negotiators to be very clear on what commitments are solicited and offered, and to sum up periodically what each party has (or has not) committed to. A negotiation that ends with an asymmetrical understanding of who has committed to what, or with carelessly made, unrealistic commitments, is unlikely to produce a deal with a point.

- *Make sure negotiators know they are not "done" until they have a clear plan for transitioning to implementation.* Too often negotiators think that once the deal is signed, they can toss it over the transom and move on. Surprising them at the end by telling them they have further obligations is neither fair nor good management. To manage negotiators well, you must be clear about what "done" means and what "good" looks like. You need to coach your team to think about the transition from negotiation to implementation and clarify what role they have in briefing and involving implementers. If you want deals worth doing, then make sure your negotiators understand that the negotiation does not end with a handshake or a signature.

Imagine a conversation between Sue, whose firm supplied defective components to Bill's company, and her manager as she gets ready to start the negotiations with Bill about how to deal with the $5 million in damages caused by the bad parts.

If her manager had not read this book, the conversation might be pretty short and sound a bit like this:

Manager: So, Sue—you are just starting your negotiations with Bill. What are you going for?

Sue: Well, we have to settle the liability question, of course. And I'd like to make sure we keep the relationship with Bill on solid footing.

Manager: How much liability do you think we should take on?

Sue: I was thinking that we ought to open with offering to take on 20 percent of the damages—they can't get too mad if we start with $1 million. If we can get out of this with the relationship intact and taking on only 50 percent of the liability, I think that would be a win. At the end of the day, of course, rather than risk the relationship with our biggest customer, we would take on the whole $5 million as long as we could spread it out in credits over a couple of years and make sure we're never in this position again.

Manager: Whoa! Let's not get ahead of ourselves. I agree that starting with an opening offer of $1 million makes sense. But don't move off of that position too quickly, or you might signal that we are willing to take most or all of the damages. Your ultimate authority here is to offer no more than $2 million, but only if they press us really hard. If that won't do it, we'll have to reassess—but be sure to sound really firm on $2 million as our maximum contribution to this mess. And don't move there too quickly—make it sound like that really hurts and we can't possibly do more.

This conversation might lead Sue to consider that the only purpose of the negotiation is to resolve the damages question, and the best outcome is to pay the least. Period. Her manager is signaling (and saying) that he cares exclusively about how much liability they take on. The "bottom line" approach the manager is taking might be excluding significant other stakeholders on Bill's side and on Sue's who either have useful information on where the problem occurred or how to prevent similar problems in the future. The positional bargaining process he is pushing for is likely to be hard on the relationship with Bill, and may well undermine Sue's credibility if she takes strong positions and then backs down when Bill pushes back (thereby training Bill that he needs to beat up this supplier to get a reasonable outcome) or escalates (thereby training Bill that he has to go over Sue's head to get a better answer if he is dissatisfied with her response). Neither is exactly the precedent one would like to set with one's largest customer. The manager is ignoring any plan for how to prevent recurrence of this expensive defect problem, keeping the door open to more costly defects and more conversations of this sort in the future. In short, he is missing the point.

If her manager really got the point, the conversation might be a bit more robust and sound more like this:

Manager: So Sue—you are just starting your negotiations with Bill. What do you hope to achieve?

Sue: Well, we have to settle the liability question, of course. And I'd like to make sure we keep the relationship with Bill on solid footing.

Manager: OK, so we need to resolve the conflict over who pays what in a way that preserves the relationship. Do we also need to develop procedures for working together to ensure that we don't have similar defects in the future?

Sue: Yes, of course that would make sense.

Manager: So, how do we do that?

Sue: Well, we might explore whether there are any other specification changes our engineering team would recommend to enhance the reliability of our components, or to simplify or improve their testing and quality assurance.

Manager: OK, good. Seems like a worthwhile set of conversations. Now let's move to the damages issue. How can I be helpful to you in thinking that through?

Sue: I was thinking that we ought to open with offering to take on 20 percent of the damages—they can't get too mad if we start with $1 million. If we can get out of this with the relationship intact and taking on only 50 percent of the liability, I think that would be a win. At the end of the day, of course, rather than risk the relationship with our biggest customer, we would take on the whole $5 million as long as we could spread it out in credits over a couple of years.

Manager: Let's back up for a minute. Who actually has knowledge about what really happened with these parts? Is Bill fully up to speed?

Sue: He has spoken with their manufacturing and QA folks, so I'm sure he is briefed.

Manager: Yeah, but might it be useful to start the conversation with them by having our engineering, manufacturing, and QA folks and theirs all in the room together to do a thorough review of procedures and get as clear a common picture as possible about what went wrong where?

Sue: Yes, of course that would make sense, especially if we are talking about how to prevent failures in the future as we work on increasingly complex assemblies.

Manager: And that might be an ideal forum to discuss any other specification changes that could help enhance the reliability of our parts or simplify testing and quality assurance . . .

Sue: But I'm worried that they will turn it into a food fight to prove that we were at fault and that we ought to pay for all the damages.

Manager: A very valid concern. Maybe it would make sense to set this up as a separate prior meeting with the engineers on how to avoid this problem in the future, and then follow it up with a meeting with Bill to talk though damages. Bill may be a little more relaxed about sorting out the damages issue if he feels that we have taken this very seriously and have worked together well to ensure that this problem doesn't happen again, rather than thinking he needs to make this really expensive for us so it doesn't happen again.

Sue: OK, so how about I start off with 20 percent of the damages for us, asking him to take 80 percent, and then move from there?

Manager: Actually, I have some real concerns about your locking into any position too early. How much of the damages we should pay depends a lot on what caused the problem, and I just don't have enough information yet to have a view on that. If it turns out that Bill's manufacturing team damaged our parts, which we delivered in good working order, or if they were damaged in shipping when we used their shipper at their request, then I am not comfortable taking even $1 million of the damages. On the other hand, if the parts were bad when we shipped them and we should have spotted it, shame on us—as the supplier we ought to take half or more of the damages, depending on whether they should have been able to catch the problem before they used them.

Sue: So what is my bottom line? How high can I go?

Manager: I really don't have enough information to know what's right. I think to resolve this you and Bill will need to understand better the causes of the problem so you can develop some solutions that will work. I am sure we'll have another opportunity to think about the numbers for past damages in the context of a solution to the problem going forward. Next time we have a problem, I want Bill to know that we won't pay an arbitrary amount just because he pushed us or threatened the relationship. Now let's talk a bit about how you can make sure that the engineers on both sides can work together well to implement whatever you decide at these meetings about new testing or revised specs.

This time around, the manager is being explicit about a vision for success that is quite different from that in the first conversation. Sue is being coached to think more fully about the real purposes of the negotiation—maximizing the likelihood of a long and mutually beneficial relationship with Bill's company and dealing with the damages issue on the merits. Sue is likely to bring in important constituents from both sides, both to resolve the existing problem and to get them invested in averting future costly problems. Sue is likely to understand the importance of precedent in how she deals with this difficult issue so that she and Bill can work through any problems they face in the future much more productively. Finally, Sue is likely to conclude the negotiations with a clear plan for who is doing what next as she and the customer move forward together, rather than simply writing a check to Bill's company and having a cranky customer no matter how large the check.

Insist on thorough preparation

You can't be in the room with them or on every phone call. You don't want to micromanage the negotiation. Being clear about what you want your negotiators to accomplish helps, but it is not enough. That's where preparation comes in.

Experience has taught us that you negotiate like you prepare. When negotiators prepare an opening offer and a fallback position, that's what they propose at the table.

The single most effective way to be an effective manager of negotiators is to require them to spend time in preparation before engaging in any significant negotiation, and to review their preparation with you. Because there are at least two parties involved, it is impossible to truly "script" a negotiation. Thinking of preparation as deciding on a "path through the woods" is likely to fail since, in the dynamic process of negotiation, the counterpart will certainly get your team off course on occasion. It is more useful to think of effective preparation as "knowing your destination and all the terrain," so that whenever your negotiators get off course, they are still able to navigate to the destination. Moreover, there's a limit to the coaching and guidance you can give negotiators and still allow them to engage their counterparts in some discovery, problem solving, and persuasion.

By requiring preparation, you let negotiators know that your expectations of them go beyond *what* they negotiate to *how* they do so. You also make it clear, however, that they are not mere messengers sent out to parrot a party line: they are professional practitioners, performing as part of a team, applying their skills and marshaling organizational resources to achieve organizational goals. The sourcing and procurement group at one large media company went so far as to state that no team or individual could spend over $2 million without having the group's senior executive review their detailed negotiation preparation. This was to review not just their signing authority, but their assessment of both sides' interests, some possible options, objective criteria for resolving critical issues, an understanding of their walk-away alternatives, clear commitments to be made and sought, and a plan for managing communication and relationships during the course of negotiation.[1] Similarly, as part of the process for preapproving travel expenses, a large reinsurer now requires that claims adjusters include a one-page negotiation preparation summary along with their travel justification. More and more organizations are recognizing that a manager's ability to influence a negotiation is at its peak during prenegotiation preparations.

Preparation sessions also provide managers with an opportunity to coach negotiators directly and model appropriate behavior. If the manager has participated in negotiation training together with the frontline negotiators, such coaching sessions serve to apply and reinforce the training. They also allow the manager to have sufficient insight into the negotiation to support the negotiators without taking over, and the manager is in a better position to challenge or introduce more discipline when that is what's needed.

Disciplined preparation also produces, as a by-product of each exercise, a valuable knowledge base that can support organizational learning. Each negotiator who prepares expresses his or her best thinking about the organization's interests on an issue and how they might be met, articulates insights about particular counterparts that can then be aggregated and generalized, and expands the organization's understanding of its own alternatives to particular deals. By capturing that information during the preparation session and then making it available to future negotiators as they prepare, each negotiator both contributes to and benefits from the organization's growing knowledge. A negotiation preparation database is an enormous knowledge asset for an organization, and most managers totally ignore or massively underutilize this asset.

A final element of preparation might include practice sessions. It has astounded us that the first time negotiators try out an argument is usually on the counterpart, when all the marbles are at stake. Very few of us would posit that we do something the best we can the very first time we try it. It is hard to imagine that Tiger Woods would refuse to practice on a championship golf course because he preferred to be surprised by the terrain during the tournament and wanted to be "fresh." Litigating attorneys are sometimes bemused by their corporate counterparts, who usually try out their argument for the very first time with the other party in the room as the audience. World-class litigators trying a high-stakes case will empanel surrogate juries and hire retired judges to hear and critique their arguments before they actually try it for real. And the more there is at stake, the more practice they will insist on. Negotiators should learn from that. Sue's saying to her manager, "I will start by asking how we can prevent this problem from recurring" does not get her ready in the same way as her manager's suggestion: "Sue, let's take ten minutes to try a few different openings for the meeting to see what is most comfortable for you. I'll be Bill. Let's hear how you might start when you come into the room and I'm seated at my conference table. Go ahead, start the meeting and we'll break after five minutes and review how it went and what you would do differently in a second try." Any negotiator who can't do it better the second or third or fourth time through is simply not paying attention.

Coach your negotiators along the way

Coaches may use lots of styles and approaches, depending on what the coach is comfortable doing and what the "coachee" most needs (which are not always the same thing). Assuming that you have provided negotiators with a clear definition of success, and you have required them to prepare before the negotiation, you have done what a good manager should to help negotiators get off to a good start. Your role as their coach comes into play next, as they fine-tune their approach or as they get into the negotiation and need to make adjustments based on what they learn during initial conversations.

We find that questions are a coach's best friend when it comes to helping negotiators make adjustments to their strategy. Rather than taking over the negotiation or making all the decisions about how to respond to a counterpart's move, a good coach helps the negotiator test his or her own assumptions, consider different perspectives, and reach a conclusion about how to proceed. For example, if we look back at the subjects of chapters 3 through 8, we can see how to construct a series of good questions a coach might ask between negotiation sessions. This will ensure that the negotiator is not missing the real purposes of the deal, ignoring important stakeholders, creating a precedent you wouldn't want to live with, suppressing concerns that ought to be aired, giving or getting unwise or incomplete commitments, or failing to plan for implementation.

An illustrative list of coaching questions is shown in figure 9-1. This is not meant to be a formulaic set of questions to be walked through in each coaching session, but rather suggestions for the kind of questions that a manager might find useful in coaching a negotiator.

Beyond practice sessions, one of our favorite techniques for coaching negotiators, whether very experienced (and sometimes impervious to coaching) or fairly new at the role (and sometimes intimidated by those with more experience), is the role reversal. Instead of the more predictable request from a less-than-helpful micromanager to "tell me exactly what you're going to say to them"—which is a great way to practice being a messenger but perhaps not much else—this coaching technique has the *manager* try out the negotiator's arguments, and has the negotiator play the role of the *counterpart*. If the negotiators have been doing their job well, they are best positioned to step into the counterpart's shoes and to understand at a fairly intuitive level how that person may hear those arguments and whether he or she would be persuaded by them. This simple exercise lets the manager work with what the negotiators know and help them improve their strategies in light of what the role reversal teaches them. It helps the negotiators focus their available time and energy on what really matters—not just what their approach sounds like, but what impact it will have. It also helps them attach words to the manager's suggestions by hearing the manager actually try playing their part—in a way that many negotiators will be able to remember more easily in the heat of battle.

Whether they mean to or not, managers constantly send messages about how they view the negotiator's role versus their own, and about the kinds of things they believe negotiators should bring to their managers versus which ones they should try to work out on their

FIGURE 9-1

Coaching questions for managers

Questions about the deal's purpose

- Why are we doing this deal?
- How will we know if we accomplished our purpose?
- What are the key interests at stake on each side?
- Are there any broader purposes we might consider integrating into this deal?

Questions about the people involved

- Who are the necessary people on our side—both for getting buy-in and for implementing the deal?
- Who are the necessary people on the other side—both for getting buy-in and for implementing the deal?
- What have we learned from the other side about their challenges in getting key players aligned?
- What should we share with the other negotiator about the challenges we may have in getting key players on board?
- Are there any blockers on either side we ought to be concerned about?
- Are there any enablers on either side we ought to engage before proceeding further?

Questions about the history we want to create

- Are we negotiating the way we want to implement?
- Does the other side understand that we see this as creating a history of working together?
- Have the parties been appropriately open in sharing information during the negotiation?
- Are the parties relying on persuasion, rather than coercion, during the negotiation?
- Has anything happened that may cause problems with trust and our working relationship going forward?

Questions about risk management

- What are our biggest nightmares about getting value in implementation?
- What might some of their nightmares be?
- What are the costs and benefits of putting these nightmares on the table?
- How do we discuss those nightmares in a useful way?

Questions about commitments

- Do we both understand our commitments and who will be doing what when?
- Which of their commitments are going to be toughest for them to meet?
- What can we do to help them deliver?
- Which of our commitments are going to be toughest for us to keep?
- What can they do to help us actually deliver?

Questions about the transition

- Have we thought through the transition from negotiation to implementation after the deal is signed?
- Is there anything we have learned during the negotiation process that might be useful for the implementation team to know?
- What might surprise the implementation team?
- What possible changes do we need to prepare for?

own. Scott Spehar, vice president of services sales at Cisco Systems, had his business leaders cofacilitate some negotiation training sessions for the firm's front-line negotiators.[2] To do so, he first had to invest and make sure those leaders were not just good negotiators, but that they were clear about their role in the process. The value to the managers of having to understand the material well enough to deliver it to their staff, and the value to the staff of engaging in role plays and real case study analyses with their managers, was unparalleled. After the training, they had a model for how managers can coach without taking over, and how negotiators can keep their managers in the loop without feeling disempowered.

Scott has also taken to heart the old principle "you expect what you inspect" and has worked with his business leaders and negotiation teams to create a set of expectations about how they negotiate and how they can improve at very specific skill sets. The negotiators know they will be held to these expectations by their managers. In figure 9-2 you will find an example of a neat device Scott is using to support managers and negotiators. It sets out clear and detailed expectations by three stages of the negotiation: preparation, conduct, and review. The expectations target specific negotiation behaviors that managers want their negotiators to exhibit, and they describe a progression over time, as negotiators get more experienced.

Welcome problems

This is hard advice for managers to follow. Most of us prefer never to have problems, and we want to hear about them only in the context of how our personnel brilliantly solved them. Sometimes explicitly and often implicitly through our reactions, we scream: "Don't come to me with problems, come to me with solutions! You get paid to solve problems, not bring them to me. If I have to fix your problems, then I am doing your job and you are superfluous."

While this reaction is understandable, if we make it hard for negotiators to raise problems because they fear it will be a career-limiting move, then we shouldn't be surprised when we hear about debacles only after it is too late to prevent or mitigate them. We had one client whose sourcing employees knew that bringing problems with suppliers to management could lead the employee to become part of what they called their "talent mobility pool"—so it was not surprising that problems were rarely brought to managers early. As that client made a concerted effort to welcome problems and reward early warning (rather than punish those who raised a red flag), they found they began to get

FIGURE 9-2

Excerpt from Cisco negotiator competencies guide

Below you will find some critical negotiation competencies, and a progression of abilities we expect you to be able to show over the next three negotiations. Please note that these reviews with managers are a critical part of your professional development, and expected whether or not you need their authorization to do a particular deal.

Negotiation competency	During your *next* negotiation, you should be able to:	During your *subsequent* negotiation, you should be able to:	During your *third* negotiation, you should be able to:
You should go beyond bargaining positions, to fully understand customer and Cisco interests.	• In your preparation, articulate who all the key parties are, and what their likely interests are. • During the negotiation, ask good questions to help you validate your assumptions about who the key players are and their interests. • When you review with your manager, report back on what you learned that was new or different than your assumptions.	• In your preparation, push yourself and others to articulate Cisco's priorities for this particular opportunity. • During the negotiation, probe further into customer interests, and to try to help the customer prioritize among them. Also, express Cisco's priorities as interests, not positions. • When you review with your manager, report back on what you learned about how various internal and external stakeholders prioritize their different interests.	• During the negotiation, engage in a thorough exploration of interests and priorities, even with a difficult counterpart who just wants your next concession. • When you review with your manager, report back on the techniques that proved most useful for getting past their reluctance to explore interests.

Source: Cisco Systems. Used with permission.

much better input from sourcing employees about potential problems with suppliers so that they could take early action to avoid expensive business consequences.

Help negotiators end it well

Many negotiators have trouble walking away from deals they should not do. Others have trouble sticking around to wrap up the details for deals they have completed. In both cases, the manager has a critical role to play as the negotiation winds down. Ending it well may mean walking out (but leaving the door open for future transactions when and as they make sense) or transitioning effectively to the implementation phase.

Not all deals are worth doing, even when they look good on paper. It's not just a question of whether a negotiator has prepared and knows his or her walk-away alternative. Even in organizations where negotiators are encouraged to think hard about their BATNA (best alternative to a negotiated agreement), there's a difference between a decision to walk away from a deal that doesn't sufficiently meet the company's interests and a decision to walk away from a deal because it's likely to fail during implementation. Part of the job of an effective manager is to help negotiators understand that reaching a deal that looks good on paper is not enough. If they cannot get a deal that they have confidence can be implemented successfully, there is likely no point in going forward.

A good manager will help a negotiator say no to deals that should not be done. Because they're not in the heat of the deal and can retain some objectivity and distance, managers have a responsibility to challenge the negotiator: Are the necessary stakeholders on board? Is there a clear purpose to the deal and do the parties understand what it will take to achieve it? Have we created the kind of working relationship and precedents that we need to be successful, and if not, how much risk does that represent to the eventual success of the deal? Managers need not be naysayers or even devil's advocates. They do have to probe and make sure that the negotiator has delivered a deal that will achieve its purposes.

The other aspect of "ending it well" is to ensure an effective transition—to make sure that negotiators are not in so much of a hurry to move on to the next deal that they fail to attend to the issues that must be addressed if the deal is going to work. If a different team is going to implement the deal, there needs to be a thorough and complete hand-off that includes these steps:

- Communicating the purpose of the deal, not just its terms

- Introducing the key people on both sides to each other, and helping each side fully appreciate the landscape of important stakeholders

- Communicating to implementers key lessons about the other side, their operating style, their communication style, how they manage relationships, and how they manage commitments

- Making sure that the precedent the negotiators worked hard to establish is transmitted to the implementers so they can benefit from it

- Working with the implementers so that plans that were started during the negotiation are more fully developed and put into action

In our experience, a handoff works best when both sides' negotiators conduct it jointly with both sides' implementers. But it has also been our experience that negotiators need quite a bit of coaxing from their managers to carry out the joint handoff. For one thing, handoffs can be difficult to schedule for big deals with big teams. The negotiations have often taken longer than expected and the negotiators have other people waiting on them; meanwhile, the implementation teams are raring to get started, so this step gets skipped. Managers can and should insist—without this transition a lot of important information will get lost, intentions will be misunderstood, and value will be destroyed.

10

Building an Organization That Does Deals Worth Doing

How so many smart companies get it wrong

Up to this point, we've focused on individual negotiators and their managers—what they do, or fail to do, that produces deals that don't deliver value. But while there's much that individual negotiators can do to make sure the deals they negotiate have a point, we would be remiss if we didn't also take a look at the environment in which the negotiator operates. After all, the negotiators (and their managers) typically get their marching orders and their applause (or boos) from someone. The organization tells them, in more or less subtle ways, what it wants them to accomplish and how.

Perils of a deal-making culture

No company, even a very large and successful one, is immune to bad decisions at the negotiating table. Here are three examples—two familiar, one perhaps less so—of the potential consequences of a deal-making organizational culture.

AOL Business Affairs story: competing to see who can do the most outrageous deals

The AOL Business Affairs team, internally known as "BA," was responsible for AOL's most complicated and important online advertising deals—deals that often closed late in a fiscal quarter to help AOL reach or exceed its financial targets just in time.[1] Given how much credibility AOL could bestow on a dot-com start up, the BA team had the leverage to pressure and make high demands on its partners. But by isolating and elevating a team of deal makers as some kind of superstars who could create money just by being tough and clever, and by insulating them from the downstream (implementation) consequences of their actions, AOL inadvertently created the conditions that produced deals not worth the paper they were written on—the epitome of deals without a point.

The culture of the BA team was one that valued a strong need to win, and winning earned wealth. As they joined the team, negotiators quickly got the message that this was a competitive environment, and that to rise—in the esteem of their managers, in pecking order on the team, in compensation—they had to do ever-more-aggressive deals. It was almost an ongoing game of "can you top this?" But when success is measured by extracting bigger concessions from your counterpart than your peers did from theirs, and closing more deals faster than your teammates, it should come as no surprise that some of these deals would drive counterparts into bankruptcy, or come under scrutiny from regulators.

Enron developers: "in the business of doing deals"

Enron International, or "EI" for short, was in charge of making Enron's global energy deals. Although the division was considered highly successful in the late 1990s, one of its inherent flaws was that though executives loved the rush of whisking around the world doing billion-dollar deals (and getting compensated for them), nobody felt responsible for managing the projects once the ink was dry and implementation was to begin. To keep their deals on track, EI negotiators often made assumptions that failed to consider the possibility of anything going wrong, no matter how remote the location or complex the implementation environment.[2]

In the aftermath of the Enron debacle, it is easy to point fingers and find fault in the way money flew around that company. It was a heady time, and it is likely that at least some of the people working there thought they really had created a new model for how companies would work and create wealth. But the way the company compensated the teams that negotiated its power development deals was a recipe for disaster. Burned by compensation structures that provided the negotiators equity in the projects, or what seemed like rich annuities out of the projects' revenues, Enron moved to paying negotiators of development projects bonuses based on the net present value of the projected future cash flows of the project—sometimes garnering as much as 9 percent of the total project value. So if developers estimated that a project was worth $100 million, they could earn around $9 million from a single deal. This meant that developers got paid when the deal closed financially, before any plants had been built or any pipe had been laid. Their incentives were clear: negotiate deals with the largest projections plausible, get them signed and funded, and move on to the next one.

EDS and the Navy Marine Corps Intranet: the lure of the "megadeal"

In October 2000, EDS signed a $6.9 billion contract with the U.S. Navy to build an advanced new network for the navy and the Marine Corps. The Navy Marine Corps Intranet (NMCI) was to be a network second only to the entire World Wide Web in its scope and reach, connecting all navy and Marine Corps users around the globe in a unified voice, data, and video system.[3] This megadeal and others like it were central to new CEO Richard Brown's growth strategy.

EDS would bill a monthly charge for each new user that came online. As the deal was initially conceived, EDS would build the network and get users on it quickly. The number of users would skyrocket and the massive NMCI would throw off positive cash flow about two years into the deal. In theory, by the middle of the eight-year contract period, EDS was to have recouped all of its initial investment and would begin to make a hefty profit from operating the network.

Unfortunately, two years into the project, the migration to the new network was already delayed by eighteen months. EDS had invested over $640 million in building the system, and not yet started to recover any user fees from the NMCI. In October 2002, CEO Richard Brown announced that, despite the company's recent setbacks with the navy deal and others, "there will be no change in our business strategy, we will still pursue mega deals."[4]

By March 2003, EDS had lost more than $800 million on the navy contract. Richard Brown was replaced by former CBS chief executive Michael Jordan, and under the new regime, EDS became more selective in the contracts it signed.

The navy was no happier than EDS shareholders, by the way. Penalties for failing to meet SLAs were no substitute for getting the global system operational for all navy and Marine Corps personnel. EDS's commitment to support "all" legacy applications without fully understanding how many there were hurt EDS without necessarily benefiting the navy. In March 2006, the contract was extended to 2010 and its value grew to $9.9 billion. Still, the profitability EDS initially hoped for in this megadeal was nowhere to be found.

Six common mistakes organizations make

The problems experienced at Enron, AOL, and EDS are not unique. They are not limited solely to large institutions or to ego-driven executives. In our experience working with companies large and small, we have noticed six common errors executives make about how they employ and organize negotiators and how they handle negotiations, especially with regard to deals where implementation matters.

Sometimes these errors are the direct result of a change made in reaction to a bad deal or to an increase in the volume of special terms the organization must negotiate. In others, these problems come as the wholly unintended consequences of actions taken for other purposes. They can arise as part of reorganizing a purchasing department, fine-tuning a sales commission structure, creating a corporate "dashboard," or creating a culture of achievement. These are important, often valid activities that many organizations engage in at one time or another for very good reasons, but which can have unintended consequences for the kinds of deals their negotiators deliver.

Creating a separate "deal department"

One of the first decisions that many executives think they need to make as they consider how to get better negotiation results is: "Where should my deal makers sit?"

In some cases, they answer that question by creating a dedicated team, concentrating negotiation responsibility. The assumptions behind such a decision are what tend to get well-meaning organizations into trouble. One of these assumptions is that specialization produces better results: in other words, if you start with relatively expert practitioners, and concentrate most of the opportunities to negotiate with that group of experts, they should get even better with experience. Unfortunately, this assumption ignores the importance of implementation. Greater and greater expertise, fueled by more and more experience at the negotiation table, does not by any means guarantee that the deals those experts negotiate will actually have a point. Unless there is a way for those who are outside and downstream from the deal team to give feedback about whether deals are working, the negotiators only learn what kinds of techniques help them get deals *signed*, not what kinds of techniques create value during implementation.

AOL's Business Affairs team, for example, was structurally removed from those who defined AOL's audiences and markets, as well as those who had to work with the other side after the deal was signed. They got their marching orders from the head of a department created to "do deals." The results included deals that called for more ad placements on AOL pages than AOL had online space for within the requisite time period; other deals took viewers from an English-language welcome screen to an advertiser's Spanish-language site, at a faster rate than the advertiser's servers could handle.[5]

It isn't only dot-com craziness that creates these dynamics. Most pharmaceutical companies have created business development teams that get better and better at negotiating a set of issues, at knowing where the potential sticking points are for their counterparts, and at when and how to exercise whatever clout and leverage they have in the negotiation. So far so good. But if they are divorced from the implementation consequences of the terms they negotiate, they have no way to know whether "winning" some of those terms is really a good thing or not.

As vice president of strategic planning and alliances at Procter & Gamble Pharmaceuticals, Tom Finn has responsibility for the postsigning relationships with the counterparts of Procter & Gamble's business development negotiators. In that role, he has acquired a different kind of experience: which terms tend to get them in trouble later in the life cycle of the partnership. That experience, which would ordinarily be outside the reach of the business development negotiators, is essential to doing deals that will create value when implemented. "It's not just a matter of a win-win philosophy. It is about incorporating our alliance managers' hard-won experience with terms that cause implementation problems and not letting those terms into our deals," explains Finn, who makes it his job to transfer those lessons learned to the negotiating teams and to make sure the battles they win don't end up costing P&G the war.[6]

Another key assumption that typically drives the creation of some kind of "deal department" is that by concentrating authority in this smaller and more expert team, fewer deals will be interfered with, undermined, or slowed down by others who are less experienced or somehow don't get it. This assumption also ignores implementation. It looks at whether something is good or bad for the negotiation by assessing whether it helps or hinders doing the deal, rather than by whether it produces deals that not only look good on paper, but are also desirable in practice.

The assumption that the best way to clinch deals is to keep people out of the negotiators' way and to vest deal-making authority in some kind of "deal department" also tends to isolate those people, often elevating them in status to what Tom Wolfe memorably named "Masters of the Universe" in *The Bonfire of the Vanities*. But that's no way to help negotiators understand the implementation implications of their actions. Rather, that's a recipe for creating the kind of deal-making mind-set that prevailed at Enron International. Indeed, that mind-set got to be so strong that even though Enron created a Risk Assessment and Control Department (the "RAC") to ride herd and assess the risk of the deals being negotiated, the RAC was unable to stand up to the deal makers or prevent them from doing any deal they wanted. (It didn't help that deals were permitted to come to the RAC at the last minute, when there was tremendous pressure to approve them, or that RAC members were evaluated at the end of the year by the same negotiators whose deals they were supposed to challenge.)[7]

What most often drives companies to create a separate deal department is the desire to do more and bigger deals faster. It tends to be true that when organizations assign a group to a narrower set of activities, people get more efficient. Fewer distractions, clearer goals, and a stronger sense of a team moving in the same direction generally do contribute to productivity. When this approach is applied to "doing deals," however, it tends to create a team of folks who see the deal as the end, rather than as a means to an end. They measure success by the number of deals they've done, how big those deals were, and to some extent, by how much bigger and better their latest deal is from their last one, or from the last one done by anyone else in the organization. They don't stop to wonder who's going to do what after the ink is dry, because their job is done and there's another deal waiting.

That doesn't make the deal makers evil, uncaring, or stupid. They believe they are doing what the organization wants them to do. After all, they are in the "deal department" and they are a well-compensated, specialist resource. To excel, they have to do deals. It's up to someone else then to do something with them.

Relying on third parties to do deals

At the other end of the spectrum from organizations that create deal-making departments are those that hire third parties to negotiate key deals on their behalf. They bring in outside help for any number of good reasons, including the need for specialized subject matter expertise for a kind of transaction they don't often negotiate, such as a complex outsourcing transaction. They may do so because they need some third-party legitimacy, as is the case when an investment banker provides a "fairness opinion" regarding a merger or acquisition. Sometimes the parties are in litigation, and they need the help of an intermediary even to talk to one another. Those are all good reasons to engage a third party's help, but not necessarily for delegating the negotiation to them.

Sometimes organizations buy into other kinds of arguments for using third parties, or they allow a third party's role to grow in such a way that the third party effectively replaces the principal in the negotiation. The most common reason for this overreliance on a third party is that the client organization accepts the premise that the negotiation will require tough tactics, and therefore in order to preserve the personal relationships between the negotiating companies, someone else (i.e., the third party) should be the one to play hardball. That way, the argument goes, it doesn't matter how much blood is spilled at the table, because when the negotiation is over and the third party exits, the principals can build a positive working relationship without any hard feelings. When organizations seek to put this approach into action, they keep their responsible executives out of the room during any discussions likely to be contentious.

Of course, that rarely works in practice. If the third party you hired to negotiate on your behalf does "bad things" at the table, your counterpart will not forget them, or take any less offense, or feel any less aggrieved because the "hired guns" have left. They will blame you for hiring the gunslingers. They will assume you knew full well what tactics they were using (and perhaps hired them precisely to use those tactics). They will believe that the "bad guys" had your blessing to push for every concession they extracted, to withhold every bit of relevant information they shielded, or to use any number of coercive tactics to close the deal.

While there is little benefit to be gained for your working relationship by hiding behind a third party, much can be lost—getting to know your counterpart, jointly exploring possible implementation issues, and creating a positive precedent for how you work together. In our experience, delegating the negotiation to a third party also effectively destroys two precious knowledge assets for the organization: knowledge about the counterpart and knowledge about the process for negotiating deals.

First, the more you negotiate through professional deal makers who do not truly represent your culture and way of operating, the less each party learns about what it's like to work with the other. By delegating the deal making, you fail to gain firsthand knowledge of what the folks on the other side really care about, what their objectives are, who their stakeholders are, and what the potential implementation barriers may be. If you consider that the negotiation is your first opportunity to see how they solve problems (and to demonstrate to them how you do so), then front and center is where you want to be.

Second, when organizations hand off responsibility for conducting key negotiations to a third party, they also fail to learn how to negotiate those kinds of deals themselves. Any lessons learned leave with the team that negotiated the deal. When you hire such third parties, you are relying on teams that get better and better at closing deals (indeed, that's often a prerequisite for their collecting their fees), but not necessarily at negotiating deals that can be implemented effectively. Next time you are considering a third party for this kind of a role, and implementation matters, ask them about the postsigning track record of the deals they have negotiated. While they will certainly be able to quote you statistics on how many deals they have done, how large they were, and what market share they have within a particular niche, few will be able to tell you any details about what happened after they left.

Using deal-making metrics

Another common mistake organizations make, often (though not always) in conjunction with creating a deal department, is to monitor and compensate the performance of negotiators by measuring their productivity as deal makers. The most common of these metrics, typical of sales or business development functions, look at the numbers or sizes of deals; others, found more in the procurement arena, consider discounts or other concessions obtained. At more process-focused companies, one may find measures of things like "time to close," number of concurrent deals in progress, or frequency of escalations.

The problem is not that keeping track of these things is bad, in itself. The problem lies in the reasons organizations create and track these measures, and in how they use them. Why do organizations develop deal-making metrics? Usually we find two related reasons: they want to use them as incentives, to drive better negotiation results; and they want to make sure they are paying people appropriately for what they are actually accomplishing. Those of us who have long argued for treating negotiation as a fundamental business process rather than just as an individual skill or an art form should applaud this trend, and we do. Negotiation should be subjected to the same rigors and analysis as other business processes, and negotiators should be expected to apply quantifiable measures to their work. The problem is not measuring negotiations, but how you do so.

Incentive systems tend to pay individuals for achieving certain outcomes or for engaging in certain activities. Both are subject to a range of familiar problems: if you pay individuals to engage in activities without requiring desirable outcomes, you may get lots of sales calls, for example, but not net new business. If you pay individuals for particular outcomes, you may find that you get them, but that they are achieved in unacceptable ways, such as business that costs more to sell than it is actually worth. Organizations that rely heavily on metrics and incentives also often find that some members of the workforce develop fairly cynical attitudes and learn to "game" the system, figuring out how to achieve those things that "count" with the least effort possible, regardless of whether they actually amount to something of value.

When it comes to negotiation metrics, these problems are compounded by the assumption that what matters are deals made, and that metrics should therefore focus on number of deals, size of deals, and time spent negotiating deals. But when the value comes *after* the deal is signed, closing more or larger deals, or doing them faster, is not necessarily a better outcome. Indeed, there will be many instances when doing the deal (which earns the reward) may be worse for the organization than walking away (which would effectively penalize the negotiator). Moreover, because the negotiation process often lays the groundwork for implementation and creates a precedent for how the organizations work together, an effective incentive system cannot afford to ignore *how* the deals are negotiated. Deals that leave the parties less able to approach implementation challenges with a collaborative frame of mind and more likely to be looking for "payback" when the tables are turned are clearly worse outcomes for the organization—any incentive system that fails to recognize this disserves the organization and sends the wrong message to individual negotiators.

When an organization is focused on how big its three most recent deals were, or how much bookings have grown since the last quarter, or the number of customers it has in a particular market segment, we can safely predict it will enter into deals it is unprepared to implement or that, even if it can implement them, will have undesirable consequences. The classic example is that of the Big Four public accounting firms, who are still reaping the consequences of taking on work for clients they could not serve well, for the sake of being able to report growth in top-line revenue and greater market share. When accounting firms heavily discount their rates in order to win business away from the incumbent, sometimes the teams assigned to those projects feel pressure to get the work done faster and with more junior staff. The Sarbanes-Oxley legislation, at least in part, was designed to ensure that accounting firms do a more thorough job of verifying internal controls instead of doing the minimum possible to still sign an audit opinion.

The problem at the leadership level lies in thinking that doing deals that "count" in the league tables actually helps the organization. EDS executives may have felt great about signing a $6.9 billion deal with the U.S. Navy. But the deal's scope was insufficiently defined: it turned out that eighty thousand applications had to migrate to the new network instead of ten thousand. Critical enabler stakeholders among navy commanders were also not on board with the deal. Without direct orders to collaborate, they were successful at stiff-arming EDS out of the way for about four years, while EDS hemorrhaged cash and prestige.

The bottom line: if the deals cannot be well implemented, net income, customer satisfaction, and staff morale will all decline even as the number of deals signed climbs.

Allowing negotiators to "protect the deal"

Negotiators probably have used as many metaphors in service of this mistake as they have for the negotiation process itself. Some talk about "too many cooks spoiling the broth." Others proclaim that there can "only be one captain in command of the ship." When it comes to deciding whom else to include in the conversations, some will object that "we shouldn't negotiate with ourselves." Whatever they call it, they are trying to assert their control over the deal process, and to keep that control from being undermined by other stakeholders. When organizations allow that to happen, they safeguard the deal, but they risk the buy-in and alignment they need for a successful implementation.

Sometimes negotiators will use confidentiality requirements from agencies like the SEC or the FDA to justify keeping a tight leash on information about the deal, or imposing a "cone of silence" around participants. They may argue that either fiduciary obligation or just good strategy demands that they limit information to those who have a "need to know." They may well have legitimate concerns about whether someone might unlawfully trade on insider information or whether a competitor might be unnecessarily alerted to the firm's plans. But often what drives the negotiators is knowing that the fewer people who know about a deal, the fewer who can raise tough questions or objections. However, by restricting the information about the deal that can go to stakeholders outside the negotiation team's inner circle, they also end up depriving themselves of potentially relevant information.

Of course, there are legitimate reasons to limit information about a negotiation to a selected group of individuals. In some circumstances the fact that a negotiation is going on could alert a competitor or affect the company's share price. In other cases, the real or imagined implications of the negotiation could impact staff morale or customers' or suppliers' reactions in ways that the organization doesn't have the time or resources to address before it knows whether there is even going to be a deal. But those legitimate organizational interests can be met without shutting out of the negotiation process stakeholders who are necessary to the implementation of a deal, or who have useful (even if negative) input about the desirability or nature of the deal.

Negotiators for vendors of complex services and solutions, for example, like to keep their delivery teams out of the room during the negotiation, because implementation managers tend to raise their eyebrows, if not burst out laughing, when they hear some of the things their sales colleagues are proposing. That kind of behavior tends to undermine the negotiators' attempt to persuade their counterparts that "of course we can fly to the moon and back, on time and on budget." Organizations that allow negotiators to exclude people who really know what implementation will take may close more deals, but they will also inevitably close more deals they regret.

Business development negotiators at pharmaceutical firms like to keep lab managers and operations teams out of the room during negotiations to codevelop new products. They know from experience that there is a certain amount of "not invented here" arrogance that will likely complicate matters at the table when they try to persuade their counterparts what a great codevelopment partner they will be. But pharmaceutical companies that end up surprising their operations staff or lab managers with newly signed alliances with biotech or other counterparts routinely disappoint their partners, and even fail in their obligations to the alliance, when those operators and lab managers turn around and say "not with my staff you don't."

Organizations that allow their deal makers to "protect the deal" by insulating it from stakeholder scrutiny or criticism do themselves a disservice. If the deal is one where implementation matters, then the resulting agreement must hold up well when examined closely by those who have to live with it. In our experience, most of those deals that looked good on paper but failed during execution suffered from flaws that could have been understood and managed if the right people had a chance to look at them sooner. This is yet another example of how the fallacy that the purpose of the negotiation is to reach agreement leads organizations to make painful mistakes.

Making it difficult for the negotiator to say "yes"

Right up there with the question, "Where should my negotiators sit?" is "How much authority should I give them?" This question is rarely raised in the context of whether the negotiator should be defining a business strategy, initiating conversations with a counterpart, or exploring possible options for resolution of some business problem. Usually what that question really means is, "How much should the negotiator be allowed to concede on his or her own?"

But asking about concessions is jumping the gun. Making a concession signifies committing to something that, at the outset, the negotiators said or implied they were not willing to do. Whether concessions result from a deliberate plan to "start high" and leave room for compromises, a counterpart's persuasive arguments, or even a feeling of desperation, *making them is about reaching closure* in the negotiation.

Far more important than whether the negotiators have the authority to reach such closure is whether they have actually engaged in a thorough exploration of both sides' interests and possible solutions before making any commitments. Far more relevant to whether the deal, once closed, will produce value is whether the negotiators have engaged the stakeholders critical to implementation and are convinced that there is a point to saying yes.

There are those who look back on the problems of the AOL Business Affairs group and argue that if that team of negotiators had been subjected to tighter controls and had been given a more limited signing authority, they would not have created the problems they did. But when AOL got itself in trouble by committing to run more ads than it had screen space for, the problem wasn't in the negotiator's authority. One could argue all day about the deal size or terms that an individual negotiator should have the authority to accept, and still miss the point that without adequately consulting the people who needed to align advertisements and screen space, a negotiator would be unable to tell whether AOL would ever benefit economically from any particular deal. A particular set of terms during a time of low inventory would produce very different consequences from the same set of terms at a different time, and focusing on the individual negotiator's signing authority would not be as helpful as creating a more consultative culture that involved downstream stakeholders more effectively.

In our experience, lots of organizations set negotiation authority in terms of the size of the deal, the size of the concession, or departure from some kind of standard or precedent. For example, sales negotiation authority tends to be based on either the absolute size of the deal or the amount of the discount that the individual negotiator can accept. The more senior and experienced the negotiator, the larger a discount that he or she can approve. On the procurement side, negotiators tend to be constrained in the size of buy they can make, or by standard bargaining positions regarding issues like discounts, warranties, indemnifications, or intellectual property ownership. Even very sophisticated organizations, in defining the authority of their negotiators for fairly complex deals, often set out a list of issues and provide the negotiation team with limits on what they may concede on each item. But one big problem with focusing on the negotiator's authority to say yes is that almost by definition, any arbitrary threshold will be "wrong" a lot of the time. There will be deals that *shouldn't be done even when they are within the negotiator's limits*, and *some good deals will be unnecessarily delayed or even lost because they are outside those limits.*

The other major problem with limiting concession authority is that many negotiators will interpret those limits as meaning that anything they can negotiate within those limits is a good (or good enough) outcome. And since many negotiators have learned that the easiest and fastest way to close a negotiation is to make concessions, they tend to jump quickly to the outcome they expect they will have to agree to eventually, by offering the most they are authorized to offer.

Of course, doing a deal at the authorized limits is not always a good thing. Closing most deals at or about the authorized limits, so that the worst deal you'd be prepared to accept becomes your average deal, is downright awful. Thus managers learn to pad their limits, not actually authorizing the negotiator to reach the "real" limits. But negotiators tend to learn that their authority is artificially limited, and that there's generally more room to move after they reach that limit. So they make their concessions all the faster, knowing more back and forth will come later. Counterparts, too, learn that when negotiators say they can't agree, that's just a signal to move on to the next stage of the negotiation, escalate, and send them back for more authority. Auto dealers aren't the only ones who have taught us that we shouldn't accept a salesperson's deal until we have heard from the manager that it really is their "best, last, final" offer.

None of this is to say that negotiators should not have limits to their authority. We are certainly not advocating betting the company on an individual's judgment at the table. What we are saying is that in seeking to structure negotiation teams and processes and develop the capability to negotiate deals worth doing, simply circumscribing the negotiator's authority is one of the bluntest, and least helpful, instruments available to management. Isn't it actually somewhat backwards to allow a negotiator to set a precedent—without supervision or review—for exaggerating a problem, hiding its true cause, or making the most of temporary leverage, but tightly constrain his ability to make small changes to the value (on paper) of a complex deal requiring joint implementation?

Making it difficult for the negotiator to say "no"

Some organizations have developed a very customer-centric culture and business model that makes it very difficult for their negotiators ever to say no to a customer. Others have a similar taboo against letting a corporate function (e.g., procurement) ever say no to an internal business unit. Yet others warn relationship managers never to let things get so bad that their counterpart escalates a conflict. Regardless of how and in what context they do so, organizations that make it impossible for a negotiator to think that they can walk away from a bad deal without "facing the music" internally end up with a lot of deals they do not want.

Most experienced negotiators are familiar with the concept of a "walk-away alternative." Many, if not most, negotiation texts refer to what's known as the negotiator's best alternative to a negotiated agreement, or BATNA, a concept popularized in *Getting to Yes: Negotiating Agreement Without Giving In.* The importance of the walk-away or BATNA lies in giving negotiators a benchmark to which they can compare possible deals, so that they never take a deal that is worse than what they could accomplish by walking away, and they never mistakenly abandon a solution that is better than their best walk-away alternative. The negotiator's BATNA is a reality check. The stronger it is, the more confident negotiators can feel at the table. But when it's weak, and they can come up with no way to improve it, the BATNA serves to keep egos in check and help negotiators make good choices within real-world constraints. Organizations that effectively take away the negotiators' sense that they can say no to an offer—even if they have a reasonable alternative—disarm their negotiators and keep them from being as effective as they need to be.

Organizations can leave negotiators feeling chained to the table in a variety of ways, but they tend to share one principal characteristic: they treat the absence of an agreement as a failure. Few organizations visit any negative consequences on a negotiator who does a deal that fails during implementation. Yet most will treat the lack of an agreement not as a choice, but as the consequence of the negotiator's inability to conjure up something better. That kind of pressure creates serious problems when it comes to negotiating deals that are likely to fare well during implementation.

A negotiator who is led to believe that not reaching agreement is a "failure" is less likely to devote any time or energy to reasons for scuttling a deal, or to issues that might slow down or interfere with reaching an agreement. Any advice we might give a negotiator about raising difficult issues or working with stakeholders to understand fully what implementation requires will fall on deaf ears if the organization has made it clear that what matters is getting the deals done. When the organization identifies heroes and goats at the time the deal is concluded or rejected, instead of when value is created or destroyed later, it focuses the negotiators' attentions on the signing (or not) of the deal. But that is the wrong time frame in which to evaluate whether the negotiation has been successful.

If walking away from a deal is never applauded, but derided as a failure, why would a negotiator ever think about walking just because the conditions were not there for a successful implementation? An organization that makes it hard for a negotiator to say no should not be surprised when, after the deal is signed, "yes" turns out to have been a bad answer.

So, we have seen some of the reasons why even smart companies get it so wrong. What should an organization do to increase the chances of getting it right?

How do you build an organization that does deals worth doing?

The problems outlined in the first half of this chapter are not the result of a lack of good intentions. Even when organizations recognize they need to improve their negotiation results and set about building their teams, parceling out approval authority, and creating incentive systems, they make some flawed assumptions about what really matters in negotiation, what management ought to control, and how best to align business needs and negotiation processes. Those assumptions lead them to make some poor choices and to suffer a host of unintended consequences.

To do better, negotiators and those who send them off on their quests must recognize that negotiation is more than an individual skill. While it is easy to fall for the old stereotypes about supremely skilled practitioners who, without breaking a sweat, can persuade anyone to do anything, the reality is that negotiation is a discipline that can be practiced by an individual or by an organization. But when an organization seeks to do it well, and to get better and better at it over time, it must treat negotiation like any other critical function or process and build up its organizational capabilities. Nearly ten years ago, when we started making this argument, it was somewhat controversial. Today there are many examples of entities in both the public and private sector treating negotiation like the organizational capability it should be— from the majority of the top twenty pharmaceutical companies, who have mapped out detailed business development negotiation processes, to newly founded Negotiations Centers of Excellence at organizations from Accenture to the United States Air Force.

But how does an organization build up its capability to do deals worth doing?

When it comes to influencing the behavior of individual negotiators—people who negotiate deals on behalf of the organization, either as their full-time job or in addition to other responsibilities—organizations have a variety of ways of "telling" them to do or not do certain things, or to do or not do them in a particular way. Organizational theorists sometimes refer to these as "levers" that management can use to make sure that its intentions are understood and acted upon, and they vary in size, shape, form, and relative effectiveness from organization to organization.

We know from experience that negotiators will respond to the following practical levers. As you consider these strategies, compare them to what you have seen work in your own organization. How do you rally a large and diverse set of people to shift the way they carry out a critical business process? How do you get them to leave some bad habits behind, and embrace an approach that may require them to view their own role differently? How do you lead them to change?

Orient your negotiation process toward implementation

Scott Adams and his creation, Dilbert, have taught us to laugh at consultants descending with their process maps, which often do little more than complicate the obvious. He gets no argument from us. Using large (and often made up) words to describe everyday activities does not add any clarity to what was obscure or help individuals do a better job. That said, it is also not helpful to tell individuals to just "go negotiate" with the "other side" or to depict the entire negotiation process as one big box in the middle of a chart that says "reach agreement," as if by divine intervention or magical incantation.

If you want to change how individuals and teams in an organization negotiate, one important lever to use is to describe, in some detail, the steps or activities involved in a negotiation, articulate what roles negotiators should be playing, and define the responsibilities that go along with those roles. Whether you call this a process, a road map, a blueprint, or just a description doesn't matter. What does matter is whether it is sufficient to help negotiators understand what they are supposed to be doing and why, and how their role relates to what others are doing.

Draw a road map

If you want to keep it simple, just break the negotiation into three big steps: preparation, conduct, and review. Preparation includes the things negotiators do to clarify who their stakeholders are and what they are trying to accomplish, and to anticipate the major issues their counterparts will raise. Within conduct are activities negotiators engage in with their counterparts to set the tone and create the kind of relationship necessary to a successful outcome, and to achieve what each is trying to accomplish. This step also includes those things negotiators must do away from the table to develop a good choice between a possible deal and a walk-away alternative and then present it to their organizations. At review time, the focus shifts to a few key questions: what have we learned, and how do we ensure a smooth transition to implementation? This simple framework is described in figure 10-1.

The road map does not have to anticipate every turn and fork along the way. The purpose of the road map is not to steer the negotiation as

FIGURE 10-1

A basic negotiation road map

	Preparation	Conduct	Review
Key activities	• Clarify stakeholders • Anticipate and analyze key negotiation issues	• Set the tone and create appropriate relationship • Explore each other's interests and possible options • Explore external benchmarks, norms, and precedents • Develop a good choice between the deal and our best walk-away alternative	• Identify lessons learned • Ensure smooth transition
Ongoing activities	• Set stakeholder expectations about their involvement • Manage stakeholder involvement accordingly		

if by remote control or autopilot. The idea is to give negotiators some signposts to help them understand what to expect, how to recognize their progress, and when and how to call for assistance.

Consider your own organization and its culture. How "process-driven" are you? How much detail is usually spelled out in critical business processes, where the organization wants not only good results, but also the ability to learn from experience and improve those results over time? We have found that when you put your mind to it you can describe negotiation activities in tremendous detail. However, when compared to a wholly undefined event, even a very simple outline or process can be very helpful. Regardless of the level of detail you include, the fact that you've decided to develop such an outline or road map need not complicate life or lead to absurd metaphysical discussions about when the negotiation begins and ends. Figure 10-2 illustrates some of the typical blocks of activities we include in more robust negotiation road maps as we work with our clients—the level of detail within each block can range from a few simple steps to a complex decision tree varying by type of negotiation.

FIGURE 10-2

Enhanced negotiation road map

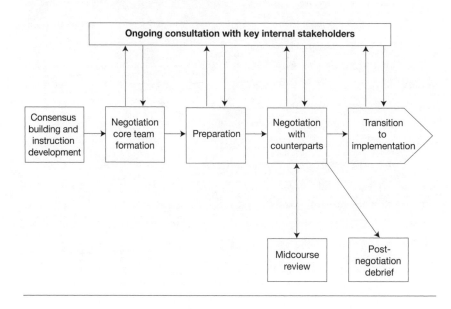

Link deals to their purposes

An organization that seeks to ensure that its deals have a point should insist on business unit sponsorship for every deal, and an articulation, however brief, by the negotiator of how a particular deal furthers the strategy of the business. This seems fairly obvious; it would be highly unusual to see a corporate development team, for example, out creating an alliance without a business unit sponsor. But in other contexts this is a step sometimes missed. When a negotiator is discounting product to close deals by the end of the quarter, one might ask whether the business unit might not be better off breaking the cycle of teaching customers to wait until the end of the quarter to make their purchases. When a procurement specialist is squeezing that last nickel from a vendor, one might ask whether the business unit receiving the goods might not prefer a bit higher level of customer service, flexibility around delivery schedules, or early access to innovation. Your road map should include check-ins with key stakeholders to ensure that negotiators have the right instructions before they start, and that they don't get to closure without checking back in to ensure the deal is serving its purpose.

Similarly, an organization that wants only to do deals worth doing should make it explicit on its negotiation road map that prior to concluding a deal, a comparison is required to the organization's walkaway alternative or BATNA. Although most negotiators would say that they always consider whether to take a deal or walk away, the reality is that this is something they usually do implicitly and, frankly, very sloppily. What negotiators usually consider is whether the deal on the table is as good as what they had decided (or were told) was their bottom line. But a bottom line is not the same thing as a well-understood walkaway alternative. A bottom line is the least you'll take from this counterpart. It does not tell you what you'll do instead if you don't get it. Too often, we find, bottom lines are either too high or too low, when compared to the value of a realistic alternative. By requiring an explicit comparison of a deal on the table against a well-defined alternative, organizations introduce a little discipline into what might otherwise be a somewhat emotional decision in the "heat of the deal." They also ensure that every deal serves a valid business purpose.

Build stakeholders into the road map

When negotiators fail to do the necessary work to engage the right decision makers and to seek input and buy-in from critical implementers, it is usually the result of a combination of factors. They may lack the knowledge or awareness of who the right stakeholders are. They may lack the skills to engage those stakeholders in a constructive way. They may find themselves unable or unwilling to devote the time and energy required to build that alignment, because of how they view their role, the directions they get from their managers, or the incentives built into their compensation system.

Thus understood, the answers to how the organization can encourage its negotiators to engage in the activities necessary to build alignment practically jump off the page. Any negotiation process for complex deals where implementation matters must explicitly call for identifying stakeholders and understanding their respective roles in any critical decisions or for effective implementation. Who are the essentials? Who are the enablers? Who are the blockers? Who will play what role in making which decisions? How do the various parties influence each other? Who defers to whom? Who antagonizes whom?

Clarify where implementers are involved in negotiation

One way of making sure that negotiators understand the importance of the precedents they create is to bring into the negotiation those who will have to live with them: the implementers. An effective negotiation road map should provide clear opportunities for implementers to have a voice in what precedents are created and what relationships are built. That does not have to mean that a delivery executive or an operations manager has to run the negotiation. But it does mean they have to play a role and influence the tone of the discussion.

In the outsourcing arena, this has become an accepted truth. Customers or would-be buyers of outsourcing are demanding to meet program managers and delivery leaders and insisting that they participate, at least toward the end of the negotiation process, and service providers are acquiescing. Initial reluctance to bring in "billable" resources too early in the process is giving way to the realization that the implementation teams need to participate in the crafting of the commitments they will later be expected to keep, and in creating the shared picture of what a successful implementation looks like.

Clarify where negotiators are involved in implementation

Similarly, effective negotiation road maps should feature an explicit role for the negotiators after the deal is signed, so that they too feel personally affected by and accountable for the precedents that are set. At the bare minimum, they should play a significant role during a formal handoff and joint review of the results of the negotiation. Ideally, they should have some ongoing obligation to be responsible for what they created.

Make sure negotiators have tools adequate to the job

It is a well-known truism that if you only have a hammer, every problem looks like a nail. When negotiators believe that their principal tools are lists of possible concessions and perhaps an economic model for valuing them, they tend to negotiate by making (and demanding) concessions. Their thinking about negotiation strategy focuses on when to make which concession, how reasonable a position to start with, how large a concession to follow with, and so forth. If you want to help negotiators change how they view the process and their role in it, providing them with a larger and more diverse toolbox is an important part of the overall solution.

Create a negotiator's toolkit—and make sure it's used

To be clear, we are not suggesting that you simply throw a bunch of tools at negotiators and expect much to change. The last twenty years have seen too much "shelfware" developed by companies who promised us the workforce would make better decisions, be more productive, and be more stimulated and satisfied in their jobs, only to find that employees almost uniformly refused to play along. Whether we are talking about software, paper and pencil forms, or just conceptual "tools," these can at best be only part of the answer. And yet it is hard to imagine how the modern, decentralized organization, with lots of individuals carrying out lots of negotiations in different places, at different times, and with very different stakes, can truly expect to change how people negotiate without relying to some extent on such devices to support consistency and transparency.

To be most useful (and most likely to be used), a negotiator's toolkit should be well matched to the road map people are expected to follow. If the tools do not help the negotiator to more effectively carry out the activities in the road map, then what purpose do they serve? In our experience, the place where negotiators often have the greatest need for, and can get the most benefit from, a well-thought-out set of tools is during preparation. Here tools can help them benefit from lessons learned by others. Tools can ensure that key stakeholders are sufficiently connected to the negotiation and their perspectives adequately considered. Some of the most effective organizations we have seen use tools to identify and map relationships among key external and internal stakeholders, to help generate and assess a range of different solutions that meet different individual and organizational interests, to help negotiators "get in the other side's shoes," and to help negotiators choose general strategies and specific tactics to use once they engage.

Equally useful in the longer term are tools that help during the review step. Once negotiators have completed the negotiation, spending a few minutes, either individually or as part of a team, reflecting on some of the lessons learned is extremely valuable. Not only does it help the original negotiators develop an awareness that will be useful when those lessons apply in the future, but it also helps all those negotiators who follow them into similar situations and can benefit from their insight as they prepare. If preparing well beforehand is the single most important thing an individual negotiator can do to improve his or her results, reviewing afterward is the most important thing an organization can do to continuously improve its results over time. However, it can be very difficult to persuade negotiators that they should take the time, especially if they are anxious to move on to the next deal.

A number of years ago, executives at one of our clients decided that while they had a pretty darn good set of individual practitioners, they wanted to see if they could improve how they negotiated as an organization. They implemented a number of changes, but one that has had tremendous payoff is their investment in harvesting and applying lessons learned. When they embarked on this project, their teams were quite isolated. They are in the insurance business, and each team adjusted different kinds of claims—some were maritime, some were aviation, others health, pollution, and so on. Those teams were fairly certain that nothing one of them did or learned was at all relevant or worth sharing with other teams, since the nature of the risks involved, the contracts at issue, and the legal rules under which they operated were all so different. They generally dealt with different kinds of claimants, typically represented by different law firms, and were used to following different procedures. Nonetheless, management decided that they would make the effort to gather and share some insights.

The question was how to get negotiators to make the time to debrief. They were all working quite hard already, and the reality was that many of the claims they settled were fairly routine and indeed held few new lessons. After some discussion, management decided that they would put the key decision about whether a particular negotiation was worth debriefing in the hands of the individual negotiators, entrusting them to make the right call for the organization. They went about it in a rather clever way, however, that helps illustrate how a little analysis can help support change in the organization.

The organization adopted a multilayered approach to reviews. The nature of the debrief and the obligation to share lessons learned grow along with the importance and relevance of the lessons. Only one step is required for all negotiations, and that step literally takes no more than five minutes. To close out a file at the end of a negotiation, the claims adjuster must answer four or five simple questions, along the lines of "Did you try anything new in this negotiation?" "Did you observe your counterpart to be doing anything particularly interesting or effective?" "Did you learn anything in this negotiation?" and so forth. Senior management also made it clear that it was perfectly acceptable to answer no to all four or five questions and move on. But they also made it clear that it was not acceptable to say no *every* time, and that if someone answered no to every question about their last dozen negotiations, it was fair game to tap them on the shoulder and ask if they were sleepwalking. Once someone answered yes to a particular question, that did not automatically trigger a major, time-consuming process. It just required the individual negotiator to have a conversation with his or her manager about the nature of the lesson learned and whether it warranted a simple write-up for the organization's "Knowledge Tree" (as they called their knowledge data base) or merited a debrief session, large or small, with a report either to that person's immediate team or to a larger group.

The organization equipped negotiators with simple templates for debriefs of varying durations and complexity and a simple form for adding lessons learned to the Knowledge Tree. The templates and the structure that described when to use each one were designed to encourage negotiators to use them. Management also set clear expectations that these tools should be used, and that monthly unit meetings and quarterly divisional meetings would include presentations on lessons learned by the different teams. After an initial launch in which management sponsored some contests to encourage teams to submit lessons and populate the Knowledge Tree, the program developed a life of its own, and teams not only submitted lessons but reported that they consistently found useful tidbits when they consulted the Knowledge Tree as part of their preparation.

Supply tools to map stakeholder relationships

Negotiators can be left to their own devices to identify stakeholders, but tools that guide them with good questions, a visual representation of the stakeholders, and some advice about how to sequence their approach can help ensure that they neither miss critical stakeholders nor waste time seeking unnecessary consensus. In our consulting practice we have come across a variety of tools for mapping relationships, from the fairly simple to the highly complex. Some are more conceptual and can be sketched on the back of a napkin, whereas others leverage extensive data in corporate information systems. One of our favorite examples is a simple software tool (named the "Sourcerer's Apprentice") that we helped the corporate sourcing and procurement team at a global media and entertainment client to design. It enables a user to input three variables (the commodity sought, the approximate size of the purchase, and the business unit purchasing the commodity), then channels the user into one of twenty-eight different road maps with a complete list of stakeholders to be involved and tips on what kind of involvement each class of stakeholder ought to have.

The more complex your organization, the greater the need for tools to "navigate the network" effectively. The old days when people stayed in an organization for an entire career, worked in silos, and could rely on personal relationships for the right connections are largely gone. With highly matrixed teams that frequently form and reform with great fluidity and rapidity, the need for tools to set the right decision-making roles and facilitate appropriate alignment is steadily increasing in importance.

Incorporate precedent setting into your strategy playbook

We have helped many organizations to create strategy playbooks as part of their negotiator's toolkit. Some of these are very informal, high-level, and impressionistic. Others are much more detailed, tactical, and specific. If the organization wants the negotiator to intentionally create precedents that will serve the organization well during implementation, it makes sense to include precedent-setting considerations into the standard moves of the organization's negotiating teams. Effective negotiation tools require negotiators to think about what kinds of challenges they should anticipate during implementation, and what kind of precedents they could create during the negotiation that would be helpful later.

The more you believe, for example, that relative power between the parties may shift later, the more important it is to create a precedent for dealing with each other through persuasion rather than coercion, and for relying on objective standards or criteria. The more you believe that effective implementation will require agility, the more important it is to create precedents for rapid decision making, as close to the problem as possible, and with limited escalations. The more you believe that effective implementation will require creativity and innovation, the more you'll want to look back on situations where the two negotiation teams jointly analyzed problems and brainstormed solutions. An effective playbook should help negotiators explore these and other possible implementation needs and develop a negotiation strategy that takes the importance of precedent into account.

In creating any kind of negotiation strategy playbook, ensure that the consequences of certain strategies and tactics are elaborated. Beware of prescribing strategies that, if deployed by the other side, would lead to devastating consequences. We say this not out of some mushy notion of the golden rule ("Do unto others as you would have them do unto you"), but rather because the precedents you set for how to behave during the negotiation may lead your counterpart to feel fully justified in behaving that way toward you when the going gets tough during implementation.

Encourage dealing with risk by supplying risk management tools

Some negotiators have a tendency to ignore risks and march blithely forward with deals that are unlikely to succeed. Others try to do everything they can through the terms of the deal to push the risks onto everyone else, and to insulate their organization through representations, warranties, exceptions, true-ups, claw-back clauses, SLAs, default provisions, liquidated damages, and more. But neither of these extremes is actually helping create the desired product: a deal that works and produces value. What negotiators need is to apply some well-established principles for risk management. Some simple tools or templates to guide them will make that process easier.

Our friend and colleague Howard Raiffa, the father of decision theory and one of the foremost proponents of bringing rigorous analysis to negotiation, years ago taught us a very simple framework for managing risk. When faced with a substantial risk, follow a three-part strategy:

1. *Learn*—Reduce the uncertainty. Seek ways to gather more information to improve your decision making.

2. *Prevent*—Reduce the likelihood of the hazard. Look for ways to make it less likely that the problem will come to pass.

3. *Mitigate*—Reduce the impact of the hazard. Do those things that will minimize the damage if, despite your prevention efforts, the problem does occur.

Applying such a tool to potential risks to effective implementation can help negotiators better understand what questions to ask of their counterpart, what options to consider for preventing the problem jointly, and what joint or separate measures to plan on for mitigation. Part of the negotiator's toolkit ought to be a simple template for analyzing likely difficulties in implementation and planning to maximize the likelihood of effective implementation.

Enhance their skills—in context

You'll find lots of negotiation training courses out there, and like everything else, some are better than others. Aside from the obvious recommendation—take a close look at what they are proposing to teach, what their material is based on, how closely the materials match your environment, and who is delivering the training—our advice is that you focus beyond the training itself to how it will be connected to and integrated with what your negotiators actually do every day.

Training, no matter how well rated by participants, is not likely to change how they negotiate unless you succeed in conveying to the participants that this is not "just a workshop" but an effort to equip them with immediately relevant skills that the organization views as critical to their day-to-day responsibilities. If they come back from training and discover that their managers don't know or don't care what they were taught or encouraged to do, participants will soon get the idea that the training and real life are two different things. If after training they have nowhere to turn for reinforcement of lessons learned or for coaching, negotiators will conclude that the techniques they learned were "nice to know about" but not something they are expected to use regularly. If they come back from training enthusiastic about things like good preparation and building alignment but find that those activities are neither rewarded nor even permitted by their actual work circumstances, they will become cynical and consider the training a waste of time.

To have an impact on how negotiators behave and whether they incorporate effective implementation in their deals, training should be connected to the road map negotiators are expected to follow. If the road map calls for extensive stakeholder involvement, for example, negotiators need skills that will help them identify and engage stakeholders, listen and learn without getting locked into a particular stakeholder's position, and build buy-in around possible solutions. But in a different context, where the stakeholders are few and are directly involved at the table, such skills may be less important than ones that will help negotiators engage in difficult conversations with their counterparts (or perhaps their teammates) about whether their commitments are realistic. Time is precious. Priorities must be set and trade-offs made among all the things for which it might be nice to offer training. Make sure that what training you deliver is well suited to what you are asking negotiators to do.

Negotiators rarely work in a vacuum. To improve the implementability of your deals, therefore, you should involve not only the negotiators themselves but some of their peers, their managers, and those who play important supporting roles. By having managers participate in some way during the training, you assure that they understand the concepts, the models, even the vocabulary that negotiators are learning and can use it as they work with their direct reports on upcoming deals. By also including individuals who may not be at the table but nonetheless play other important roles, you surround the negotiators with people who understand both what the negotiators will be doing and how they will be doing it. Those individuals can then be more supportive, reinforcing the training, and can contribute more effectively, whatever their own role.

A great example of this practice is the one at Procter & Gamble Pharmaceutical's Regulatory Affairs Department, where Lynne Tracey, the head of the group, trained her entire team.[8] As a result, not only did the individuals who actually negotiate details of clinical trials, submissions, and labeling with the FDA have the opportunity to improve their skills, but so did those who support them in the background and those who ultimately have to answer for the negotiated outcomes. Together, they all explored what was challenging about those negotiations and developed strategies for dealing with those challenges. Because the training has the participants play both the role of the company and the role of the regulator, the participants developed a better appreciation of each other's roles with regard to negotiations, and of a way to help each other continue to improve. Now, when managers check in with front-line negotiators, they can rely on a common vocabulary and a repertoire of models and tools for coaching.

Create a mind-set conducive to deals that can be implemented

Changing a mind-set is one of the thorniest parts of building real organizational capability to do deals worth doing. The question is not so much what kind of a mind-set to create—we've certainly spelled that out here—but how to do so. Because of the nature of negotiation—at some point, individuals have to be off on their own, engaging in critical activities without hands-on supervision—you really need to persuade your negotiators of what you want to accomplish and how; you need to win their hearts and minds, because without those, you will fail. Libraries are filled with volumes on how to exercise leadership, create organizational cultures, and drive organizational change. We won't even pretend to summarize or compete with that body of work. Rather, we will briefly describe some things we have seen work. In our experience, some of the most effective organizations incorporate several of these approaches.

Tell 'em what, why, and how

If you want negotiators to change their behavior and negotiate as if implementation mattered, you must be explicit about that objective. There is simply too much emphasis in our popular and business culture on hotshot deal makers and the importance of closing the deal. So if you expect negotiators to have a different objective in mind, you need to make that clear. Executives at all levels in the organization consistently need to send and reinforce the message that the objective of the negotiation is *not* to sign a piece of paper. It is to benefit from the actions the parties will take *after* the paper is signed. They need to articulate why implementation matters and how the way the deal is negotiated is likely to impact the eventual success or failure of that implementation.

Measure critical business outcomes and activities along the way

For better or worse, we live in a society where things either "count" or they don't. Generations of managers have been taught that "if you can't measure it, you can't manage it." So if you want to instill a mind-set that implementation matters, it seems pretty obvious that you should develop metrics that are tied to successful implementation, rather than to a successful close. But when organizations seek to do that, they often encounter some resistance from the negotiators. Negotiators don't typically control implementation. They often don't even play much of a role in it. Negotiators (be they in sales, purchasing, corporate development, or other functions) uniformly consider it downright unfair that they should be measured on whether someone else successfully picks up where they left off and does a good job.

The answer to us seems twofold: avoid the temptation to go from one extreme to another and be clever about how you measure not only *what* the negotiator produces, but *how* they did so. It would be unfair to measure a negotiator's performance entirely by what happens during implementation. It should feel equally unfair to completely *ignore* implementation when considering how good a job the negotiator did in creating the conditions for implementation. The goal should be to develop a balanced view, incorporating some things directly under the negotiator's control and others that they influence indirectly by how they negotiated. The components of such a scorecard that relate to the negotiation itself look not only at the agreement reached, but also at whether their activities are conducive to a deal that can be implemented. Did they prepare well? Did they engage critical stakeholders? Did they raise tough issues to ensure that any commitments were realistic?

Use carrots and sticks, but in moderation

Rewards (and penalties, where appropriate) are closely related to the question of metrics. Our advice about making sure that you measure the things that matter (like implementation results, or negotiation activities conducive to good implementation) as opposed to the things that are easy to measure (number of deals, size of deals) applies equally to incentive systems. Rewarding implementation is an important part of an organizational effort to change the behavior of negotiators, as is rewarding behaviors that help position the deal well for implementation. Indeed, some firms have started making sure that part of their negotiator's compensation is dependent on whether the deal produces value. For example, in the outsourcing arena, some of the top-tier service providers, like IBM and HP, make the incentive pay of their lead negotiators dependent on whether the deal is doing well during its first eighteen months or so. This is based on the assumption that it is the negotiator's responsibility to position the deal for success as the relationship is launched, but recognizes that too many variables outside the negotiator's control influence implementation years later.

Perhaps as important as creating new appropriate incentives in support of the desired behaviors is making sure you *eliminate disincentives* that deter negotiators from doing the right thing. Compensation systems that reward closing deals or signing contracts, without regard to whether those deals are realistic, have the necessary buy-in, or will ever produce value, do considerable damage. Asking negotiators to do things against their own interests—like walking away from bad deals, or pushing hard to make sure commitments are realistic before accepting them—is a very tall order for any change management program. Better to take the time up front to at least remove the biggest obstacles than to fight lengthy battles later over why negotiators resist clear directions from management, fail to use the tools provided, or neglect to invest time working with stakeholders. The answer is that they are just doing what the company pays them to do.

While incentives are without a doubt an important lever available to management, also take care not to become overly reliant on them. Individuals in an organization that is driven entirely by incentive systems quickly learn how to score highly on those measures without necessarily accomplishing what the organization hoped. To the extent that you treat your negotiators as if they were "coin-operated," they will behave that way. But we have yet to see an incentive system that couldn't be gamed, or where all the desired behaviors could be measured and compensated. Negotiation, particularly in the case of complex deals where implementation matters, requires more engaged, and more subtle, management systems.

Walk the talk

"Do what I say, and not what I do" really doesn't work when it comes to managing negotiators who do a lot of their work behind closed doors, without the benefit of direct management oversight. Negotiators need to believe that those things the organization is telling them to do are the same things that, when push comes to shove, their managers would do. In the context of negotiating as if implementation matters, this means that negotiators need to know their managers support analyzing their walk-away alternatives. They need to see their managers invest time in gaining stakeholder alignment. They need to see them asking the tough questions when the need arises.

Negotiating as if implementation matters will feel risky to some negotiators. They will perceive, and be at least partially right, that when they follow some of the advice in this book, they are putting in jeopardy some deals that might otherwise have closed. If they do not see their managers and their managers' managers also taking similar risks, and if the managers don't seem to be analyzing the deals in jeopardy for whether they are deals worth doing, they will quickly get the message that the risks are not worth taking. If you cannot "walk the talk," don't bother with all the rest of it, because you won't succeed.

Get the structure right

Of all the ways that management can seek to influence negotiator behavior, organizational structure is not our favorite approach. We find too many companies use structure as the answer to all problems, and just as often, people take the wrong message from an organizational chart (or changes thereto). Unless carefully managed, some particular structures, like negotiation departments, have a tendency to create more problems than they solve. Throwing a group of deal makers together and making them responsible for just getting deals signed can lead to situations like the ones that developed at AOL and Enron International.

We think it is much more useful to clarify the steps negotiators should follow and their roles and responsibilities, to equip them with the right tools and the right skills to carry out that process, and to ensure that management supports (and monitors) them as they follow the process. Structure is often a proxy for whose directions you follow and who pays your bonus. There are simply better levers to use to enable an organization to leverage resources.

This is not to say that any particular structure is invariably an impediment, just because that structure is sometimes problematic. A well-managed team of full-time negotiators can be very effective if they have close ties to the business units for whom they negotiate deals, a clear process that involves critical stakeholders and requires discussion of difficult issues, and metrics and incentives focused on implementation and the negotiation activities that lay a good foundation for it. It is indeed worth examining whether restructuring where your negotiators sit and who they report to will help you get deals that are better implemented. The key is making sure that all those other pieces are in place, rather than relying on structure alone to carry the burden.

An organization ought to consider whether any structural mechanisms can encourage negotiators to keep the purpose of the deal in sight. Accenture, for example, established a Negotiations Center of Excellence in the middle of 2006. Part of the mandate for that organization is to ensure that big engagements are crafted through a careful negotiation process and serve the company's purposes well, including the ability to deliver profitably with a high level of client satisfaction.

The center is focused on improving Accenture's negotiation capabilities and effectiveness. Critical parts of their strategy include creating tools and processes to support negotiations at Accenture and ensuring that management supports and reinforces negotiation dynamics that maximize chances for durable agreements.

Some structures are more likely to encourage negotiators to involve at least some stakeholders. For example, embedding negotiators in the business units who will own the deal or be responsible for implementing it creates some powerful incentives and even peer pressure to make sure the interests of those stakeholders are well represented. Similarly, even within a dedicated negotiation function or department, associating individual negotiators with specific business units can have a similar effect. Finally, in some highly matrixed organizations, we have seen dotted-line reporting structures work well to ensure adequate advance consultation with the units key to implementation. What none of these approaches actually addresses, however, is the involvement of other stakeholders who are unrelated to the business unit or function in question.

Even though we don't recommend overestimating the power of restructuring to fix problems of alignment, we do suggest checking for structural impediments to alignment. If you find such impediments, whether caused by geographical distance, different reporting chains, different metrics, or any other factor, it is worthwhile to ask yourself how to break down these barriers most effectively. Will changing the structure do it, or might you have more impact by pulling other levers? Instead of yet another reorganization, might it be more effective to work on a better road map that identifies and engages stakeholders? To give negotiators better tools or better skills for getting consensus? To support them with a corporate mind-set that values alignment as a virtue?

In summary, an organization has several levers to enable, exhort, and incent its personnel to do deals with a point. Leaders can create self-fulfilling prophecies. If they assume that negotiation is an art and cannot be approached in an organized, systematic matter, then it will be difficult to achieve across-the-board improvements. On the other hand, if leaders assume that they have several levers by which to create the context for deals with a point, they and their shareholders are likely to be rewarded by deals that deliver more value over time.

PART III

Critical Deals in Which Implementation Matters

Bet-the-Company Deals

Mergers, alliances, and outsourcing

As we all well know, there are negotiations and then there are Negotiations. Some deals feel like they are one-time events. They are momentous for the organization. They might involve an acquisition, a joint venture or alliance, or the outsourcing of a significant back-office function like information technology, human resources, or finance and accounting. The seriousness and formality with which organizations undertake these negotiations and the people directly involved in them give this work a very different feel from that of the day-to-day negotiations with a customer, supplier, or established business partner.

In our experience, these relatively infrequent negotiations, despite the greater attention they receive, are not necessarily more important than the many daily negotiations that can either grease the wheels or gum up the works with critical suppliers or key customers. But they do have somewhat different dynamics, and they tend to involve different people in the organization (and often external advisers), so to do justice to those differences, we'll look at them in two different chapters.

Business combinations: mergers, acquisitions, and joint ventures

Not every organization goes through one of these, and that may be a very good thing for those that don't. These kinds of deals bring together two companies to create a new one, whether through a full-blown merger or acquisition where one of the original companies ceases to exist, or by creating a joint venture, where the parent companies go on as before but also create a new shared offspring. Regardless of which approach you take, they are very difficult to do well. So difficult, in fact, that more than half of these deals destroy value.

The facts can be a bit sketchy, because not everyone is eager to air dirty laundry. The very definition of success or failure for a merger or a joint venture is debatable. But among those who do debate these things, it is fairly well accepted that from the perspective of the shareholders of the acquirer, *the success rate is less than one in two.*[1] You need only look as far as the business page of your local paper. Pretty much every time an acquisition is announced, the stock price of the buyer drops because the market knows what many CEOs seem to ignore.[2]

In our experience, these failures are more often about implementation than about whether the deal was a good idea: computer systems that fail to operate well together; cultures that conflict; turf battles among managers; unrealistic time lines; and often painful failures to reach out to and work with key stakeholders, including customers, suppliers, and other business partners who rightfully get nervous about how they will be impacted by the deal. The consequences are predictable: employee morale suffers, and those who are best able to find better positions do so. Key decisions fail to get made, or if made, receive no follow-up. Products are late to market. Customer service suffers, as does customer confidence in the new organization. Long-term suppliers get skittish and hedge their bets.

Before we dive in, it is worth making an important clarification. When it comes to acquisitions, implementation does not always matter, at least not to both parties. Buyers certainly care. But among sellers of corporate assets there will be some to whom implementation matters a great deal—for example, if it is a stock deal and the value of the shares they receive depends on how the deal is perceived by the market and how well it is implemented. But there are also sellers who have little incentive or obligation to worry about implementation. If the deal calls for payment in cash and the seller will have nothing else to do with the combined entity, implementation does not really matter to the seller. Perhaps the clearest example comes from looking at the board of directors of a publicly traded company being acquired: the obligation of those board members to the current shareholders is to get the best price they can and to maximize the likelihood the deal will close. Whether they are negotiating directly, or just instructing third-party negotiators, they have little reason to care about what happens after the close.

The advice in this chapter therefore, like that throughout the book, is focused primarily on those for whom the point is not the transaction but what comes after. We direct our attention primarily to buyers and to those involved in stock mergers and joint ventures.

The roots of the problem: doing deals for the sake of the deal

Much has been written about these kinds of deals—from the social implications for employees and the communities in which they live, to the consumer protection, competition, and balance of trade issues that follow consolidation of market share in ever larger firms. There are many writers who offer advice to those considering whether to do a deal and with whom. Others focus on how to manage through the many challenges of bringing the two firms, their processes, and their cultures together after the deal is signed. We won't try to rehearse their arguments here or to replace some of the excellent guides to these deals. Our intent is primarily to add a dimension to the discussion: how should the importance of implementation affect the negotiation. In these few pages we will focus on applying the themes of this book to the context of mergers and acquisitions and joint venture negotiations.

These "business combination" deals where two companies become one or come together to create a separate third entity don't tend to fail because the executives who came up with the idea are blind or stupid. Usually the problem is not that smart people didn't think hard about the strategy, or about the price they should pay. Yet experience and research both confirm that many deals turn out badly because of a lack of strategic fit between the buyer and the acquirer, because the buyer overpaid, or because integration and implementation broke down. The roots of all of these problems are found in how the deals are negotiated. In particular, we find that these deals suffer from inadequate consultation of important stakeholders and a rush to do the deal that ignores, if not actively suppresses, difficult questions about its real risks.[3] Finally, depending on how they play their role, external advisers can aggravate both of these problems. We'll look at each of these issues in turn.

Ignoring key stakeholders because "time kills deals" can kill implementation

"Time kills deals" is a bit of common wisdom that is both true and misleading in what it seems to imply. When negotiations drag on, the deal making loses momentum. When that happens, circumstances can change, making the deal seem less interesting. The attention of executives can wander, or critics of the deal can find time to rally the opposition. A competitor or adversary or other suitor has time to intervene. These fears tend to drive negotiators, who view it as their job to get the deal done, to do all sorts of things that later hamper implementation.

The first and most obvious consequence of rushing to agreement is that buyers overpay. The easiest way to ensure sellers will sell is to offer to pay them more or, what can be effectively the same thing, to give in on key terms and conditions. When deal makers worry about a negotiation dragging on too long, one of the first things that goes out the window is any objectivity about value. Because most acquisition negotiations require a fair amount of subjective analysis about the potential synergies a buyer may achieve through the deal, it is possible to justify a broad range of prices for any given deal. But just because the numbers can be rationalized does not mean the deal can achieve the buyer's purposes.

In the name of speed, consulting with stakeholders and building alignment are also given short shrift. These stakeholders are likely to have useful views about whether the deal really fits well with the buyer's business strategy. But deal makers often don't want to hear the answer.

Prior to the start of the negotiations, the buyer's senior management had probably been sold on some view of why this deal made sense strategically. The chances that, in the search for alignment with other stakeholders, the view will *improve* and the deal will seem even *more* strategic are quite low. More likely, those who are consulted later in the process will raise questions or challenge assumptions, which can only get in the way of closing the deal.

Of course, what these negotiators miss is that sometimes deals that tank because they took too long to close *should* have tanked, because they would not have withstood the test of changing circumstances, would have starved for lack of executive support, or would have failed for lack of buy-in among those charged with implementation. In the case of a business combination, a rush to judgment routinely causes implementation problems later.

The fear that "loose lips sink ships" can shut down needed communication

It is also true that the more people who know about a big deal, the more likely it is that someone will think of a reason not to do it. Furthermore, the more people who know about a deal, the more likely it is that someone will try to take advantage of the information. Even though there are laws against insider trading or divulging trade secrets, having too many people privy to the deal before it is done exposes the organization to unacceptable risks from regulators, competitors, the media, and all sorts of other opportunists. In the name of secrecy, however, too many stakeholders are kept in the dark.

The veil of secrecy put around these deals—whether or not it is justified by the need to protect the organization or the deal—almost guarantees that important information and critical interests will not be considered. Risks and potential implementation problems (which might have been raised by those very stakeholders who are being kept in the dark) are played down or simply deferred. Lead negotiators tend to look askance at anyone on their own team who asks too many difficult questions, calling it "negative thinking" with no place in the "war room" where strategies are being developed. The perspective that "those problems can be addressed during postmerger integration" seems to be a ready excuse for ignoring real operational challenges that often then prevent companies from achieving the synergies that were supposed to justify the premium they agreed to pay.

It's not only opponents of the deal who may not be able to raise their concerns. Among the stakeholders excluded for the sake of expediency are often people who would be supportive but who might have information critical to understanding possible obstacles and how to overcome them, who might help make time lines more realistic, or who might help deal makers seize additional opportunities. Now, it would be naïve to suggest that full disclosure to all interested parties is a sensible way to deal with this problem. In many business combinations, some of the synergies and savings come from reducing head count and eliminating redundancies, and it would be foolish to forewarn anyone who might think that they could be adversely impacted by the deal or to imply they might all have a say in the matter. Just because involving everyone would be a mistake doesn't mean that excluding all naysayers is a wise path either.

Balancing the need to carry out thorough due diligence and hear from relevant stakeholders against the risks associated with letting too many people know about the deal is not easy. We have no simple formula for how many stakeholders are too few or too many to consult. But we do know that failing to understand and anticipate integration challenges was identified as the leading cause of deal failure in a Bain & Company survey of two hundred fifty global executives, and that many of those integration challenges could be better understood with more communication with those managers who will have to make the new combined business work well. In a subsequent study, researchers at Bain looked at best-in-class corporate buyers and at the best practices of leading private equity firms for ways to help improve results. Their conclusion is that the best thing a buyer can do to make better decisions about whether to proceed with a deal or walk away is to "ask and answer the big questions in due diligence."[4] Business combinations worth doing are worth doing even when they have been subjected to criticism before being finalized. Business combinations worth doing at all are worth doing well.

Relying on "hired guns" to do the dirty work leaves parties unable to work together

In many business combination negotiations, investment bankers or other consultants take on the role of being the "bad guys" so that the relationship between the principals is not damaged. Sounds like a good plan—you get all the benefits of tough deal making with none of the consequences. They can push for the last dollar, ignore whether the commitments made are well informed and realistic, and rely on time-tested pressure tactics.

Of course, as anyone who has lived though such a deal and its aftermath will tell you, the fact that these tactics are used by a third party does not really remove their sting or change their implications for implementation. Even when the hard bargainers exit right after the final celebratory dinner, the other side still feels coerced, bamboozled, or otherwise taken advantage of.

When the other side is also represented by a third party, the dual layer may mitigate some of the potential relationship damage. After all, both sides understand that they are represented by professional "bad cops" so the principals can play the "good cops." Unfortunately, it also doubles the barrier to the parties' ability to get to know one another and create the kinds of precedents and relationships needed to help them deal with the challenges of implementation. Without that knowledge, implementation of the deal only gets harder.

The other challenge that third parties can introduce into the negotiation comes from their own set of interests and priorities. When third-party advisers get paid only if the deal is done, their incentives are clear—and somewhat in conflict with those of a principal who wants more than a signed contract.

Third parties who have no further skin in the game after the deal is signed have little reason to ask whether commitments are realistic. They also tend to impose the restrictions noted earlier to keep critics out of the room and draw a veil of secrecy over the whole negotiation. It's no small wonder. Anything that slows or jeopardizes the deal puts their paycheck at risk, whereas any problems that arise during implementation happen after they have been paid and left. Third parties have a strong legal and financial interest in doing a competent and professional job in crafting the deal. A few of the most senior and experienced advisers, especially those who have themselves been principals in acquisition negotiations, know their clients appreciate it when the adviser recommends the client *not* do a particular deal. They all want a reputation for being ethical, effective, and capable of creative deals that look good to their clients. But unfortunately, that reputational interest does not often extend to whether the deals they negotiate are successful during implementation.

Negotiate business combinations that have a point

All of the advice in this book is relevant when you are negotiating a stock merger or putting together a joint venture. There are few kinds of deals where implementation matters more, at least to the buyer, than in a business combination, yet certain actions taken during the negotiation predictably lead to trouble in such deals. It is worth paying special attention to these issues, and we have some advice aimed at the principals in these deals as well as tips for their external advisers.

Advice to principals

As the consumers of these services, you need to make clear what you are asking your advisers to do, and what role you intend to play. Even more to the point, you need to be clear how you measure success: is it just getting the deal done, or are you looking for more?

Ask Advisers About Their Approach to Implementation. When you are deciding whether to use an investment banker or consultant, make sure you ask your candidates about their approach to enabling implementation. What do they do during the negotiation to ensure that implementation proceeds smoothly? When do they check back with principals postdeal to measure their satisfaction with the outcome? Do they have a rigorous process for getting implementers involved during the negotiation process? Some of them may be surprised when you ask, and respond by showing you how well they rate on the "league tables" that indicate how many deals each bank or consulting firm has done.

But the point is not how many deals they have negotiated. The point is how many of those deals have achieved their purposes.

This conversation provides an excellent opportunity to learn about their experience with those things that tend to go wrong. They have probably seen more deals than you have and have heard more horror stories. How can they help you improve your due diligence efforts by drawing on their vast repertoire? How can they help you keep an eye on strategic fit as you both learn more about the target firm? Let them know that you expect them to articulate key assumptions underlying their price recommendation *and how you might test those assumptions* during the negotiation and due diligence.

To some extent, this is a conversation about the role you expect them to play. Make sure they understand that you want more from them than just deal execution: you want them to help you execute a deal that will work, and you believe that what happens during the negotiation has everything to do with the success or failure of implementation.

Insist on Staying Involved. After you have made it clear that implementation matters and that you expect them to negotiate with your ultimate goals in mind, you then have to remain engaged and involved. If implementation matters, then no matter how good your intermediaries or advisers, those who are critical to implementation have to play a role in putting the deal together. That does not mean you should not rely on the expertise of your bankers and consultants. They may well be indispensable to getting the deal right and doing it at the right price. It does mean that you cannot just go on autopilot and assume they can run the deal, pulling you in now and then.

You should verify that key stakeholders have been catalogued on both sides of the deal—and are being appropriately included. Raise the difficult questions and ensure that others on the negotiation team feel able to ask them as well. Be certain that careful thinking has gone into what happens after the signing and that plans are being developed in parallel to the work on the deal itself. And perhaps most important, don't delegate the creation of precedent and your "history." You must make sure that during the negotiation you are learning what it is like to work with your counterparts and to solve problems with them, and that they are learning the same about you.

Advice to advisers

As consultants ourselves, we are most assuredly not anti-advisers. However, that does not mean that we believe external advisers can't or shouldn't do better. If success rates are to improve, advisers must play a more constructive role during negotiation, leading to better implementation. It is not enough to say, "Well, they will bring in someone else to do the postmerger integration work." By then a lot of opportunities to get things right from the start will have been squandered and barriers will have been created.

Educate Clients on the Importance of Implementability. Our best advice to our friends in the investment banking and deal consultant communities is to negotiate your role or mandate to include implementability. Do not accept the client's statement that all they want from you is to strike the best deal possible and that they will worry about the rest. That is foolhardy at best and impossible in the vast majority of cases. Business combinations are not just fungible commodities. *How* they are negotiated has everything to do with how they will be implemented, and you and your client need to be on the same page about this. We have all heard the Wall Street truism that "you can only be as good a negotiator as your client will allow you to be." And yet we also know that the best advisers help their clients recognize the deals they should not do or when their insistence on particular terms or conditions is likely to come back to haunt them during implementation.

Stake your reputation and competitive differentiation on doing deals that work in the long term. Think about your portfolio of projects over that last year or two. What percentage of those were deals where you could say that implementation mattered to your client? The higher the percentage, the better the indication that if you could deliver demonstrably better deals, the world would beat a path to your door. How might you change your approach to negotiating these deals and how might you measure the impact of those changes in ways that matter to your target clients? Might you also consider putting some of your fees at risk for twelve months or so, to show that you are committed to doing deals that work?

Consider the Benefits, Not Just the Costs, of a More Inclusive Process. We all understand that there are legal and strategic reasons to keep a "cone of silence" around some sensitive business combination negotiations. And we also understand that as an adviser, the quicker you can sign the deal, the higher the margin on your engagement is likely to be. Notwithstanding those facts, as you think about how inclusive to make the process, consider the benefits, and not just the costs, of involving more stakeholders, even if you do so later in the process once the existence of the deal becomes more widely known.

Identifying stakeholders who may not be able to block the deal but who might be able to make or break implementation will mean more people to bring into the process and a broader set of interests to accommodate. We understand this makes your job a bit harder. But doing so will make it substantially more likely that the deal will succeed, which is good for your client and, over time, great for your reputation.

Not all of these stakeholders need to be in the same room with the other side during every negotiation session. You should certainly think carefully about who you tap as a resource for preparation and who should be involved in face-to-face meetings with the counterparts. Our advice is to find and encourage those who will be responsible for implementation and for delivering on the expected synergies as early as possible and have them help you test your assumptions, identify big implementation challenges, and take some ownership for implementing deal terms they helped shape. In the preparation room, naysayers and devil's advocates are your friends: they tell you what you need to think about to be successful and they allow you to address issues at the negotiation table, while you still have an opportunity to do so.

You can also leverage your extensive experience here. You and your team have collectively seen a lot of deals, based on a wide range of assumptions, and using a wide variety of structures. You know a lot of those assumptions tend to be wrong and that a lot of those structures sound better in theory than they work in practice. Share your perspectives on agreements that call for dual headquarters or co-CEOs. Where have you seen those work, or not? How well do "mergers of equals" work when they call for split boards of directors? The question is not just whether you can negotiate such provisions on their behalf, but how those terms accomplish your client's goals for the deal. Is there a point to winning such deal terms if the consequences are massive problems in implementation?

Push to Make Sure Commitments Are Realistic. Orient due diligence toward implementation and ensuring commitments are realistic, as opposed to simply validating reps and warranties. Every business combination negotiation requires extensive due diligence, carried out by teams of accountants and attorneys, and sometimes subject matter experts in engineering, quality assurance, and so on. But in our experience, the typical report from a due diligence effort is about whether the other side's contractual representations need to be strengthened, or whether an adjustment should be made to the price of the deal. Wouldn't it be better if due diligence could instead help surface possible implementation challenges so that both parties could discuss them, develop real solutions, and act on them to prevent problems, instead of relying on the ability to penalize the other party when things go wrong? How difficult would it be to fine-tune a standard due diligence methodology so that the diligence taken was really that which was "due"?

Partnerships: alliances and other "incomplete" contracts

It remains true that, popular and widespread as they have become, alliances are very difficult to do well. There are many good reasons to enter into alliances, including the ability to share risks with partners, to leverage resources they have that you might otherwise have to build or buy on your own, and to access markets in which they are well positioned. But those benefits do not come cheaply. Alliances take a lot of work to set up and to manage, and many of them fail. As with the business combinations discussed earlier, the failure rate depends a bit on how you define success, but the research, across the board, suggests that between 50 and 70 percent of alliances fail.[5] Even if you wanted to quibble with the definition of success, those are not attractive odds.

Our firm has done quite a bit of research into why alliances fail, and we won't bore you here with all the details.[6] But we will focus for a few pages on how the way you negotiate these alliances can set you up for success or failure during implementation. In some ways, the problem starts with one of our favorite definitions of just what an alliance is. Our friend and colleague Ben Gomes-Casseres, professor of international business at Brandeis University, has quite tellingly called alliances "incomplete contracts."[7] From that perspective, one way to tell whether a particular business relationship should be treated as an alliance, as opposed to a supply agreement or something else, is to determine whether it is possible to articulate all its critical terms. To the extent that there are significant issues where the obligations of the parties are inherently uncertain, you are likely to need to rely on your relationship to make the deal succeed, and that's what makes it an alliance. It is also what, in large measure, makes alliances prone to failure.

The roots of the problem: trying to avoid conflict instead of managing it

We're happy to be able to report that alliance negotiations typically do not cripple the partnership because one side tries to squeeze the other too hard or take advantage. Of all the situations where implementation matters, an alliance negotiation is one of the most obvious, and negotiators usually recognize that the outset of the alliance is not the place to engage in brinksmanship or hard bargaining. They often do worry about the impact of creating bad blood between the partners at the start and try to be their most civilized during the negotiations. Unfortunately, recognizing that the negotiation is the start of an important working relationship is not enough. Too many alliance negotiators translate their awareness of the need to get along after the deal is signed into a need to "be nice" during the negotiation.

But when you are trying to put together an alliance worth having, being "nice" is the last thing you want from your negotiators. In our experience, alliance negotiations set the stage for later failure if the would-be partners do not spend enough time figuring out how they will actually work together and don't ask tough questions about whether the partner can really deliver. Do not try to be "nice" to your potential alliance partners. Do not rely on the milestones and obligations in the contract alone to protect you. Do them (and yourselves) the courtesy of raising the tough issues. Let's consider some specific pitfalls that await the conflict-averse alliance negotiator.

Negotiators make light of the real differences between the would-be partners

Alliances, unlike some of the business combinations discussed earlier, are typically created between companies that are quite different from one another in size, capabilities, culture, and so forth. Indeed, it is precisely such differences that have brought them together: each needs something the other can provide. If the two organizations were very similar, they would be less likely to partner and more likely to compete, or perhaps consider a merger or an acquisition.

Differences are the source of value in an alliance, and they can also make life quite difficult during implementation. Each organization likely has different norms about big and small things alike: When and how do decisions get made (and are they then "final")? How much consultation is expected in advance? How quickly do calls get returned? Is a commitment an unbreakable promise, or an aspiration? Yet these and other differences are often ignored during the negotiation, except as something to be endured (and sometimes privately ridiculed) by the negotiation teams. Often, in the interest of "being nice," negotiators simply try to adapt and accommodate the other side's differences while they are putting the deal together. But as we well know, old habits die hard, and it can be difficult to pull people out of their usual ways of looking at the world and doing business.

When differences are brushed aside during the negotiation, they have a way of returning with a vengeance later, often with all the pent-up emotion of someone who feels her endless accommodations have been ignored and have gone unreciprocated.

Negotiators focus on negotiating the deal, not the relationship

Even when alliance negotiators recognize that the partners must have a strong relationship going forward and will need more than just a signed contract to enable their success, few devote any significant time or energy to how the relationship will be managed.[8] Alliance negotiators have come to expect that their role is to put the deal together, and that someone else will worry about making it work later. Indeed, they are often encouraged to get the deal signed and move on to the next one. Thus, most of their effort goes into negotiating the deal terms rather than pursuing questions like how decisions will be made, how the partners will deal with risk and uncertainty, or how they will manage the necessary changes in their respective organizations. They assume that those kinds of issues are the province of the alliance managers, who will know best how often they want to meet with their counterparts, who should be present, and the like.

Anytime you are talking about how you will hold each other accountable for the success of the partnership or how you will deal with conflict, you are talking about things that might go wrong. So even when they do address these issues, alliance negotiators tend to tread lightly. They don't want to give offense or upset their partners, much less raise the possibility that their own side might not deliver. They sometimes even shrug their shoulders and roll their eyes, saying, "I'm sorry, but the lawyers are making me address these exit issues." Everyone laughs nervously, as they rush through the "standard exit provisions" that "everyone uses" (and therefore raising them here is "nothing personal").

We often get called in to help remediate alliances that are in trouble. When that happens, one of the first things we look at is the agreement itself and how the parties agreed to manage their relationship. More often than not, what we find looks like someone grabbed a standard exhibit laying the governance terms of the last deal, ran a "search and replace" for the parties' names, and slapped it onto the new agreement. When things like the structure and makeup of governance committees, decision-making responsibilities, and conflict management protocols get treated like uninteresting and unimportant boilerplate, it is fairly predictable that the parties will have difficulties sooner rather than later.

Negotiators quit too soon

Alliances often suffer an extreme version of the handoff problem. Whether from an internal business development function or an outside firm, alliance negotiators who view their job as negotiating the deal will inevitably feel the need to move on to their next assignment. Every minute they spend on the transition to the team who will manage the alliance is a minute they are not spending on their principal responsibility, which is to negotiate deals. Since most partnership negotiations tend to be more complicated and take longer than anyone expects, it is likely that the negotiators already have someone breathing down their necks about some other deal they are supposed to be working on. Consequently, they shortchange the handoff.

What gets lost? Probably not the critical pricing information or the high-level definition of the alliance's objectives or the core responsibilities of each partner. And probably not the big milestones that trigger payments or penalties or possible unwelcome attention. "Everyone knows" that ignoring those things would be irresponsible. But a few other critical questions consistently get dropped from transition meetings, and you should know that ignoring them will cost you.

- What have we learned about our new partner that may make it challenging to work with them?
- What insights have we gained about the working style of the "enablers" at our new partner? Which of them are likely to be most challenging to engage, win over, or work with?
- What do they need from us, beyond our contractual obligations, to be successful? What do we need from them?
- What issues did we run out of time to resolve? Are there any outstanding issues from the negotiation that need to be dealt with during implementation?
- What do we and they need to do differently for this partnership to succeed, and how are we planning to drive those changes?

Remember that partnering effectively
is the point of the deal

All of the themes discussed earlier in the book are at play here: given how difficult alliances are, it simply does not make sense to enter into one without a clear purpose and an understanding that the best way to meet that purpose is through this alliance. You can't expect to succeed without having the right people in agreement regarding the terms of the deal and what it will take to achieve its purpose. And if you are to deal successfully with all the uncertainties surrounding an alliance, you without question must create a useful precedent for working together, be able to talk about and manage risk, and have a clear plan of action for what happens the day after you sign the deal. If not, why bother?

Be prepared to deal with differences and with change

Alliance negotiators cannot and should not let their sense that "this is a future partner" keep them from raising tough issues and asking tough questions. Those tough questions may be about your shared business plans, your respective capabilities, or even your approach to problem solving. You and your partner are probably going to see things differently in some significant ways, but you cannot paper over those differences. You have to harness those differences early on and put them to work for you.

If you have to partner well in order to produce the results you want, then you need to know about the stakeholders in either organization who may be opposed to the deal, and about differences in culture or in expectations that may hinder implementation. Make learning about those a priority, both during preparation and in conversations with the other side. Assume that a critical component of an alliance negotiation must be a thorough conversation about the often-ignored enablers on both sides. Make figuring out how you will jointly manage difficult stakeholders or those perceived differences between the organizations a critical element of the negotiation agenda. While you may not start there, you cannot consider the negotiation "done" unless you have addressed those issues, and addressed them well.

Integrate negotiation and implementation

In our view, some alliance teams have become overly specialized. If negotiators are focused only on putting the deal together and alliance managers are focused only on making it work, they are both failing to do all that is required for the organization's success. You cannot fumble a handoff if the team that will manage the relationship going forward was sufficiently involved in the negotiation to learn firsthand what it will take to succeed. That does not mean that there is no distinction between those whose primary goals are to imagine, structure, and plan alliances and those who work with the partners to create value after the deal is signed. But it does mean that there needs to be more overlap in activities and more dialogue between the two. Have negotiators stay loosely connected to the alliance after the ink has dried so they can see the consequences of their handiwork. Bring alliance managers into the negotiation process before the deal is done. Learn from their experience dealing with partners and with things they wished had been discussed earlier.

When you are ready for a handoff, there is no better way to do it than jointly with your counterparts. Think about the power of a joint transition meeting, where individuals who were principally involved in the negotiation—on both sides—help brief those who will be principally involved in the implementation—again on both sides. Such a kickoff meeting also provides a wonderful opportunity to fine-tune your governance model and make sure it will be implemented. Steering committees don't steer if they never meet. Innovation committees don't innovate if they aren't staffed. And escalation processes only raise blood pressures unless both sides bring similar assumptions to what things should be escalated and in what manner.

Outsourcing: when a vendor is more than just a vendor

Over the last fifteen years or so, outsourcing has become an increasingly common feature of the business landscape. Businesses of all sizes now have to consider whether they are well served by doing everything themselves, or whether to be competitive they should contract with a third party to deliver, at a lower cost or a higher quality or both, some services that were previously handled internally. Other objectives commonly cited by buyers of outsourcing services include benefiting from the ongoing improvements of a market-facing provider (as opposed to an internal department), shifting from a fixed to a variable cost model for these services, avoiding large capital expenditures to upgrade technology or improve processes, getting "nonproductive" assets out of their capital structure to improve their return on assets, and refocusing management time and attention on their core business. To date, outsourcing has most often been used when business functions rely heavily on information technology (IT) or when developments in IT enable the delivery of that service by others. When the contract permits the service provider to base some of its workforce in a country with a lower labor cost, outsourcing becomes "offshoring," but it is worth noting that whether to outsource and whether to offshore should be separate questions.

As with the other kinds of complex deals addressed in this chapter, reported failure rates for outsourcing are high: about a third fail to deliver the expected benefits. As many as 70 percent of firms renegotiate significant terms during the first two years.[9] Another similarity: we believe that the seeds of these failures are often sown during the negotiation.

The roots of the problem: thinking that it's all about the contract

A bit of history may help put the challenges of outsourcing negotiations in perspective. Early on when large IT providers started offering outsourcing services, they had something of an information advantage. They had more information than their customers did about the costs of providing these services and about upcoming advances in technology. They also had more leverage as repeat players—negotiating with multiple customers, learning from each deal, and choosing what precedents to create (or not). In addition, they were able to buy from their suppliers at ever increasing scale, driving down costs. The market quickly remedied that imbalance, spawning a new industry of outsourcing advisers, some of whom came from the service provider world and could help customers negotiate with their IT providers. In the process, these advisers saw lots of deals and learned what different service providers would or would not generally agree to do. Balance achieved. Or so you would think.

What appears to have happened in practice is that some negotiators of outsourcing deals—whether third-party advisers or internal procurement teams—took their mandate to negotiate the best deal possible a bit too narrowly, ignoring the fact that to create real value these deals have to be implemented in a way that works for both parties. Otherwise providers lose money and buyers fail to achieve their objectives.

To overcome the information advantage and gain some bargaining leverage, outsourcing negotiators have historically pushed hard to commoditize what service providers were offering. The more their services could be analyzed on an "apples to apples" basis, the easier it was to comparison shop and find the best deal. But unlike apples, complex outsourcing arrangements require significant implementation efforts to be enjoyed. Recognizing that we paint with a bit too broad a brush here because not all outsourcing negotiators—be they customers, providers, or advisers—negotiate this way, we see a few typical problems during the negotiation that often interfere with effective implementation later.

Outsourcing negotiators lack enough information and access to reach good decisions

Despite often taking nine months or more to negotiate these deals, both buyers and providers end up making their decisions at the negotiation table with insufficient information and without fully understanding the perspectives of all the right people. If you have never experienced one of these negotiations, you might well ask, how does that happen? The bottom line is that because the parties approach the exercise with a generally adversarial mind-set, both sides limit the people involved in the process and the information they share. As we have seen, the results can be disastrous. This is the kind of process that led EDS to sign up for transferring "all" the navy and Marine Corps' applications to the NMCI, believing it would have to migrate ten thousand applications instead of the eighty thousand applications there turned out to be.

Buyers and their advisers, on the one hand, believe that competition among providers will produce the best price and often invite many providers to bid on the business. This in turn creates a perceived need to standardize what providers are bidding on, and to apply some kind of process to limit the sheer volume of incoming information. There is also a need to manage providers' requests for time with business and functional stakeholders and to avoid giving any one provider an unfair "inside track." Providers, on the other hand, fearful about educating the competition, wasting the time of costly expert resources on deals they may not win, or appearing pushy and difficult to work with, tend to answer only those questions asked and channel all their interactions with the buyers through their sales team. The result is a game of hide-and-seek, where buyers try to get providers to commit to delivering a very detailed set of generic services at the lowest price possible, and providers try to figure out whether there is any way to differentiate their offering on something other than price.

The result, after an arduous and expensive process (for both sides), is often a deal struck with no meaningful dialogue between the parties about their purposes (beyond buying or selling a set of specified services for a specified fee). The process has excluded many key stakeholders, who are likely to be fairly unhappy about whatever decisions were reached. Moreover, the process by which the deal was negotiated has created a terrible precedent for how the companies will work together in the future (especially if the bargaining leverage is ever reversed). The parties never engaged in a meaningful conversation about obstacles to effective implementation. And despite all the time that went into the process of defining what would be outsourced, to whom, and at what price, precious little time has been spent to plan how the parties will work together. Indeed, after a long and drawn-out process, it is amazing how many critical decisions get made in the last thirty-six hours, when all concerned are running on caffeine, adrenaline, and scant sleep, and have little chance of getting them all right.

Buyers place too much reliance on service-level agreements and penalties to protect them

Because outsourcing a significant function can be scary, buyers and their advisers make considerable efforts to protect themselves from a service provider's failure to live up to promises made in order to win the business. They start by trying to define a baseline—everything they are currently doing for themselves, with some metrics to measure how well they are doing those things. They then ask providers to commit to those same tasks at that same level of service or better, and they insist that providers agree to pay penalties if they fail to live up to those commitments.

Providers, understandably, are a bit skeptical about some of the claims made by internal departments (who are often resisting the entire outsourcing exercise) regarding the quantities and quality of the services in the baseline. They insist that only those things that are highly objective and quantifiable be used, enabling them to verify the baseline and feel confident that they won't be penalized later over differing perceptions of what "good enough" looks like. The result is often a long list of service level metrics covering things like the number of rings it takes for a call center to answer the phone, the percentage of time that a set of servers is down, or the number of paychecks issued that have an error. There is an entire industry of firms that help define these service level agreements, pull data from the many different systems where it is measured, validate and cleanse the data, and create reports for buyers to use to determine whether the service provider is meeting obligations.

With reports in hand, buyers can then confront providers with objective evidence that they are not living up to their obligations and threaten to impose financial penalties provided for by the contract. Of course, those conversations are never easy, and providers often have their own interpretations of whose fault it was that certain service level agreements were not met. ("Your other suppliers didn't cooperate." "Your power was fluctuating too much." "Your people made more calls than were anticipated because they were not trained adequately or encouraged by their managers to use the Web site.") After much discussion and frustration, some accommodation is typically reached.

But collecting penalties rarely is a good substitute for actually achieving the kinds of savings, business process improvement, and improved management focus that companies outsourced to accomplish in the first place. And when providers are penalized for failing to meet these service level obligations, they get the message that their most important goal is to fix that problem and make sure they don't get penalized again next month—instead of putting their resources toward other activities that might add more value to the customer, but are not as easily tracked.

The result tends to be a tense, adversarial relationship, and more often than not, both sides are unhappy with the way the deal they negotiated is playing out in practice. We wish we had a nickel for every time a provider has said to us, "I'm meeting all my SLAs and my customer still isn't happy!" The parties can negotiate the deal. Maybe they can even live up to its terms. But that doesn't mean the deal creates value.

Providers place too much reliance on scope limitations

Because they believe that the buyer's ultimate decision will be made on the basis of price at contract time, providers try to "skinny down" their offering and come in with what seems like the lowest price. To protect their margins, they reduce the price by trying to limit the definition of what's "in scope." Anything else the buyer requests later will cost extra.

Sometimes the intense focus on completing the deal causes the parties to omit things that are critical to a successful implementation. One of the most jarring examples, sadly, happens fairly often. Providers include in their proposals significant resources for carrying out change management activities, because they know that outsourcing can be disruptive and that some of the savings they are committed to delivering to their customers require employees to do some things differently. Take the use of Web-based self-service, for example. When employees use the Web for things like address or beneficiary changes on their benefits plans, it costs a lot less than faxing a form or calling a processing center, which in turn costs less than walking down the hall to an administrative office and getting someone to make the change for them. If employees don't change old habits, the provider will not be able to deliver the cost savings that are the point of the deal.

Under pressure during the bidding process, providers will look for things to cut from their proposal to reduce the price. They look at the buyer and suggest that they can reduce their price if the customer's internal HR department will drive the change effort required to move to self-service. The buyer looks them straight in the eye and says: "Sure, we can do that." The item comes out of the provider's scope, the price is reduced, the contract is signed, and everyone pats themselves on the back. Win-win, right?

Unfortunately, what happens in many cases is that the customer never had the necessary change management resources, or actually eliminated those resources as part of the overall cost-reduction effort. Without the necessary communication and education, employees resist change, and look for ways to continue old habits—for example, to make their requests on paper or via phone. But the processing center is not staffed to handle the volume of requests they get. They are supposed to work only on the handful of exceptions that can't be handled through the Web site. In one case where we were asked to help remediate a damaged relationship between the customer and the service provider, the processing center received something like three hundred sixty thousand fax requests over a time period when they were expecting a fraction of that number.

The results of this kind of problem are predictable: Service levels drop. Customer satisfaction is terrible. Employee morale at the service provider suffers. And the blame game ensues. The fact that the customer agreed during the negotiation that change management was not in the provider's scope of services does not help the service provider much at this point. The provider missed an SLA and there is a contractual penalty. There was no corresponding SLA for the customer's HR department, which was supposed to drive the change effort. The customer alleges an SLA was missed and a penalty is due. The service provider says it is really the customer's own fault. Whether a penalty payment is made or not, this is not a story with a happy ending for anyone (least of all the poor customer end-user, who is trying to use the new system).

Remember that signing the contract is *not* the point of the deal

Outsourcing as a business model is mature enough by now that most companies involved understand that when they are negotiating a deal, implementation matters. Nonetheless, many of them still approach the negotiation as if their objective is simply to write a good contract. Our advice, regardless of which side of the table you are on, is to take a big step back and ask yourself: "What is the point of this deal? What can I do to ensure that my purposes are well met?"

Advice for buyers of outsourcing

If you're a buyer of outsourcing, remember these tips to help ensure successful implementation.

Keep Your Eye on the Purpose of the Deal. Keep in mind that you're not just negotiating a contract, you are handing over an important function to an outside company. Just because you think that someone can provide those services more effectively or at a lower cost doesn't mean that your employees and your customers are no longer relying on you to make sure those services are delivered well. Remember also that part of the deal may involve transferring a number of your employees to that outside company. The way that transition happens and what your former employees have to say about working at their new employer while providing services to your organization will have an impact on the morale of both your former and your remaining employees and on the quality of the services you receive.

What this suggests is that you cannot choose a provider solely on the basis of which one put the lowest numbers on your RFP spreadsheet, and then rely on the contract to protect you. If suppliers failed to bring their key delivery stakeholders into the conversation to make sure that they really could do what was promised, it's not just going to be *their* problem. If they made foolhardy commitments that they can't live up to, you will feel the pain at least as much as they will.

Make the Deal Discussion a Precedent for Implementation. Make the process of coming up with a deal that works a shared responsibility: Do you both understand what your stakeholders care about, and what it's really going to take to implement? Do the provider's implementers know what they are committed to delivering? That kind of dialogue requires that you engage those stakeholders and fully understand how a particular provider's solution will meet your needs. You are not looking for the deal that is easiest to compare; you are looking for the deal that will best meet your purposes in outsourcing. You are also trying to learn what it is like to work with a provider, and to create a model for how you will work together for the next five to ten years.

It is absolutely understandable that you cannot engage in this kind of time-intensive process with a dozen different providers. But when you have narrowed the list of real candidates to a manageable number, treat each of them as if they were going to be your provider, and make sure that you have clarified all of your purposes for the deal. Introduce the stakeholders who are going to be critical not only to the decision but also to its eventual success or failure. Build their perspectives into the negotiation and gain their buy-in from the outset. Negotiate the initial deal like you want to negotiate later over scope changes, performance challenges, and regulatory and technological changes. Wittingly or not, those are the precedents you are creating. Make sure you have a clear plan for what is going to happen after the contract is signed, including how you are going to manage this very complex relationship. If you wait to figure out how you are going to make decisions, resolve problems, deal with surprises, and manage change until you are in the midst of transition, you will inevitably fall further and further behind as decisions take longer, follow-through is spotty, and conflicts fester.

Advice for providers of outsourcing

It may not surprise you that a lot of our advice for providers mirrors that for buyers, and there is little reason to repeat it all here. But a few things are worth highlighting for providers, who may feel that only the buyers can change how the negotiation unfolds.

Insist on Getting the Information You Need to Be Successful. Keep in mind that you too are entering into a long-term relationship and that to be successful in any sustainable way, that relationship must not only be profitable for you, but must also provide your customer with the benefits that your scale and experience can provide. For your customer to be able to redirect resources and management attention to the core business, they must first be able to rely on you. Even if you meet the letter of the contract, you will fail to meet expectations unless you ask the hard questions about what kind of change the buyer's organization must undertake to accomplish its purposes—versus the kind of change it is ready to handle. If your customer cannot or will not engage in those conversations, ask yourself what that means for the risks you will incur during implementation. You may not want to do deals where the other players have no reasonable prospect of accomplishing their purposes; they will also likely keep you from accomplishing yours.

Push for more and better information and access. If you cannot get it, and you are far enough along in the process that a buyer who recognized the importance of implementation would provide it, consider whether you should devote your scarce sales resources to a client that assumes that what you don't know won't hurt them (or you). What kind of precedent are you allowing them to create about how you will work together during implementation? Will they expect that they can withhold information and deny you access to critical stakeholders during implementation? Can you possibly succeed under those conditions? If not, why go into such an arrangement?

Focus on Both Profitability and Relationship. Beware of the "winner's curse."[10] If the bidding process feels like an auction where the ultimate decision will be made on price alone, the service provider who wins often regrets it. If there are any significant uncertainties, it is usually the provider who is most optimistic about all of them who will offer the lowest price. But is that optimistic provider likely to be right?

Service organizations are notoriously bad at making decisions to walk away from a negotiation. Sales negotiators are paid to close deals, not to make good business choices about how best to deploy resources. But consider for a moment a typical portfolio of accounts. Plot them on a graph as in figure 11-1, where one axis measures the quality of the relationship and the other measures account profitability.

There are only two stable quadrants on such a graph: the upper-right high profit/excellent relationship quadrant we all want to be in, and the lower-left low profit/poor relationship sector we all want to avoid. The other two quadrants have a natural tendency to decay to the low/poor scenario. Here's why: consider first those accounts that are very profitable, but with which you don't have a strong relationship. What happens there? Over time, competitors threaten your position

FIGURE 11-1

Profitability and relationship in a typical service provider portfolio

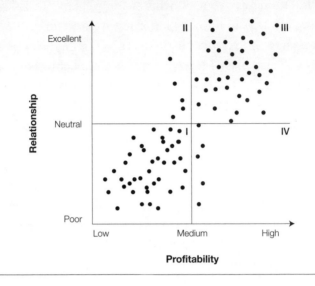

and, lacking a relationship to defend it, you end up having to reduce your margins, moving them toward that low/poor quadrant. Now consider those good relationships where you are not making much money. What happens there? You look for ways to cut costs, and in the process, your service quality drops, you invest less in the relationship, and you end up in the low/poor quadrant once again.

What should we make of this tale of woe? How do you get to the high/excellent quadrant? Well, that comes from working with accounts in the other two unstable quadrants so that instead of decaying, they improve. Let's go back to the high-profit but low-relationship accounts. Investing time in better understanding your clients and their needs and in building your relationships can move you up to the high/excellent quadrant. Consider the low-profit but good-relationship accounts. Leveraging those good relationships by working together to ascertain how to deliver more value or deliver it more cost effectively will let you improve your margins, and again move you toward the high/excellent quadrant.

But where will all that time and energy come from? It comes from making the decision to walk away from deals that are bound for the low/poor quadrant, because you know from the start you are chasing an unachievable purpose, you lack the stakeholder alignment needed to be successful, or you are creating a terrible precedent for working together. If you walk away from those deals, you can devote resources to improving the "high/low" mixes. If you don't, you are dooming not only this deal, but several others, to the low/poor quadrant. And once you are in that box, it is devilishly hard to get out.

Integrate Delivery Teams into Negotiations. Last but not least, we offer a piece of advice that may be much easier to act on, even if it requires some difficult conversations internally. Integrate some of your delivery resources into the negotiation process. Don't exclude them for fear they will blanch at what's being promised. If that's the case, you really want to understand their concerns and discuss them, not bury them. We know that these delivery resources are considered billable, and therefore it can be difficult to get them assigned to a deal before it is done. We also know that some of your delivery people are not as "polished" as those in sales. We are not suggesting that you make them your lead negotiators. But if you don't include them and give them an appropriate role and voice during the negotiation process, you are less likely to come up with a plan that can achieve your purposes.

Advice to advisers

As in other kinds of big deals, third-party advisers have a critical role to play in making outsourcing deals that work. You have both the knowledge and the role in the process that should enable you to help your clients reach deals worth doing if you view the objective as effective implementation.

Help Your Clients Focus on Governance. Use your expertise and experience to give your clients the benefit of hindsight. Don't let them give short shrift to governance and the management of the relationship just because the deal is "almost done." You know from experience how important it is that they hit the ground running during transition with an effective governance model. Make sure they put in place the processes for dealing with all the things they can't anticipate and put in the contract. Help them manage the relationship by building a strong partnership rather than relying on penalties. You have seen many deals go sour because your client and the service provider were unable to deal with difficulties or cope with change after signing the deal. Ensure that every client you have benefits from your best advice on how to set up structures to meet the challenges that you know will come during implementation.

Embrace and Evaluate Differentiated Solutions. Leverage your databases and continue to extend your methodologies to allow your clients to make good choices among dissimilar solutions. Anyone can force hungry providers to contort their products and services into a common structure that's easy to compare. It takes real insight to help a client choose among very different solutions that play to each provider's unique strengths. Yes, the initial winnowing down may need to be done on some fairly objective basis; unless providers know they have a legitimate shot at being selected, they have little incentive to participate in an expensive process. But after you have narrowed the list sufficiently, shift gears. Facilitate a process that is more open and welcomes solutions that play to each provider's strengths, instead of asking all providers to come up with the lowest price for the middle-of-the-road solution.

When those varied solutions are put forward, push providers hard to articulate what they need from the customer to be successful. None of them can really do it alone. Make sure buyers understand what is expected of them, and uphold their end of the bargain.

Manage Communication, but Don't Stifle It. Facilitate, rather than constrain, communication. Sure, it's important to help your client manage the process and avoid manipulation by aggressive salespeople. But there is no point in going into these deals without the information needed to support effective implementation. Service level agreements will not protect your client if they were based on incomplete information or if they measure things that in the end are not that important. Nominal "business case" savings that cannot be sustained because they were based on faulty assumptions about the client's readiness to hold up their own end of the bargain or to reduce their consumption of some services do not deliver value. But they do set clients up for a contentious and adversarial relationship that will cost them over time.

In the next chapter we will consider smaller, but no less important deals. The negotiations that organizations carry out every day, with customers and with suppliers, collectively represent at least as much potential value as the large, headline-grabbing deals discussed in this chapter.

Bread-and-Butter Deals

Customers and suppliers

As we said in the last chapter, there are negotiations and there are Negotiations. Even though the big deals referred to in chapter 11 capture headlines, the imagination, and your attention, they happen much less frequently than day-to-day negotiations with a customer or a supplier. It is the myriad (small n) negotiations where value can be captured or squandered that can make the difference between success and failure in the business world and in your personal life.

In this chapter we provide advice specific to bread-and-butter deals—those involving suppliers and customers. You might expect that our recommendations for negotiating such deals would be fairly consistent with the advice throughout this book. Surely, given the emphasis we have already placed on joint gain, collaboration, long-term value creation, and the like, we cannot now slip into an asymmetrical approach to advice for each side—telling the seller to start high, haggle hard, and feign indifference about closing the deal, and telling the buyer to start low, haggle hard, and fabricate lowball bids from fictitious competitors.

Of course, that is correct. We are not providing tactical, adversarial, short-term advice to *either* side. It is also correct in the sense that we are not providing "secret" advice to buyers that we don't want sellers to know or vice versa. However, it is incorrect to assume that what we have to say does not vary at all based on whether you are doing the buying or the selling. Our best advice to buyers is somewhat different from that for sellers, based in part on how and why implementation matters to them, and on differences in their specific purposes for a negotiation. Even though buyers and sellers are two sides to the same coin, it misses an important nuance to assume that the approach ought to be the same regardless of which side of the transaction you are on.

The point of negotiations between buyers and sellers

Negotiations between buyers and sellers are the most classic ways to create value. I have something you want (i.e., goods or services) and you have something I want (i.e., money) and we exchange one for the other. When that simple exchange is all that is required to produce value, then implementation does not matter very much. But when the signing of the deal only signals the beginning of those activities that really produce value for the parties, then you have to think about the point of the deal.

Buyers care about more than just price

Any company negotiating with its suppliers usually wants to get the best terms and conditions possible. Traditional vendor management and supply chain management theory and practice offer many useful insights into ways to reduce the cost of procuring goods and services, and numerous negotiation tactics can be used to implement those strategies. The problem is that many people negotiating with suppliers assume the task is to get an agreement for the lowest price possible. Period. To achieve real value, however, we suggest you take a step back and ask the simple and more basic underlying question—what really is the point of doing a deal with a supplier?

The answer, equally simplistically, is that the point of a deal with a supplier is ultimately to improve your bottom line. Getting a contract that has a great price does not help your bottom line if the supplier cannot deliver the goods at that price. The value of litigation against a defaulting supplier rarely is so great that you can buy sustainable competitive advantage with the proceeds of the lawsuit (even if you ultimately prevail on the merits and can collect on the judgment). Getting a contract that has a great price also does not help your bottom line if your sole supplier goes bankrupt trying to get you goods at that price, and you miss important delivery dates to your customers while finding a new supplier. Getting a contract that has a great price does not help your bottom line if your "low bidder" supplies products that fail to meet your minimum quality standards, and your production line closes down or you end up producing defective products and get sued by your customers. Getting a contract with a great price does not help your bottom line if your supplier nibbles you to death with change orders because the base price you negotiated was so low that they did not have a sustainable margin.

Even getting the goods or services promised at the low contracted price is not necessarily a victory for a procurement team. If negotiators look only at the initial purchase price, they may miss other aspects of the total cost of ownership that their company must bear. The true total cost of the product includes acquisition costs, carrying costs, service and repair costs, and end of life/disposal costs. There may also be re-sourcing and reprocurement costs to consider, unless the deal is sustainable for the supplier. The traditional procurement perspective of focusing on "price at any cost" misses a more robust focus on lowering total cost and gaining competitive advantage.

At the end of the day, the point of a deal with a supplier is to procure goods and services on the terms and conditions that best support your business. As you consider what a supplier can do for you to enhance your own competitiveness, you should be looking not only at lower prices, but also at lower acquisition costs, improved operational efficiencies, greater quality, innovation, speed to market, brand positioning, and more.

Sellers care about more than just volume and price

On the other side of the coin, any company negotiating with its customers wants to sell as much as possible under the most favorable terms and conditions possible. As with procurement, traditional sales management theory and practice give many useful insights into ways to drive bookings, and a salesperson can choose from among a range of tactics for putting those strategies into action. The problem is that many negotiators assume the task is to get an agreement for maximum volume at the highest price. Period. Sound familiar? To achieve real value, we again suggest you ask the simplistic and more basic underlying question—what really is the point of doing a deal with a customer?

The answer is that the point of a deal with your customer is ultimately to improve *your* bottom line business results. Getting a contract that has a great price and great volumes does not help your bottom line if the buyer defaults and cannot accept delivery of your goods at that price after you have paid to manufacture and ship them. That contract does not help your bottom line if your largest customer becomes uncompetitive in the market and stops buying from you. And that "great" contract does not help your bottom line if your customer figures out that you hoodwinked them into a one-sided contract, cancels future orders, and shares their dissatisfaction with your entire customer base.

Even getting paid for a large sale at a high price may not be a real victory for the sales team. If the salespeople are looking at the revenue line only, they may miss other aspects of the deal or account profitability that are critical to the health of the business. Some customers are just more expensive to serve than others—high rejection or return rates, slow payments, and disproportionately high support needs can all play havoc with the value of a deal or customer relationship. One-time purchases that are not repeated because the customer concludes you are too expensive or drive too hard a bargain tend to increase the costs of sales. Unexpected fluctuations in demand can whipsaw production schedules and facilities. Customers who fear that information they share with you will be used against them during the negotiation are less likely to help you learn about or anticipate market shifts.

At the end of the day, the point of a deal with a customer is to sell goods and services under the terms and conditions that best support your business. In some cases, the real objective in dealing with your customer is not just better prices, but some combination of lowering your cost of sales, lowering your costs of delivering on the contract and providing after-sales support, improving the predictability of your revenues, gaining reference accounts, improving your brand image, and learning to anticipate this and other customer's needs.

Common problems faced by negotiators for both buyers and sellers

Unfortunately, many purchases and sales are negotiated without much attention to factors besides price and perhaps a couple of other basic terms. As might be expected, much value is left on the table when that happens. For example, in a study done by Vantage Partners and the International Association for Contract and Commercial Management, we found that only 13 percent of companies said that they realized all of the anticipated value from their supply contracts.[1] We think there are two main contributing causes to this broadly felt dissatisfaction among buyers and sellers, both of which relate directly to focusing more on the art of the deal than on its point.

Negotiator as diva

Many organizations assume that they can get the best deals by employing a team of expert negotiators who take over after the parties have reached some critical point in their discussions. To some extent vendors have brought this on themselves by the way they train and compensate their salesforces. Fearing that the customers are not used to negotiating for a living the way salespeople are, companies created the role of procurement negotiators to protect their line managers from "those super negotiators" on the sales side. The procurement negotiators see themselves as experts, brought in to make sure that naïve buyers don't get taken advantage of. Indeed, putting buyers with expertise, experience, discipline, analytical tools, and structured approaches against professional sales teams that negotiate sales contracts day in and day out is likely to improve the outcome for the buying organization. All that makes perfect sense.

The challenge is that in many large organizations, the procurement professionals have gotten increasingly remote from the constituents for whom they are buying. This is especially true in large, multiunit, multi-location businesses, where the sourcing and procurement function has been centralized. To make sure that they are doing their job as effectively as possible, procurement organizations have created fairly tight and disciplined processes to prevent wily salespeople from sneaking around the professional negotiators and to keep "rogue" buyers from ignoring corporate policies. The result is that in many cases critical stakeholders are left out of the picture during the negotiation. (In fact, some procurement processes actually forbid the salesperson from speaking to his or her customer from the time procurement is engaged until the purchase order is issued.)

It is not only the procurement negotiator who hogs the stage. On the sales side of the table, negotiators are often doing everything they can to keep anyone who has anything to do with delivery out of the scene. Delivery people, after all, tend to blurt out things like "but we've never done that" or "that would take time," which puts the deal signing at risk. They are not trained in the art of closing deals. They can be prone to rethinking or reinventing what the deal should be as they hear more about the situation. They tend to worry less about discounts or volume (indeed, they might find it easier to implement a smaller deal) than about requirements and timetables (they always want more details and more time).

But without the participation of the internal customer and the delivery team, it is much more difficult for the negotiators to explore ways to collaborate to improve operational efficiencies, reduce costs for either side, or create new solutions to business problems. Depending on how well integrated the negotiators are with the business unit of the internal customer or the delivery team of the supplier, they may not know enough about possible trade-offs or creative ways to solve specification, quality, timing, or logistics problems. All they can really talk about is price.

Painting by numbers

Organizations that tend to exclude the individuals who really understand the underlying business purposes of the deal also often set themselves up for failure by then measuring (and compensating) the negotiators on the wrong things, measured at the wrong time. Procurement negotiators tend to be compensated for obtaining discounts and concessions. And if they are responsible for a particular supplier over time, they will be expected to achieve not only a discount when they first negotiate a deal, but to obtain some further reductions each year. But rarely would a businessperson say that her primary purpose in a negotiation is to get a discount. Discounts, in and of themselves, tell you nothing about value. They tell you nothing about the appropriateness of the starting point from which the concession was made. They tell you nothing about any of the other factors that impact operational expenses, profitability, or competitiveness. And if you reward procurement negotiators on the basis of discounts achieved *at signing*, you are certainly not taking into account any of the costs the buying organization will experience later in the life cycle of the goods or services they've acquired.

Sales negotiators, too, tend to get paid "by the numbers"—usually the volume of sales they achieve on the size of the discounts they had to give (or successfully avoided giving). But the picture they can paint by achieving those numbers may have nothing to do with the real point of the deal. Depending on how goods and services are bundled into the contract, how and when they have to be delivered, and what the customer is responsible for regarding scheduling, forecasting, adjustments, design reviews, quality control, and so on, a sale may or may not prove profitable. Depending on how well the customer's expectations have been managed, the buyer may or may not be a good reference account. Depending on how the deal has been characterized, it may create a more or less desirable precedent for pricing for similar customers. And similarly, if you reward salespeople on the basis of the sales achieved at signing, you are not taking into account whether, with the benefit of hindsight, those were sales worth making.

Advice for buyers negotiating with suppliers

Our advice for a buyer's negotiators is compatible with, but a little different from, our advice to the seller's negotiators, which will be detailed later in this chapter. In both cases, however, it begins with clarity of purpose.

Structure the negotiation around your business purposes

As the buyer, you often have a fair amount of flexibility in defining the basic structure of the negotiation: Are you going to get bids from multiple suppliers or negotiate with just one party? Are you going to say "jump" and expect them to ask "how high?" Or are you going to ask them to put on their thinking caps and help you figure out an answer based on their experience with other customers? Are you going to explore each side's interests and brainstorm possible options, or will you just ask for a quote? Will you try to get an auction going among potential competing suppliers and use each one's "confidential" bids against the others? There isn't necessarily a right or wrong answer to these questions: it depends on what your purpose is. The good news is that as the buyer, you often get to go first in signaling how you want to proceed.

For buyers, one of the principal purposes of the negotiation is to obtain savings. When implementation does not matter very much, one of the first and most obvious routes to savings is to persuade the supplier to offer a lower price per unit. In terms of simply extracting the best price possible, basic laws of supply and demand will generally prevail. The more competitive the supplier set and the lower the barriers to entry, the more their margins will be driven down over time. The more attractive the BATNA a buyer has, the more power the buyer will have in negotiating with a supplier. Procurement teams use requests for proposal (RFPs), requests for information (RFIs), requests for quotations (RFQs), various e-procurement mechanisms, competitive auctions, reverse auctions, and other means of driving down the unit price. Auctions of some form will tend to drive prices down to the lowest possible point, and buyers are advantaged by playing one seller against others. Even after a well-structured RFP process in which a buyer seeks to get bids from multiple suppliers, the buyer will attempt to parallel track two or more finalists to ensure that the suppliers know that the buyer has at least one other alternative in play.

When implementation matters a lot, however, the value to the buyer is not just in favorable quotes or contract terms, but rather in a supplier's ability to deliver the requisite goods or services on time, on spec, and at the contract price. We have all heard about deals that are "too good to be true." Our experience tells us that more often than not, the buyer won't get the benefit of the bargain—the deal was, indeed, too good to be true. Deals with suppliers who can't deliver according to the terms of the deal miss the point.

Beyond simply getting better pricing, there are other routes to cost savings for the buyer; these require exploring ways to reduce the "total cost of ownership" for the customer. The costs of buying from and dealing with suppliers, which are quite significant for large corporations, can sometimes be reduced. By working together with engineering and manufacturing resources at both the buyer and supplier organizations, sometimes the parties can redesign product specs for more efficient manufacturing. Procurement teams may work with their suppliers to reduce inventory levels, get just-in-time delivery, and thus lower their carrying costs. Service and maintenance costs can be reduced if the parties work together to design products that are easier to service and then train staff accordingly.

Achieving those kinds of savings tends to require a different negotiation process than what is required to persuade a supplier to cut its unit price. But the processes that are most effective at driving suppliers to cut prices may be counterproductive if you are seeking savings that can be achieved only by working together. You need to make a choice based on the purpose of the deal.

Beyond cost savings, buyers sometimes want help from their suppliers in developing new products or reaching the market faster. In markets where demand can change rapidly, suppliers can be critical to a buyer's ability to adjust their own product mix quickly. In highly regulated markets, buyers may want more transparency of information through their supply chain to satisfy their own compliance obligations. In the new, more global economy, where competition takes place not so much between companies but between supply chains, buyers may want suppliers that can not only provide a good price today but also demonstrate that they will continue to improve their efficiency and responsiveness over time.

As a buyer, you must exercise some leadership and help your supplier counterparts understand what you are trying to achieve. Then structure the negotiation process in such a way that you can involve the necessary stakeholders, define the precedents you want to create, and develop the implementation plans that will help you achieve your purpose.

Aim to get the best of both worlds: align procurement professionals with their internal constituents

Getting savings from procurement teams is wonderful for buyers. A buyer with a 10 percent margin will feel that the bottom-line result of saving $10 million in purchases is essentially the same as finding another $100 million in sales—and in some saturated marketplaces, cost cutting may feel much easier than finding new customers. But it can be very hard to be successful in business if procurement professionals believe their *only* job is to reduce cost at any price, while the business unit requiring the product is much more concerned about quality, timely delivery, and engineering support. Companies must ensure that their procurement community doesn't lose sight of the goal of meeting the needs of their constituents—of the point of doing a deal.

Be careful how you measure and compensate procurement teams. Incentives that lead them to focus entirely on obtaining discounts may not produce the outcomes you desire. Much more useful are metrics that reward procurement teams for obtaining savings that are indeed realized, not just contracted for, and that look to the total cost of ownership and not just contract prices.

Define procurement processes that keep key business stakeholders engaged throughout the negotiation. It is critical that you involve enablers within both the customer organization and the supplier organization during negotiations. They are key to determining sources of value that might not be completely obvious and to ensuring that you get the full value of your deal with your suppliers. All too frequently, however, we see the negotiation with a supplier driven by purchasing on one side and sales on the other, and the people who will actually work together to implement the deal are sitting on the sidelines waiting for the outcome.

A buyer negotiating a contract for just-in-time delivery of product critical to its manufacturing operations is wholly dependent on the supplier's ability to deliver consistently on time. That supplier's ability to meet the customer's need, however, may in turn depend on the quality of the customer's forecast and the frequency with which it is updated. If, in order to create "competitive tension" and achieve the best discount possible, procurement keeps key enablers out of the negotiation until the contract is done, savings due to reduced inventory needs may prove to be illusory when the supplier is unable to deliver or the customer is unable to provide sufficiently reliable and timely forecasts. The more creative and unusual the solution being crafted, the more critical it is to involve enablers in the process. They will have insights into operational details that other functions will likely be blind to.

Create precedents that encourage suppliers to collaborate with you

In working with procurement organizations, we have been surprised how infrequently they sit down with stakeholders on the supplier team and simply ask: "How can we help you keep your costs down?"

In an often-cited example, a major aerospace company had had a series of very difficult negotiations with its suppliers, trying to squeeze cost out of their supply chain and bolster an ailing bottom line. After several successive rounds, eventually the Japanese OEM could give away no more margin. As the aerospace buyer pushed for more price concessions, it became apparent that no more blood could be wrung from that stone. At last the buyers threw up their hands in despair and said: "Isn't there anything you can do to help us out here?" A dialogue somewhat like the following ensued:

> *Supplier:* Actually, if you would be willing to let us talk to your engineering team, we believe that there are many areas where your parts could be redesigned so that it would be more efficient for us to manufacture them and probably easier for you to use them in your fabrication process as well.

> *Buyer:* Why didn't you raise this before?

> *Supplier:* We tried several times. In each of the last three years of negotiations we tried to broach this subject. Each time your engineers told us we were just a supplier and should keep our noses out of their business.

Had the procurement team for the aerospace company made the effort to find out how they could help the supplier drive down costs, they would have had assistance in reengineering their parts and been able to realize lower prices (with increased margin to the suppliers) years earlier.

Some buyers not only fail to take advantage of this sort of collaboration when it is offered by their suppliers, they actually make it nearly impossible for a supplier even to consider offering it again. Across many companies and many industries, we have heard stories of customers who ask suppliers to help them design product improvements, develop prototypes and drawings, and so forth. The supplier works closely with the customer's engineering or R&D or manufacturing team and comes up with an innovative design that will produce some savings or other benefit to the customer. As a thank-you, the supplier sees the customer's procurement team then send their design and their specifications out to multiple competitors, with the work going to the lowest bidder. A supplier may let that happen once, maybe even twice if they are slow. But after a while they catch on to the rules of the game and learn to stop playing.

Advice for suppliers negotiating with their customers

Our advice for a seller's negotiators closely parallels our advice for buyers. So much so, in fact, that we would encourage buyers and sellers who expect to continue to work together beyond a single deal to read all of this advice and discuss what they might do to help each other follow it. As with our suggestions for buyers, our advice to sellers starts with clarity of purpose.

Recognize that all customers are not alike

A seller should start with a clear idea of the purpose of a deal with a customer. By definition, one purpose is to sell goods and/or services to the customer. But is that all there is? Why do you want to sell to this particular customer?

The answer may be as simple as "to increase our revenue." Or it might be the somewhat more demanding "to increase our profit." Or it might be more strategic, as in "develop a new market" or "gain some reference accounts in a new industry." An important question to ask yourself as you ponder your purpose is "in what time frame?" Are you trying to sell a lot today, or are you trying to create a sustainable revenue stream? To achieve your goals, does the customer also need to be successful in its endeavor?

In our experience, if you are negotiating deals in which implementation matters, it's likely that simply getting the order is not enough. You need to make sure that your customers get what they need to be successful and that they can use it appropriately. You need to make sure that serving them is not so costly to you that you lose money with every order you ship. And you need to be thinking about where tomorrow's orders (and profits) are going to come from.

We often hear our clients say that they want to "partner" with their customers or clients. What does that mean? When we ask, the typical sales rep will say something like "they buy a lot from me" or "they don't beat me up on price." Of course, what's missing from those kinds of statements is what's in it for the customer. Why would a buyer want any part of a partnership that is primarily about their buying more, at a higher price? When a buyer says, "We're looking for you to partner with us on this," most suppliers know to grab their wallets or run for the hills, because that phrase is so often a preamble to a request for yet another discount, rather than a promise to buy a lot at high prices.

The purpose of a typical negotiation with a customer, then, is not to "partner" with them. Just because the purpose of a negotiation has to be more than just reaching a deal does not mean that the "end" is some ill-defined and often-illusory state called "partnering." Even when you really want a partnership, it is usually for the purpose of doing something you cannot manage on your own, rather than just to have a partnership. To do deals worth doing, you need to work a little harder up front to be clear about your purposes. What are you trying to accomplish with this deal, with this customer?

Don't do it alone—align internal resources early

Sales teams are sometimes isolated from the realities their delivery and service teams face. Failing to get appropriate input from those who will be charged with implementation is a sure-fire route to unhappy customers. As a customer-facing representative of your company, it is important to think though the myriad touch points likely to unfold during implementation.

In crafting complex relationships with customers and creating deals that have more value over time, it is useful for the sales executive to ensure close contact with the teams of enablers within the supplier organization who are in touch with that customer. Arranging for their involvement early will enable the sales team to rally the resources necessary to deliver on promises to the customer and avoid making promises the delivery team probably can't keep. In a growing, long-term relationship, sales execs have to be able to overdeliver on their promises, rather than consistently overpromising and underdelivering.

Don't let them do it alone—avoid the procurement trap

Recognize that procurement has a role to play and that, if not for the behavior of some of your predecessors, your customer might not have created these often cumbersome and expensive processes. And now that the procurement negotiators are in place, they too have incentives that drive some of their behavior. Think of procurement as potential blockers, people who have a critical role to play up front and almost none during implementation. Blockers generally care a lot about whether they are seen as making good decisions, based on whatever criteria apply to the situation. If the only criteria that apply are the size of the discount and the perceived pain the discount is causing the supplier, you can only "win" (get the deal) by losing.

To ensure that you and your customer can do a deal worth doing, you must find ways to involve other key actors. For example, consider the enablers, who, although they may have no role to play in the decision, will have a very important role during implementation. What would they say *if* they had an opportunity to get involved during the negotiation? What errors might they help you or your customer avoid that would otherwise cause problems for one or both of you during implementation? Although often ignored in procurement processes because they have no formal decision-making authority, enablers can bring a great deal of legitimacy to a process. They can also be credible allies in a discussion with procurement about, for example, what things are true comparables, or why a particular set of delivery conditions makes a difference in the value the customer receives or in the cost of doing business with them.

Other critical players to identify are the essentials—those whose interests are most aligned with the point of the deal. They are often important business buyers who procurement must try to satisfy *and* they care deeply about implementation. The key with essentials is to figure out how to help them give their representatives at the table (in this case, procurement) the right instructions.

By the time you get to the actual negotiation with procurement, it is often too late to reach out to those individuals. Your actions will be seen as trying yet another end-run around procurement. But earlier in the process, perhaps even as early as the implementation of a prior deal, you can and should try to build a working relationship with essentials that helps you understand what really matters to them, and that allows you to educate them on what your needs and challenges might be. Show them (note this will require doing as much as talking) that you are a trustworthy counterpart, that you care about implementation, and that you are looking beyond getting this order. If you do so, you will be better able to persuade them that the criteria by which they should measure procurement's performance are less about discounts or your level of pain and more about the value that you can deliver through product innovation, process improvements, speed to market, reliability, and other benefits.

Invite your customers to help you create the precedents you need

Good precedents can be difficult to create entirely on your own. Suppliers and their customers tend to be part of a classic "act and react" loop. We've often heard exchanges between senior buyers and sellers that boil down to, "We can't stop treating you like a vendor until you stop acting like one!" with the obvious retort being, "We can't stop acting like a vendor until you stop treating us like one!"

It is extremely hard to step back and say: "We want the way we behave today to inform how you behave tomorrow." Sadly, the reality is that how we behave today *inevitably* affects how others will act tomorrow. But we rarely take the future ramifications into account when we consider our next move.

Put the question of precedent squarely on the table. For example, you can always ask this simple question: "If we were implementing the way we are negotiating, would we be well served?" If the answer is no, that should serve as a good signal to rethink a bit, review your agenda, reconsider the makeup of your teams, and try again. A similar question could be: "If supply became short, or another key supplier was suddenly acquired by your competitor, and the contract did not provide all the answers, how would you want us to respond to your requests?"

It takes some skill to engage in such difficult conversations, and it is a different sort of skill than many negotiators have been encouraged to develop. The idea is not to pressure (or even persuade) the other side just to say yes, but rather to work with them to create a history that will help ensure the deal they strike today is still worth doing tomorrow.

Conclusion

When "yes" is not enough

We decided the most useful framework for concluding this book would be a Q&A with a hypothetical reader. We imagine someone having this kind of response: "I think the ideas in the book make sense. Some seem compelling and some seem at least reasonable—but as I grapple with my real-life negotiations, how do I assimilate the ideas from the book and make them part of how I think and act?"

Excellent question. Ensuring that you achieve deals with a point may take more than just assimilating the ideas. It may require internalizing them and turning them into behaviors. This book isn't just a descriptive model that outlines desirable outcomes. Rather, it is filled with prescriptive advice. As an individual you have to work on these behaviors and improve over time. This may involve careful preparation, self-reflection and review, training, and other actions on the path to self-improvement. Moreover, as a member of an organization, much of the advice in this book can't be fully operationalized if you act alone. It may require some buy-in from senior leaders and organizational changes over time. If that is the case for you, then your challenge is obviously more significant than just changing what you do and say during negotiations—it involves changing what your whole company does when it negotiates. As a reader who is excited by these ideas, you need to make them more than ideas. You need to turn them into practice.

What big messages should I take away from *The Point of the Deal*?

If we had to narrow down our message to just a few key take-aways, we'd offer the following summary.

"Yes" is not enough in most deals

In the vast majority of negotiations, simply getting the counterpart to "yes" is a useful step along the way to creating value, but not the end in itself. In most cases, getting the handshake, nod, or contract signature is only the beginning of building value. Implementation matters any time there is something that one, both, or all parties must do (or refrain from doing) after the deal is "done" in order to get the benefit of their bargain.

In our experience, most negotiators *underestimate* the importance of implementation to the success of whatever it is they are negotiating about. As a result, they often engage in strategies and tactics that may undermine their ability to achieve their desired goals during the implementation phase. The negotiation tactics designed to push the counterpart to agreement as efficiently as possible may actually limit the value the deal can ultimately deliver. And the tragedy is that even experienced negotiators often fail to consider whether implementation will be important as they design their strategy for the negotiation.

When implementation matters, how you negotiate is critical to your ultimate success

When implementation matters, there are many ways that the manner in which you and your counterparts negotiate will set you both up to fail:

- The real purpose of the deal is unclear.

- Key stakeholders have been left out of the process.

- Constituents on each side are not sufficiently aligned.

- Hard issues have been avoided and finessed.

- The parties have dealt with each other in a way that will be problematic if they continue the behaviors during implementation.

- Significant implementation risks have been ignored.

- There is ambiguity about who is doing what when, or how the transition to implementation will happen.

And this is only a partial list. If the value of your deal comes from implementation, you need to think hard about how you manage the negotiation process to maximize the likelihood that you will be able to extract that value over time. The choices you make will have a big impact on your ultimate success. Success is determined by how you position yourself to capture value, not just by getting them to "yes."

In short, when implementation matters, you must:

- Negotiate like the deal is a means to an end.

- Consult broadly.

- Use the negotiation to create a positive history of working together.

- Air your nightmares and work together to manage risk.

- Make sure both of you are making commitments you can live up to.

- Keep going when the deal is "done."

What should I do next to ensure I achieve the point of the deal?

Here are a few simple suggestions (at least, it is simple to suggest them; actually putting them into practice will take work!).

Prepare, prepare, prepare

When you're in the room with the other side, negotiation is always a dynamic, interactive process. It is very hard, when the pressure is on and the counterpart is waiting for your next response, to think carefully about what you might do differently in the moment. During preparation, you generally have more time to think and less pressure, plus you can try out an argument and then decide that you don't want to use it.

Practice, practice, practice

How you implement the advice in this book will have a huge impact on its effectiveness. In negotiation, as in any skill, practice will lead to improvement. No one who is an expert at what they do got there simply by being born great. World-class athletes spend years practicing. The amount of time they spend practicing is huge compared to the time spent competing. And no matter how good they are, they can only continue to improve through practice.

Getting your counterparts to step outside their comfort zone may be a negotiation in itself. You can safely assume that you will not get an overwhelming response if you start your next negotiation by telling your counterparts: "I just read a great book on negotiation. It says we have to share all of our concerns about implementation as we negotiate—go ahead, tell me what concerns you have about implementation." You are more likely to get (well-founded) looks of bewilderment.

You will more likely evoke a positive response if you start with something like this: "We are making very good progress toward a deal that seems to make sense. However, even when a deal sounds good on paper, we sometimes have challenges in actually making it work. We do things that make it hard for our counterparts to get their job done, or they do things we didn't expect. Sometimes we find that, although we thought we each had a clear idea of what to do as we move to implementation, certain areas are still ambiguous and would benefit from further clarification. It might be useful if we took a little time to look at where we expect execution of our deal will be most challenging. After all, it is in both our interests to make sure we each get the benefit of our bargain."

A great way to get your team aligned is to practice together. Remember, though, you are not learning a script. That doesn't work in negotiation because you can't write your counterparts' lines, or count on them to stick to your libretto. But you are working on your lines. And that never hurts.

Review, adjust, review

To really improve over time, you have to review what worked well and what you might do differently next time. These lessons will allow you to replicate successful strategies and adjust your performance where things need improvement. Getting into the cycle of review, adjustment, and further review will improve your skills over time.

While it is tempting to simply move from one disaster to the next without pausing for reflection and debriefing, it is a formula for yet more disasters. If you don't learn from your mistakes, you are doomed to repeat them. People who are world class at what they do have a system for reviewing their performance and adjusting it to improve. Anyone who doesn't do that will not remain world class for long.

What if my organization just doesn't get it?

If you live in the C-suite, as a senior executive, the advice in chapter 10 will give you some guidelines for action. As you think about helping your troops do deals worth doing, it is within your power to get the structure right, build a road map, make sure they have tools adequate for the job, enhance their skills, and use your bully pulpit to create a mind-set conducive to deals that can be implemented. This is certainly not an easy set of tasks, but we have offered some specific operational advice for you.

Of more concern to us here is how the organizational challenge feels to the masses who are not masters of their own destiny with final decision-making authority over big corporate issues. We are thinking of the executives, managers, and rank and file who feel that organizational change must be someone else's problem. We are looking at those who think that until someone else fixes the organizational impediments, perhaps it's not worth trying to do anything differently. We are thinking of the readers who feel that the ideas in this book resonate with them, but who may be having doubts like these:

- "I could end up looking for a new job if my boss heard me start a conversation with the other side about 'nightmares' we each have about implementation; I'm supposed to close deals, not prevent them!"

- "The legal department will go into convulsions if I start talking about how *we* might fail to implement our end of the deal."

- "We have an incredibly huge savings target for the year. If I start thinking about total cost of ownership instead of just price, we will miss our targets and I may get fired!"

- "I might miss my performance bonus this year if I let anyone here know that the buyer can't possibly take all of our product that they are signing up for!"

We have advice for all of you.

Ask questions

Don't underestimate the power of asking good questions. No matter what your position in your organization, consider asking those above you questions about the purpose of the deal, who ought to be involved at what stage, what precedent they think you'll need to really capture the value you are negotiating for, which risks ought to be discussed, whether commitments ought to be examined more carefully, and what the transition plan is.

As people ponder how to answer those questions, many of the points raised in this book will occur to them on their own. After all, what we have laid out here is not rocket science—it's just organized experience and common sense. If the answers they give to your questions don't make sense, then follow up with another set of questions about why they see the issue that way.

There are, of course, some limits to our exhortation to ask questions. Obviously if you are a professional athlete in a play-off game, asking the coach "why" when he gives you a play may not be prudent. And if you serve in the military, asking "why" on the battlefield when you get a direct order may not be much appreciated by your commanding officer. But for most of the rest of us, just saying "yes sir!" or "yes ma'am!" when asked to do something that may not be in the best long-term interests of the organization may not be the best course. In trying to do our jobs to the best of our abilities, we owe it to our employer to ask questions if we are told or incented to do things that may not make much sense at the end of the day. Asking good questions is the best way to get managers thinking about their own assumptions and whether change would benefit the organization.

Be the change you desire

Cribbing from Gandhi, we suggest that you be the change you desire (or, we suppose, the more modern and direct version of this suggestion would be Nike's "Just do it!"). Many of the suggestions in this book are contagious. By modeling some of the behaviors we prescribe, you may encourage others to follow suit, both within your organization and on the other side of the table. Perhaps you can create a bit of a grassroots movement to negotiate more effectively when implementation matters.

For example, if you choose to consult with the implementers during the course of negotiation, even though your corporate culture is to exclude them until the deal is done, you might be surprised by the results. Not only might they help you refine some pieces of the operational plan so that you get more value in implementation, but they also might be more positive about the deal you negotiated and convey that enthusiasm to senior people at your organization, which will certainly reflect well on you. Moreover, when those implementers are doing something that you will have to work on at some point, they are much more likely to bring you in at an earlier juncture if you have done the same for them.

Negotiate to get the right instructions

Your organizational context is not immutable. In fact, it is likely changing all the time (perhaps at a pace where you don't notice it on a regular basis). You have the power, to a greater or lesser extent, to encourage change in your organization, regardless of where you find yourself on the org chart.

A key way to encourage change is to negotiate explicitly for the change you want. These internal negotiations happen all the time, although they are rarely framed as "negotiations" per se. Think of them more as "influence" or "persuasion." From making simple suggestions to building a robust business case, they effectively are, at the end of the day, negotiations.

Start off small. Tackling your corporate compensation system or overall organizational structure would probably not be wise as a first step. However, starting with the instructions you get from your boss as you are sent out to negotiate a deal is very sensible indeed. Make sure you discuss purposes, stakeholders, precedent, risks, commitments, and transition plans with your boss as you prepare to negotiate. If you hear anything that does not make sense to you in terms of achieving a deal with a point, push back. Push back gently or vigorously, depending on your relationship with your boss and organizational tolerance for "insubordination." If it is not clear to you how the negotiation leads to real value, ask about it. If you feel that you lack some critical tools or would benefit from additional skills training, talk about it with your boss.

At the end of the day, your job is not just to follow orders from your harried manager, but to enable your organization to get to deals with a point. If you are currently co-opted into doing pointless deals, you owe it to your organization to give them better deals over time. After all, why negotiate with a counterpart and bring them to "yes" if that doesn't really get you the value you are bargaining for? That would be pointless, wouldn't it?

Notes

Chapter 2

1. We refer to "salient" differences in the calculation of the importance of implementation (figure 2-1) because it would not make sense to consider differences in a vacuum, regardless of how those may impact your interactions during implementation. Your small company might have huge differences with the IBM corporate culture, but if the total interaction with IBM involves buying some new computers from it over the Web, then the fact that you have cultural differences is not in the least relevant to implementation. On the other hand, even small differences, if they go to the heart of how you must work together during implementation can be critical and require you to take them into account during the negotiation.

Lots of deals are done between very different parties, in part *because* of differences such as competencies, interests, or resources. If not for those differences, they might not have a lot to offer one another. However, those differences bring with them some challenges when it comes to working together after the deal is signed.

The more aligned the parties are in perceptions and interests, the more they share common goals and objectives, the more they have the same performance plans and metrics, the more they report in to a common group of executives, and the more their work styles are consistent, the more likely they are to "play well together" during implementation. On the other hand, the greater the differences in how the parties see the world, in how they do business, in what gets rewarded (or punished), and in how they work, the greater the implementation challenges are likely to be. We don't mean to suggest that you shouldn't do deals with companies that are different from yours. Differences are often the key to value. But if you don't effectively address some of those differences during the negotiation, they may interfere with the implementation of your deal.

Chapter 3

1. Lewis Carroll, *Alice's Adventures in Wonderland* and *Through the Looking Glass* (New York: Signet, 2000), 64–65.

2. Art Wilson, who spent twenty-three years with IBM and much of his life in the oil patch before he founded Critical Path Strategies of Boerne, Texas, shared with us several stories about how major oil companies were sometimes short-sighted both on the commodity side ("rope, soap, and dope" for drilling rigs around the world) and on the well services side of their businesses. When costs are insignificant compared to the revenue side, according to Wilson, you get perverse incentives for procurement teams to save money, even if they risk exploration and production activities that are huge in comparison to any possible savings from procurement. Authors' interview with Art Wilson, Brighton, MA, February 23, 2006.

3. Authors' interview with Ken Wolf, March 8, 2006.

4. Telephone interview with V. N. Tyagarajan, March 27, 2007.

Chapter 4

1. David A. Lax and James K. Sebenius, *3-D Negotiation: Powerful Tools to Change the Game in Your Most Important Deals* (Boston: Harvard Business School Press, 2006), 2.

2. Ibid., 66.

3. Mike Beals and Frank Conway, "E. I. DuPont de Nemours & Company and the Value of Outsourcing Governance: Observations, Lessons Learned and Success Factors," May 18, 2006, https://equaterra.webex.com/ec0507l/eventcenter/recording/recordAction.do?theAction=poprecord&confViewID=286470727&siteurl=equaterra.

4. Authors' interview with Brett Pauly, August 17, 2005.

Chapter 6

1. Douglas Stone, Bruce M. Patton, and Sheila Heen, *Difficult Conversations: How to Discuss What Matters Most* (New York: Penguin Books, 1999).

2. A tool that can be used for interpreting data and drawing conclusions is the Ladder of Inference, based on the work of Chris Argyris and Donald A. Schon. See C. Argyris, R. Putnam, and D. Smith, *Action Science: Concepts, Methods, and Skills for Research and Intervention* (San Francisco: Jossey-Bass, 1985).

Chapter 7

1. William Ury, *The Power of a Positive No: How to Say No and Still Get to Yes* (New York: Bantam Books, 2007), 10–15.

2. Telephone interview with Paul Cramer, May 18, 2007.

3. Telephone interview with V. N. Tyagarajan, March 27, 2007.

Chapter 8

1. David A. Lax and James K. Sebenius, *3-D Negotiation: Powerful Tools to Change the Game in Your Most Important Deals* (Boston: Harvard Business School Press, 2006), 74.

2. Ibid., 149–157.

Chapter 9

1. For some examples of the kinds of tools, techniques, and worksheets that negotiators (and their managers) can use to be better prepared, take a look at Roger Fisher and Danny Ertel, *Getting Ready to Negotiate* (New York: Penguin, 1995).

2. Authors' meeting with Scott Spehar, September 12, 2006.

Chapter 10

1. Alec Klein, "Creative Transactions Earned Team Rewards," *Washington Post*, July 19, 2002, http://www.washingtonpost.com/wp-dyn/articles/A28624-2002Jul18.html; Gary Rivlin, "AOL's Rough Riders," *Industry Standard*, October 30, 2000.

2. Bethany McLean and Peter Elkind, *The Smartest Guys in the Room: The Amazing Rise and Scandalous Fall of Enron* (New York: Penguin Books, 2004), 76–77.

3. Simon London, "EDS Finds Sea Legs After Navy Storm," *Financial Times*, May 4, 2005.

4. Tom Foremski and Richard Waters, "Companies & Finance: The Americas: EDS May Seek to Renegotiate $6.9bn US Navy Contract," *Financial Times*, October 3, 2002; Tom Foremski, "Second SEC Probe Adds to EDS Troubles," *Financial Times*, May 16, 2003.

5. Klein, "Creative Transactions Earned Team Rewards."

6. Danny Ertel, "Getting Past Yes: Negotiating As If Implementation Mattered," *Harvard Business Review*, November 2004.

7. McLean and Elkind, *The Smartest Guys in the Room*, 115–116.

8. E-mail from Lynne Tracey, April 30, 2007.

Chapter 11

1. According to several studies, the success rate of mergers and joint ventures is less than 50 percent. See Mark L. Sirower, *The Synergy Trap* (New York: Free Press, 1997), 6. Further research continues to support this finding: Michael Arndt, Emily Thornton, and Dean Foust, "Let's Talk Turkeys; Some Mergers Were Never Meant to Be," *BusinessWeek*, December 11, 2000, 44–46; J. Robert Carlton and Claude Lineberry, *Achieving Post-Merger Success: A Stakeholder's Guide to Cultural Due Diligence, Assessment, and Integration* (San Francisco: Pfeiffer, 2004), 8; Eugene G. Lukac, "Will Your Merger Succeed?" July/September 2006, http://www.csc.com/cscworld/072006/fa/fa004.shtml; David Harding and Sam Rovit, *Mastering the Merger: Four Critical*

Decisions That Make or Break the Deal (Boston: Harvard Business School Press, 2004), 3; KPMG, "Unlocking Shareholder Value: The Keys to Success," KPMG M&A Global Research Report, November 1999. There is a contrary view that argues that mergers and acquisitions do pay, on average. They certainly pay for sellers and, when adjusted appropriately for other business factors and benchmarks, there is data that suggests that value is at least conserved for most buyers. Even so, the author concludes, "Many buyers in M&A transactions should prepare to be disappointed." There is much about these deals that can be improved. See Robert F. Bruner, *Deals from Hell: M&A Lessons That Rise Above the Ashes* (Hoboken, NJ: John Wiley & Sons, 2005), 24.

2. Carlton and Lineberry, *Achieving Post-Merger Success*, 8; Sirower, *The Synergy Trap*, 6.

3. For more information on the importance of stakeholder consultation, refer to David Harding and Sam Rovit, *Mastering the Merger: Four Critical Decisions That Make or Break the Deal* (Boston: Harvard Business School Press, 2004), 172–174.

4. Ibid., 62–63.

5. Stephen M. Dent, "Partnering Intelligence," *Executive Excellence* 19, no. 11 (November 2002), 10–11; Robert E. Spekman, Lynn A. Isabella, and Thomas C. MacAvoy, *Maximizing the Value of Your Partnerships* (New York: John Wiley, 2000), 27.

6. Danny Ertel, Jeff Weiss, and Laura Judy Visioni, "Managing Alliance Relationships—Ten Key Corporate Capabilities: A Cross-Industry Study of How to Build and Manage Successful Alliances" (Cambridge, MA: Vantage Partners, 2001); Jeff Weiss, Sara Keen, and Stuart Kliman, "Managing Alliances for Business Results: Lessons Learned from Leading Companies" (Cambridge, MA: Vantage Partners, 2006).

7. The "incomplete contract" is used to describe alliances in Benjamin Gomes-Casseres, *The Alliance Revolution: The New Shape of Business Rivalry* (Cambridge, MA: Harvard University Press, 1996). This term originally comes from economics and was used in R. Coase, "The Nature of the Firm," *Economica* 4 (1937), 386–405.

8. Weiss, Keen, and Kliman, "Managing Alliances for Business Results," 24–28.

9. Seventy percent renegotiate significant outsourcing terms during the first two years, according to results from 2002–2004 surveys of U.K., North American, and continental European buyers conducted by Simmons & Simmons and presented by David Barrett at the February 2005 Outsourcing World Summit. David Barrett, "Building Win:Win Strategic Partnerships" (research presented at the Outsourcing World Summit, San Diego, CA, February 2005). Fifty percent of outsourcing deals fail to deliver expected value, as seen in David Craig and Paul Willmott, "Outsourcing Grows Up," *McKinsey Quarterly*, February 2005.

10. Thomas Kern, Leslie P. Willcocks, and Eric van Heck, "The Winner's Curse in IT Outsourcing: Strategies for Avoiding Relational Trauma," *California Management Review* 44, no. 2 (Winter 2002), 47–69.

Chapter 12

1. According to 2004 survey of eighty-two companies, coconducted by Vantage Partners and the International Association of Contract and Commercial Management (IACCM).

Analytical Table of Contents

Chapter 1—Introduction: *What's the point?*   1

How the point of the deal gets lost   3

Your counterparts never intended to perform   4

Both sides intended to perform, but had different
interpretations of what that meant   4

Everything was clear, but one party couldn't follow through   4

Everything was clear, but the circumstances changed   5

Everything was clear, but the contract requirements were
not enough   5

Why negotiators often get themselves in trouble   6

Why managers don't steer negotiators
in the right direction   8

Why smart organizations fail to get it right   9

Creating a separate "deal department"   9

Relying on third parties to do your deals   10

Using deal-making metrics   10

Allowing negotiators to "protect the deal"   10

Making it difficult for the negotiator to say "yes"   11

Making it difficult for the negotiator to say "no"   11

Applying an implementation mind-set   11

Bet-the-company deals   12

Bread-and-butter deals   12

Before we go on—meet our cast of characters   13
  Resolving a conflict—buyer and seller   13
  Creating economic value—alliance partners   14
  Working together—internal negotiations   14

Chapter 2—The Deal-Making Mind-set:
Why "yes" is often not enough   17

Calculating the importance of implementation   17
Conventional wisdom, assumptions, and behaviors   19
  "Avoid disclosing information when you don't have to"   20
  "Limit the number of people in the loop"   21
  *"Treat the negotiation process as distinct
    and separate from implementation"   23*
  *"Lock them in early and often" (a.k.a. "Always
    be closing" or "Time kills deals")   24*
  *"If you don't have something nice to say, don't say
    anything at all" (a.k.a. "Silence is golden")   25*
  "Keep them off balance"   27
  "Create strong sanctions to ensure they will perform"   28
Less convention, more wisdom   29

Part I: The Implementation Mind-set   33

Chapter 3—Treat the Deal as a Means to an End:
What do you need beyond a "yes"?   35

What is the point of your deal?   38
  Resolving a conflict   38
  Purchasing, exchanging, or creating economic value   39
  *Making organizational or interpersonal arrangements
    for working together   40*
How do you ensure your deal has a point?   41
  Ask in advance: what will be different "the day after"?   41
  *Challenge your team: what kind of relationship do you
    need to implement well?   43*

How do you make sure the point is clear
to your counterpart too?   45
Engage others in the purpose discussion early on   45
Try a little "backwards thinking"   46

Chapter 4—Consult Broadly:
Who do you need to get beyond "yes"?   49

How do you line up the right people for the negotiation?   52
Identify different types of stakeholders   53
Bystanders   54
Blockers   55
Enablers   56
Essentials   57
Set and manage expectations about roles   58
Delineate roles for decision making   58
Assign different roles for different decisions   59
How do you get sufficient buy-in?   60
Set expectations early   61
Consult early and often   62
Help your counterparts make sure their stakeholders are on board   64
Ask about their enablers and essentials as well as their blockers   64
Ask about the time and place for some joint meetings among
key implementers   64
Describe your own consultation process   65
Consider a joint effort to build the necessary alignment   65

Chapter 5—Make History:
How do you set the right precedent for implementation?   67

How do you anticipate the history you need?   70
Let the point of the deal define the precedents you need   71
Align your team on the precedents you want to create   75
Benefit of the doubt   76
Respect   76
Creativity   77
Commitments   77

Information sharing   78

Use of power or leverage   79

How do you get others to see your view of history?   82

Chapter 6—Air Your Nightmares:
How do you discuss risk without risking the deal?   85

Are there risks to avoiding risk discussions?   86

How do you decide which risks to raise?   88

How do you minimize the risk of talking about risk?   91

Make joint risk management a natural part of the conversation   91

Be a little humble about risk management   92

Separate intent from impact   94

Help your counterparts understand your thinking   95

Express your concerns as *hypotheses*, to be tested jointly   96

Acknowledge the difficulty of raising the topic   97

Make it easier for others to raise their nightmares   97

Chapter 7—Don't Let Them Overcommit:
How do you help make sure your counterparts can deliver?   99

Overcommitment in different types of deals   100

Stretch versus overcommitment   101

How do you keep the other side from overcommitting?   102

Avoid extracting pointless overcommitments   102

Adopt an implementation mind-set   103

Take the 80/20 hindsight challenge   106

Engage with all the enablers and essentials   108

Chapter 8—Run Past the Finish Line:
How do you stay focused on the real goal?   111

Don't let up   111

Pay attention to momentum and handoffs   112

How do you move from "yes" to implementation?   114

Make transition a part of the negotiator's role   114

Consider a joint handoff meeting   114

How do you maintain momentum to carry you
through change?   117

Part II: Negotiating and the Organization   121

Chapter 9—Managing Negotiators:
How do you steer them toward deals worth doing?   123

Why don't managers steer negotiators in the right direction?   124

Oversteering: micromanaging the negotiator   124

Understeering: lacking a clear process for managing negotiators   125

Backseat driving: negotiators resist being managed   126

The checkered flag: incentives make the problem worse   126

So . . . what's a manager to do?   128

Use the implementation mind-set to define success   129

Insist on thorough preparation   135

Coach your negotiators along the way   137

Welcome problems   140

Help negotiators end it well   141

Chapter 10—Building an Organization That Does Deals Worth Doing:
How so many smart companies get it wrong   145

Perils of a deal-making culture   145

*AOL Business Affairs story: competing to see who can do the
most outrageous deals   146*

Enron developers: "in the business of doing deals"   146

*EDS and the Navy Marine Corps Intranet: the lure
of the "megadeal"   147*

Six common mistakes organizations make   148

Creating a separate "deal department"   149

Relying on third parties to do deals   151

Using deal-making metrics   153

Allowing negotiators to "protect the deal"   155

Making it difficult for the negotiator to say "yes"   157

Making it difficult for the negotiator to say "no"   160

How do you build an organization that does deals
worth doing?   161

Orient your negotiation process toward implementation   163

Draw a road map   163

Link deals to their purposes   165

Build stakeholders into the road map   166

Clarify where implementers are involved in negotiation   167

Clarify where negotiators are involved in implementation   167

Make sure negotiators have tools adequate to the job   167

Create a negotiator's toolkit—and make sure it's used   168

Supply tools to map stakeholder relationships   171

Incorporate precedent setting into your strategy playbook   171

Encourage dealing with risk by supplying risk
management tools   172

Enhance their skills—in context   173

Create a mind-set conducive to deals that can be implemented   175

Tell 'em what, why, and how   176

Measure critical business outcomes and activities along
the way   176

Use carrots and sticks, but in moderation   177

Walk the talk   178

Get the structure right   179

Part III: Critical Deals in Which Implementation Matters   181

Chapter 11—Bet-the-Company Deals:
Mergers, alliances, and outsourcing   183

Business combinations: mergers, acquisitions,
and joint ventures   184

The roots of the problem: doing deals for the sake of the deal   185

Ignoring key stakeholders because "time kills deals" can
kill implementation   186

The fear that "loose lips sink ships" can shut down
needed communication   187

Relying on "hired guns" to do the dirty work leaves parties
unable to work together   189
Negotiate business combinations that have a point   190
Advice to principals   190
Ask advisers about their approach to implementation   190
Insist on staying involved   191
Advice to advisers   192
Educate clients on the importance of implementability   192
Consider the benefits, not just the costs, of a more inclusive
process   193
Push to make sure commitments are realistic   194
Partnerships: alliances and other "incomplete" contracts   194
*The roots of the problem: trying to avoid conflict instead of
managing it   195*
Negotiators make light of the real differences between
the would-be partners   196
Negotiators focus on negotiating the deal, not the
relationship   197
Negotiators quit too soon   198
Remember that partnering effectively is the point of the deal   199
Be prepared to deal with differences and with change   199
Integrate negotiation and implementation   200
Outsourcing: when a vendor is more than just a vendor   200
The roots of the problem: thinking that it's all about the contract   201
Outsourcing negotiators lack enough information
and access to reach good decisions   202
Buyers place too much reliance on service-level
agreements and penalties to protect them   203
Providers place too much reliance on scope limitations   205
Remember that signing the contract is not the point of the deal   206
Advice for buyers of outsourcing   207
Keep your eye on the purpose of the deal   207
Make the deal discussion a precedent for implementation   207
Advice for providers of outsourcing   208
Insist on getting the information you need to be successful   208
Focus on both profitability and relationship   209
Integrate delivery teams into negotiations   211

Advice to advisers   211
  Help your clients focus on governance   211
  Embrace and evaluate differentiated solutions   212
  Manage communication, but don't stifle it   212

Chapter 12—Bread-and-Butter Deals: *Customers and suppliers*   215

The point of negotiations between buyers and sellers   216
  Buyers care about more than just price   216
  Sellers care about more than just volume and price   217
Common problems faced by negotiators for both buyers and sellers   219
  Negotiator as diva   219
  Painting by numbers   220
Advice for buyers negotiating with suppliers   221
  Structure the negotiation around your business purposes   222
  Aim to get the best of both worlds: align procurement professionals with their internal constituents   224
  Create precedents that encourage suppliers to collaborate with you   225
Advice for suppliers negotiating with their customers   226
  Recognize that all customers are not alike   226
  Don't do it alone—align internal resources early   228
  Don't let them do it alone—avoid the procurement trap   228
  Invite your customers to help you create the precedents you need   229

Chapter 13—Conclusion: *When "yes" is not enough*   231

What big messages should I take away from *The Point of the Deal?*   232
  "Yes" is not enough in most deals   232
  When implementation matters, how you negotiate is critical to your ultimate success   232
What should I do next to ensure I achieve the point of the deal?   233
  Prepare, prepare, prepare   233
  Practice, practice, practice   234
  Review, adjust, review   234

What if my organization just doesn't get it?   235
   Ask questions   236
   Be the change you desire   237
   Negotiate to get the right instructions   237

Index

Accenture, 105, 162, 179

acquisitions. *See* mergers, acquisitions, and joint ventures

action plan for organizations

developing an implementation mind-set, 176–178, 232

facilitating change in the organization, 235–238

negotiation behaviors that impact implementation, 232–233

practice and, 234

preparation and, 233

review and adjust plans and results, 234–235

Alice's Adventures in Wonderland, 35

alliances. *See* partnerships

AOL Business Affairs, 146, 149, 158

assumptions and behaviors in deal making

avoidance of saying negative things, 25, 27

commitments, 104

creation of strong sanctions, 28–29

creativity, 82

deal closure timing, 24–25, 26, 105

desire to keep the other party off balance, 27–28, 104

grabbing value, 81

information disclosure and, 20, 82

keeping negotiation separate from implementation, 23

limiting the number of people involved, 21–23

surprise, 104

BATNA, 142, 160, 166

blockers, 55–56

Bonfire of the Vanities, The (Wolfe), 150

Brown, Richard, 147, 148

buyers negotiating with suppliers

business purpose at forefront, 222–224

keeping procurement and implementers talking, 224–225

mutually beneficial precedents creation, 225–226

buyers negotiating with suppliers
(*continued*)
problems related to compensation
schemes, 220–221
problems related to use of professional procurement negotiators, 219–220
ultimate goal for buyers, 216–217
bystanders, 54–55

Cisco, 60, 141
Confluence, 42
counterparts in negotiation. *See* participants in deal making
Cramer, Paul, 105
creating a history. *See* precedents in
negotiations
culture, deal-making, 145–148

deal-making mind-set
calculating the importance of
implementation, 17–19
characteristics of good outcomes,
30
consequences of a deal-making
culture, 145–148
conventional wisdom (*see*
assumptions and behaviors in
deal making)
vs. implementation mind-set
example, 131–135
key variables, 19
precedents in negotiations and,
80, 82

EDS, 147–148, 155
enablers, 55, 56–57
Enron International, 146–147,
150–151
essentials, 55, 57–58

Finn, Tom, 150

Genpact, 46, 107
Getting to Yes, 23, 43, 160
Gomes-Casseres, Ben, 195

Harvard Negotiation Project
(HNP), xii

implementation mind-set
80/20 hindsight, 106–107
agreeing on the ultimate purpose,
45–46
backwards thinking, 46
continuum of a deal, 38
creating in a company, 176–178,
232
vs. deal-making mind-set
example, 131–135
described, 7–8, 11–12
managing negotiators and,
129–130
precedents in negotiations and,
80, 82
prenegotiation focus and disclosure importance, 41–43

principles, 30–31
reasons for implementation troubles, 3–6
relationship building and, 43–45
seeing the deal as a means to an end, 35–38
staying focused on the real goal (*see* postnegotiation plan)
using backwards thinking, 46–47
when negotiation is to resolve a conflict, 38–39
when the purpose is to create value, 39
when the purpose is to make working arrangements, 40–41
willingness to discuss risks (*see* risk discussions)

joint ventures. *See* mergers, acquisitions, and joint ventures

knowledge sharing, 169–171
Kurosawa, Akira, 82

Lax, David, 51–52, 118

managing negotiators
coaching approach, 137–140, 141
common manager mistakes, 8–9
deal-making vs. implementation mind-set example, 131–135
implementation mind-set and, 129–130
joint handoff meetings, 141–143
misdirected incentives, 126–128
negotiators' resistance to being managed, 126
openness to hearing about problems, 140–141
oversteering, 124–125
preparation and, 135–137
raising postdeal issues, 141–143
understeering, 125–126
Matsushita Electric, 52
mergers, acquisitions, and joint ventures
advice to advisers, 192–194
advice to principals, 190–192
consequences of using of third parties, 189–190
failures due to poor implementation, 184
outsourcing (*see* outsourcing)
partnerships (*see* partnerships)
problems from ignoring key stakeholders to save time, 186–187
secrecy that impedes communication, 187–188

Navy, U.S., 147–148, 155, 202
Navy Marine Corps Intranet (NMCI), 147–148, 202

negotiation
  common manager mistakes, 8–9
    (*see also* managing negotiators)
  common organization errors,
    9–11 (*see also* organizations'
    negotiation mistakes)
  implementation mind-set, 7–8,
    11–12 (*see also* implementa-
    tion mind-set)
  postnegotiation considerations
    importance, 1–3 (*see also*
    postnegotiation plan)
  reasons for implementation trou-
    bles, 3–6 (*see also* assump-
    tions and behaviors in deal
    making; implementation
    mind-set)
  reasons for negotiation troubles,
    6–7
  typical negotiation contexts, 13–15
Negotiations Centers of Excellence,
  105, 162, 179
negotiations between buyers and
  sellers. *See* buyers negotiating
  with suppliers; suppliers negotiating with buyers

organization-level aspects of
  negotiating
  changing to an implementation
    mind-set (*see* action plan for
    organizations)
  consequences of a deal-making
    culture, 145–148

  managing negotiators (*see* manag-
    ing negotiators)
  negotiation seen as a critical func-
    tion/process, 162
  negotiators' toolbox (*see* toolkit
    for effective negotiation)
  road map creation (*see* road map
    for negotiation)
  support through the company
    structure, 179–180
  training connected to the road
    map, 173–175
organizations' negotiation mistakes
  closure made difficult, 157–160
  closure made too easy, 160–161
  common errors, 9–11
  involvement kept low, 155–157
  metrics use, 153–155
  separating the deal department,
    149–151
  using third parties to do deals,
    151–153
outsourcing
  advice for buyers, 207–208
  advice for providers, 208–211
  advice to advisers, 211–213
  overreliance on scope limitations,
    205–206
  overreliance on service-level
    agreements, 203–205
  profitability and relationship
    matrix, 210
  typical lack of useful information,
    202–203
overcommitment avoidance, 100–109

participants in deal making
  alignment with counterparts,
    64–65
  blockers, 55–56
  bystanders, 54–55
  decision-making roles delineation,
    58–59
  disadvantages to leaving people
    out, 50
  enablers, 55, 56–57
  erroneous assumptions made by
    negotiators, 58
  essentials, 55, 57–58
  getting team alignment on key
    issues (see team alignment)
  helping counterparts not over-
    commit (see overcommitment
    avoidance)
  matching roles with decisions,
    59–60
  negotiation climate used to define
    precedents (see precedents in
    negotiations)
  rationales for limiting partici-
    pants, 49
  risk discussions and (see risk
    discussions)
  setting expectations early,
    61–62
  stakeholder buy-in importance,
    51–52, 53
  stakeholder involvement, 62–63
  stakeholder types, 53–54, 55
  understanding how your counter-
    part works, 67–68

partnerships
  alliance criteria, 195
  attempts to avoid conflict,
    195–196
  failure to define the relationship,
    197–198
  failure to discuss differences, 196
  focus on partnering effectively,
    199–200
  questions that should be asked, 198
Pauly, Brett, 60
Perry, William D., 105
postnegotiation plan
  importance of having, 1–3
  joint handoff meeting, 114–117,
    141–143
  keeping momentum into the
    handoff, 112–114, 117–119
  necessity of looking past the deal
    close, 111–112
  raising postdeal issues, 141–143
  transition identified as the nego-
    tiator's role, 114
Power of a Positive No, The (Ury), 105
precedents in negotiations
  benefit of creating positive prece-
    dents, 79–80
  creating based on the negotiation
    purpose, 71–73
  deal-making vs. implementation
    mind-set and, 80, 82
  precedents and questions to con-
    sider, 73
  precedent-setting nature of nego-
    tiations, 68–70

precedents in negotiations
(*continued*)
   process questions to consider,
      80–82
   team alignment on key issues (*see*
      team alignment)
   transparency in precedent-setting
      moves, 82–84
Procter & Gamble Pharmaceuticals,
   150, 175

Raiffa, Howard, 173
Rashomon (Kurosawa), 82
right to cure clause, 117–118
risk discussions
   costs and benefits of raising
      potential problems, 90
   deciding which risks to raise,
      88–90
   effective risk management conver-
      sations, 92–94
   receptiveness to others' risk issues,
      97–98
   risks in avoiding, 86–88
   techniques to use, 94–97
   toolkit for dealing with risk,
      172–173
   treating risk as ordinary to the
      negotiation, 91–92, 93
road map for negotiation
   basic elements, 163–165
   implementers involved in negotia-
      tion, 167
   linking deals to their purpose,
      165–166

negotiators', involved in imple-
      mentation, 167
   stakeholders inclusion, 166–167
   training connected to, 173–175
role reversal for preparing for nego-
      tiations, 138

Sebenius, Jim, 51–52, 118
sellers. *See* suppliers negotiating
   with buyers
social contract, building, 118–119
Spehar, Scott, 139–140
suppliers negotiating with buyers
   creating mutually beneficial
      precedents, 229–230
   involving all enablers, 228–229
   keeping purpose of the deal at
      forefront, 226–227
   problems related to compensation
      schemes, 220–221
   problems related to use of profes-
      sional procurement negotia-
      tors, 219–220
   ultimate goal for sellers, 217–219

team alignment
   benefit of the doubt, 76
   commitments, 77–78
   creativity, 77
   information sharing, 78–79
   respect, 76–77
   use of power or leverage, 79
3-D Negotiation (Lax and Sebenius),
   51–52, 117–118

toolkit for effective negotiation
  for dealing with risk, 172–173
  making sure kit is adequate,
    167–168
  for mapping stakeholder relation-
    ships, 171
  postnegotiation knowledge shar-
    ing, 169–171
  precedent-setting incorporation,
    171–172
  value from creating, 168–169

Tracey, Lynne, 175
training in negotiation,
  173–175
Tyagarajan, V. N., 46

Ury, Bill, 105

Wolf, Ken, 42–43
Wolfe, Tom, 150

About the Authors

Danny Ertel and *Mark Gordon* have worked together for nearly twenty years advising governments, organizations, and individuals around the world on negotiation, how to deal with conflict, and how to manage relationships. Their work has ranged from assisting clients on significant strategic negotiations to working on the cessation of armed conflicts. They have helped organizations in both the public and private sectors structure and launch new alliances, remediate troubled partnerships, and systematize their processes for negotiation and relationship management. Both are founding partners of Vantage Partners LLC, a management consulting and training firm that specializes in helping companies achieve breakthrough business results by transforming the way they negotiate and manage their most important relationships with key customers, suppliers, and business partners. Vantage is a spin-off of the Harvard Negotiation Project, and its partners are authors of numerous books and articles on relationship management. To learn more about Vantage Partners, visit www.vantagepartners.com

Danny Ertel leads the Outsourcing practice area at Vantage and focuses on helping buyers and providers improve the way they negotiate and manage complex outsourcing arrangements. In addition, Danny is the chairman of Janeeva, Inc., the industry leader in outsourcing relationship management software.

Prior to cofounding Vantage Partners, Danny was a senior researcher at the Harvard Negotiation Project, taught negotiation at the University of Toronto Law Faculty, practiced law with Debevoise & Plimpton, and served as a law clerk to the Hon. Justice Harry A. Blackmun on the U.S. Supreme Court. In his public-sector work, Danny worked with both the government and the rebel high command to help end a decade-long civil war in El Salvador, and with government leaders throughout South America on privatizations, sectoral reform, and efforts to improve public-private interactions on regulation, labor relations, and violence reduction.

Danny's first book, *Beyond Arbitration* (1991, coauthored with Ralph Ferrara) was selected by the CPR Legal Program as the winner of its 1992 Book Award. He is also the coauthor, with Roger Fisher, of *Getting Ready to Negotiate* (1995), and editor of *Negociación 2000* (1996). Danny has written for and has been quoted in *Harvard Business Review*, *Sloan Management Review*, the *Economist*, *Purchasing Today*, and *Financial Executive*, among others. Danny is a graduate of Harvard College and Harvard Law School, where he was managing editor of the *Harvard Law Review*. He can be contacted directly at danny_ertel@vantagepartners.com.

Mark Gordon works with leading companies across a range of industries including financial services, entertainment, health care, information technology, manufacturing, and telecommunications to help develop and implement strategies for maximizing the value from both intraorganizational collaboration and relationships with alliance partners, customers, and suppliers. Mark has worked on every continent except Antarctica, and much of his work focuses on enhancing cross-cultural communication and relationship management.

In addition to his work at Vantage Partners, Mark is a cofounder and has been chairman of Conflict Management Group (CMG), a nonprofit organization focused on disputes of international public concern, and currently serves on the board of Mercy Corps after CMG's merger with Mercy Corps. During his more than twenty years of experience in the public sector, Mark has worked with President Daniel Ortega of Nicaragua on negotiations between the Sandinistas and Contras, President Jose Napoleon Duarte of El Salvador on negotiations between the government and the FMLN, and the PLO negotiation support group reporting to the late Yasser Arafat, Mahmoud Abbas, and Saeb Erakat, as well as Israeli negotiators from the IDF, police, foreign ministry, and prime minister's office. In addition, he has worked with the ANC in South Africa on the constitutional negotiations led by Cyril Ramaphosa and Roelf Meyer, taught at the NATO Defense College in Rome, and conducted training for numerous foreign ministries around the world.

Prior to specializing in negotiations full-time in 1984, Mark practiced law as a corporate attorney with the firm of Cravath, Swaine & Moore in New York, worked for the U.S. State Department's Arms Control and Disarmament Agency on U.S.-Soviet strategic arms reduction negotiations, the Democratic National Committee, Senator Hubert Humphrey, and Ralph Nader. Mark has a JD from Harvard Law School and an AB from the Woodrow Wilson School of Public and International Affairs at Princeton University. Mark can be contacted directly at mark_gordon@vantagepartners.com.